ESSENTIAL
WORSHIP

ESSENTIAL WORSHIP

A HANDBOOK FOR LEADERS

GREG SCHEER

BakerBooks

a division of Baker Publishing Group
Grand Rapids, Michigan

Published by Baker Books
a division of Baker Publishing Group
P.O. Box 6287, Grand Rapids, MI 49516-6287
www.bakerbooks.com

Printed in the United States of America

Library of Congress Cataloging-in-Publication Data
Names: Scheer, Greg, 1966– author.
Title: Essential worship : a handbook for leaders / Greg Scheer.
Description: Grand Rapids, MI : Baker Books, a division of Baker Publishing Group, [2016] |
    Includes bibliographical references and index.
Identifiers: LCCN 2016017642 | ISBN 9780801008283 (pbk.)
Subjects: LCSH: Worship.
Classification: LCC BV10.3 .S34 2016 | DDC 264—dc23
LC record available at https://lccn.loc.gov/2016017642

16 17 18 19 20 21 22   7 6 5 4 3 2 1

This book is dedicated to my sons,
Simon and Theo.

Love God.

Stay weird.

Contents

PRELUDE

Acknowledgments

It takes a village to raise a book. My village included:

- The wise folks who gave me feedback on the manuscript: David Bailey, Jordan Clegg, Maria Cornou, Laura de Jong, Scott De Young, Eric Mathis, Neal Plantinga, Ron Rienstra, Samuel Tandei, Howie Vanderwell, and Michael Weller.
- The good people of Richmond, where I began this book on a too short but very sweet sabbatical: East End Fellowship, David Bailey and his Arrabon community, the Urban Doxology interns, and Danny and Mary Kay Avula, who opened their home to me.
- My fellow staff at the Calvin Institute of Christian Worship, whose sharp minds are surpassed only by their open hearts, especially John Witvliet, who took a chance on me.
- The staff, musicians, artists, and congregation of Church of the Servant, especially Maria Poppen, who somehow keeps everything running smoothly even when I'm writing a book. You have provided a gracious church home in which I could develop as a worship director and as a worshiper.
- The many mentors, teachers, and fellow worship leaders who have been a part of my journey, especially Michael Hawn, who has been all three. I am always grateful for the gifts you've been in my life.
- My Three Muskabeers, Todd Kapitula, Matt Plescher, and Scott Yonkers, who have done their best to keep me on the straight and narrow.

About Me

(Or, Confessions of a Failed Pentecostal)

My formative years were spent in a small Pentecostal church in Rhode Island, a place where, my father used to brag, you could tell the Spirit moved because of the handprints on the ceiling.

The church was full of characters: Vietnam veterans, university professors, Southern belles, and African immigrants. Pastor Gooding was a straight-shooting hellfire-and-brimstone preacher, accompanied by the accordion-playing, white-patent-leather-shoe-wearing Brother Nash. Sister Rankin, even at ninety years old, would get so excited that she'd stomp up and down screaming "Praeese ya Jeezus!" "Praeese ya Jeezus!" while Brother Kwame would let out a long, regal "Halleloooooooyah." College students tried to avoid Sister Reid because she'd grab them by the forehead and pray out the demons of education. (She also prayed demons out of my dog and spoke in tongues while driving—I learned much about prayer myself during those car rides.) Young women tried to avoid Brother Keith because he'd likely tell them that God had told him they should get married. Everyone tried to avoid "the world," which included movies, rock music, long hair (for men), pants (for women), and jewelry (for anybody).

From the outside it might have seemed strange, but that church laid the spiritual foundation of my life. I grew to love Jesus there, learned the Bible (I can still quote many Scriptures in the King James Version), and came to expect the Spirit to be at work in the world. However, once I left for college I found an increasing disconnect between my faith and my life. There was my "spiritual life"—reading the Bible, praying, and going to church—and then there was my "life life"—making music, learning German, and hanging out with friends. In an effort to bridge that gap I attended a variety of churches, but the chasm only grew wider and I was soon a functional agnostic. I may have been an unsuccessful Christian but I was even worse as an agnostic, because I still had the nagging feeling that there was, indeed, a God, and I couldn't shake Jesus's claim to be the Son of God.

By my early twenties I was a failed Pentecostal, then a failed Baptist, and then a failed agnostic. At that point in my life I was introduced to the Reformed faith, with its focus on Christ's reign over the arts, civic life, and "every square inch" of the earth.[1] I discovered that I could be a Christian and a human simultaneously. I've been both ever since.

Shortly after this, I began leading worship. It turns out that my pop music background, classical training, and love of God were exactly what I needed for the job! My first church was in a Presbyterian (PCUSA) church in Pittsburgh. From there I moved to a Presbyterian (PCA) church in Florida. While teaching at a Christian college in Iowa (affiliated with the Reformed Church in America), I wrote a book called *The Art of Worship*. It focused on leading praise bands. In a deliciously ironic twist of fate, that book was released right as I moved to my current church, Church of the Servant in Grand Rapids (Christian Reformed), which has no praise band.

In the last decade, I've become convinced that modern worshipers benefit when deeply connected to the roots and rhythms of the historic, global church. My work has focused on the psalms, global worship songs, and the ways worship and culture intersect. Yet even with all these changes, I still can't shake my inner Pentecostal. The young, Pentecostal Greg is always questioning the current Greg: *Are all your highfalutin' ideas taking away your ability to worship from the heart? Is global, ecumenical worship simply a way of keeping things from getting too intimate? Does structured worship keep you from hearing and responding to God in the moment?*

This personal history is included here not because my life is particularly interesting but rather because it is important for readers to know the perspective from which this book is written. We each have our own faith story. Mine is the story of a spiritual mutt adopted into a Reformed home. I believe that my convictions are well-founded but don't want to ignore the wisdom of other perspectives. It's a tricky balance, and I pray that God's grace shines through in the pages that follow.

About This Book

This book began to take shape on trips to Indonesia, Uganda, and Ukraine, where I've taught and learned from a wide variety of brothers and sisters in Christ. The common denominator in all of these situations was that local musicians and pastors were lacking adequate training materials. Topics I assumed would be a review turned out to be a revelation for leaders who were patching together their worship philosophy from whatever they came across on YouTube or saw in other local churches. Closer to home, a friend who worked in a prison congregation asked if I could recommend a book on worship that would provide a simple overview of worship and worship leading. There are lots of great resources but nothing that laid out all the basics in one book.

What is missing is a primer on worship. Whether we're in Peru, Peoria, or prison, we all need to learn the fundamentals. It took me over twenty years of leading, reading, and teaching to slowly piece together my worship theology and practice. I hope I can save you some time by putting it all into one book.

As a starting point, *this book is biblical*. "All Scripture is inspired by God and is useful for teaching, for reproof, for correction, and for training in righteousness, so that everyone who belongs to God may be proficient, equipped for every good work" (2 Tim. 3:16–17). Scripture is the foundation upon which we build. (I'll be using the NRSV translation throughout, unless otherwise noted.)

Second, you will quickly notice that *this book gives special consideration to historical worship forms*. This is not some strange nostalgia for the "good old days," but instead a conviction that we need to allow the "cloud of witnesses" (Heb. 12:1) to speak into our modern context. The longer a worship practice has been a part of Christian worship (psalm singing, for example), the more likely we should continue its practice today. This doesn't mean we shouldn't look to the future or try new things; it simply means that each new generation doesn't need to reinvent the wheel.

Third, *this book is for worship directors*. I use the term "worship director" throughout to denote someone who is responsible for worship decisions, planning, and leading leaders. Many musicians will read it, of course, but this book is written for anyone who is involved in a church's worship leadership, from pastors honing nonpreaching worship skills, to worship committees providing direction, to dancers who want to learn more about the context in which they contribute their choreography.

Finally, *this book is personal*. I wish I could tell you that the Holy Spirit dictated these chapters directly into my laptop or that this book defines, once and for all, the right way to worship. But instead you will find my best attempt at boiling down everything I've learned from the Bible, the church of yesterday and today, and the fellowship of worshipers throughout the planet. Some of this will be my own story, but I hope it will also be *our* story. I have tried to discern the unity underlying a variety of worship traditions, allowing readers to apply the ideas to their own cultural or denominational context.

No single book can be the *last* word on worship, but I'd be honored if God would use this book as a *first* word on worship, opening a door for those who serve local congregations by leading worship.

Beginning with a Funeral

Before you begin: Plan your own funeral.

Before you start reading this book, I'd like you to do something that might strike you as unusual: I want you to plan your own funeral. You don't have to work out all the details, but I want you to make a list of elements you'd like to include. What Scriptures would you use? What verses have sustained you throughout life? What passages summarize your life's mission? Which are appropriate for a funeral? (For me, Psalm 103 would be at the top of the list.) What songs would you want people to sing? Do you have a theme song, a hymn that reflects your life and faith, or music used at a spouse's or grandparent's funeral you would want your loved ones to sing at your funeral too? Would there be a sermon? Who would you like to preach it? Are there any other things you would want included in your funeral service?

At the start of each chapter, spend some time with each "before you begin" section, alone or in a group, writing down your thoughts. These are meant to prepare you to engage each topic more deeply and more personally.

It might seem odd or morbid to begin a book on worship by planning our own funeral, but beginning with the end in mind helps clarify what is most important. It helps us think beyond the ever-changing styles and mundane disagreements that occupy our minds on a day-to-day basis, asking the question: *What kind of worship do I want to take to the grave with me?*

Once we know where we want to go, it becomes a lot easier to take steps in our weekly worship that bring us closer and closer to our goal.

Unfortunately, there are many forces competing for our attention, keeping us from focusing on life-sustaining worship that leads us ever nearer to Christ. Instead of shaping us into Christ's image, our worship too often looks just like us and our personal preferences. I once gave the "plan your own funeral" assignment to a group of seminarians, and one of them decided he would lead most of the service via prerecorded video, the sanctuary would be decorated with hunting pictures and his favorite guns, and his casket would be transported to the gravesite using his pickup truck. This has the makings of the world's creepiest funeral. More importantly, a future pastor should have deeper, more substantial thoughts about his final worship service.

But this man is not alone. Most of us, whether worship directors or worshipers, become so focused on the details of worship that we lose sight of the big picture. We ask all the wrong questions: What would my people like? Who will get upset about it? How long will it take? Instead, we should be asking questions that will help us go deeper: What does the Bible say? How have Christians worshiped in the past? What do my people need?

We need to get back to the basics. We need to lay a strong foundation built on Scripture and the saints who have gone before us so that we can lead worship that will sustain a healthy faith in our cultural context. This book is written for, and dedicated to, those unsung heroes who love God and want to help their churches worship well but are not quite sure how to get started.

For Discussion

1. Share a few highlights of your funeral plan with a group, a friend, or family.

2. By spending some time on your "final" worship service, did you gain any insight into the worship services in which you're currently involved?

3. Make a list of recurring questions you have about worship. What is it you'd like to learn from this book?

PART 1

PRINCIPLES

1

What Is Worship?

Before you begin: How do you define worship?

You might have a working definition of worship, but it's likely that your actual worship leading is far more developed than any definition you've come up with. That's okay. But it's important to periodically take a step back and consider the big picture of what we do on Sunday morning and beyond. Take a quiet ten minutes to carefully consider your definition of worship. Do your best to capture your thoughts in a paragraph or less. Bonus points if your definition would fit on a bumper sticker! If you're in a group, take the time to share your answers with one another.

Defining Worship

Worship is just as difficult a word to define as *love*. No definition will ever capture all its facets. Like love, it is far better to experience worship than to define it. On the other hand, without reflection we may find ourselves going through the motions week after week without any real vision of what we're doing or why. Spending time looking at the big picture of what worship is—or could be—may just transform our weekly worship in our local congregation.

While thousands of worship definitions have been written, a handful in particular bear repeating. One of the most profound definitions comes from Archbishop of Canterbury William Temple:

Worship is . . .
> the quickening of conscience by His holiness;
> the nourishment of mind with His truth;
> the purifying of imagination by His beauty;
> the opening of the heart to His love;
> the surrender of will to His purpose—
> and all of this gathered up in adoration, the most selfless emotion of which
> our nature is capable and therefore the chief remedy for that self-centeredness
> which is our original sin and the source of all actual sin.[1]

See how Temple shows each part of our being transformed by God's very nature. Worship is not something we try to manufacture out of nothing; instead, it is a response to who God is. Because God is beautiful, our imaginations are purified. We magnify God by squealing like children, "I want to be like that!"

My pastor, Jack Roeda, came up with a definition of worship that gives keen insight into the relationship between the Christian life and Christian worship:

> Worship is the essence of our faith in ritual form.

Jack's definition shows us that any joy or sorrow, any triumph or tribulation we could experience in our life with Christ is distilled into an hour of time on Sunday morning. We don't leave our "real" life behind when we come to worship; we give it to God in prayer, song, and preaching. Also implied in Jack's definition is that worship—the compact version of our whole faith—can be lived throughout the rest of the week.

My own definition may not add much to the above, but it would be unfair to make readers write down a definition of worship if I weren't willing to take part in the same exercise. For years I had either relied on definitions like William Temple's or had simply been satisfied with a *functional* definition of worship—we worship when we do XYZ. My lack of reflection came to a head in a meeting with my church's youth group in which they were free to ask questions about our church's worship. The youth group leader, Trent, began the meeting by turning to me and saying, "Let's start with Greg: Greg, what is worship?" I stammered and stalled, said something about worship being hard to define—like love—and pretty much wiped away any confidence the youth may have had in me being able to answer their questions.

I kicked myself all the way home and determined I would not miss an opportunity like that ever again. Later that night I came up with this:

Worship is tuning ourselves to the Trinity.

This bumper sticker–sized bonbon is not only pleasingly poetic but also gathers meaning as it's unpacked. The word *tuning* has musical connotations, of course, but I used the word mostly for its spiritual meaning. Paul admonishes us, "Do not be conformed to this world, but be transformed by the renewing of your minds" (Rom. 12:2). One of the things worship does is remind us of who God is. When we come to worship we hear God's perfect pitch and we recalibrate our lives to that pitch. Once we're in tune, we vibrate sympathetically to God's perfect pitch. This tuning happens at a deep, intuitive level and is nothing we can do on our own—it is all in response to God. I chose the word *ourselves* because it's important to remember that both worship and the Christian life must be done in community. *Trinity* is a word too infrequently used when considering worship. At the heart of the divine nature is God's united three-ness. If we are to worship the true God, it must be as the Father, Son, and Holy Spirit. If we are to be tuned to God's character, it must be in harmony with the Three-in-One.

None of these definitions do worship justice. Worship is a profound experience of God that will only be fully revealed in eternity. However, our attempts at defining worship will hopefully open us up to a more profound, more expansive vision of worship. It is too easy to trivialize worship with functional definitions ("three songs and a sermon") or slogans ("get your praise on"). It reminds me of the recent trend for couples to write their own wedding vows: "I, Julie, take you, Brad, to hug and snuggle . . ." Having never been married, these couples have no way of imagining the joy and pain of "in sickness and in health, until death do us part." In the same way, we want to make sure to set our sights on worship that is ever deeper and more satisfying. God will not disappoint us but will fill us "abundantly far more than all we can ask or imagine" (Eph. 3:20).

Worship: One Word, Many Meanings

One of the difficulties of defining worship is that we're often talking about different things. The word *worship* can mean a worship service—a specific time, often on Sunday morning, when we gather to take part in a group ritual called *church*. It can mean the worship we offer God with our whole lives as "a living sacrifice, holy and acceptable to God" (Rom. 12:1). Recently the word *worship* has come to refer to the music time at church, as in "praise and worship." This creates confusion when we discuss worship and we often end up arguing about definitions of entirely different things!

For example, you might describe worship as passionate and joyous. That may be a positive trait for a set of worship music, but what about preaching? Should that always be joyous? What about a funeral service? Is that not also worship? What about Scripture, which shows us examples of worship being terrifying, heartrending, or focused on the law of God?

Some people point out that a walk in the woods is worshipful because they are immersed in God's good creation. Or they say they worship God by feeding the hungry. Certainly, these are good examples of worshiping God with our lives, but should they take the place of meeting with God's people to remember God's work in Christ and hear Scripture preached?

As Bob Kauflin, music director of Sovereign Grace, recounts in *Worship Matters*, "I once heard a woman describe how Bono and U2 taught her more about worship than any Sunday morning worship leader."[2] Similar statements have been applied to Sufjan Stevens, Brahms, and Bruce Springsteen. In fact, I was at a Sufjan Stevens concert when, during intermission, the guy who came to the concert with me said, "This is what worship should be like." (Point of etiquette: don't unfavorably compare a concert to worship when you know the person you're talking to is a worship director—especially when that worship director bought your ticket.) Even though I found the concert absolutely soul-stirring, I was offended that this person used it as an opportunity to denigrate worship at the local church. Though both involve music, they are fundamentally different experiences. I'm with Bob in his response to that woman: "That's an alarming statement. Our goal as worship leaders is unlike that of any concert and is far more significant. We're seeking to impress upon people the greatness of the Savior whose glory transcends our surroundings and technology."[3]

Confusion arises because Bob and I are working with a definition of worship that means "worship service" or "music in the context of a worship service." These other people are working with a definition of worship as "music that moves me deeply."

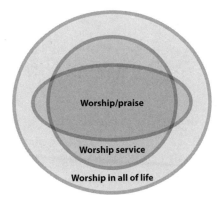

So how can we clarify these three meanings? John Witvliet, director of the Calvin Institute of Worship, shows these three definitions as three concentric circles.[4] The outside circle is "Worship in all of life." This is our Romans 12 living sacrifice worship. Inside that is the "worship service," the hour we spend together on a Sunday morning. "Worship/praise" is a circle within the worship service. It is the music and singing part of the worship service; in common usage it often connotes a modern praise and worship style. This gets us started in understanding how the different types of worship relate to each other, allowing us to quickly narrow our discussions to the specific meaning we intend.

However, one of the difficulties in discussing the various meanings of worship is that while we need to separate the definitions for clarity, as humans we experience these three separate aspects of worship in fluid and overlapping ways. Yes, there is danger in equating a U2 concert or working at a soup kitchen with a Sunday morning worship service, yet they are all part of our lives as Christians.

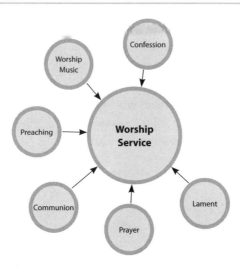

How could John's diagram be adapted to show the dynamic relationship between these three types of worship—not only the *meaning* of worship but also our *experience* of worship? Let's begin with the worship service. As we see in the diagram, worship music is naturally part of the worship service. Of course, we all know that it's not the only part of a worship service. Worship services also include preaching and other elements such as communion, prayer, and confession. All of these are "worship" just as much as the worship music.

While worship music is, theoretically, a neutral term, it often connotes a musical style—modern praise music led by a band. While modern praise music is great, we want to be careful not to exclude other expressions. For example, we don't want to focus so much on joyous praise that we lose the ability to lament—to bring our sorrows to the Lord in prayer and song. We also don't want to restrict our music style to one genre but rather remain open to the multitude of musical expressions Christians have used throughout the history and geography of the church: chant, hymns, psalms, and folk songs from around the world.

Now let's look at life worship. This is the way we offer ourselves to God every day with our whole lives. When we assess our spiritual health, we may quickly think about how consistent we've been with our "quiet time," the time we've spent with the Lord in prayer and Bible study. Or we may think about spiritual aspects of our lives such as evangelism or fellowship. All of

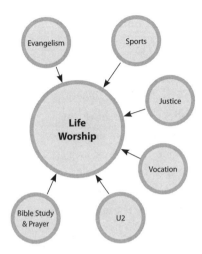

these are good and important but they are only a small part of life worship. God wants our whole lives, not just the specifically religious parts of them. For example, if we work in law or engineering, are we serving God any less than a pastor or missionary? I hope not! If we are working for justice for the oppressed, is that any less spiritual than attending Wednesday night prayer meeting? I would suggest that the prayer meetings and justice work are inseparable, like breathing in and breathing out.

Still, our lives consist of so much more than serious things such as vocation, prayer, and justice. Much of our time is spent with recreation, entertainment, and the mundane stuff of life. Is our understanding of our place in God's world big enough to incorporate sports? Can we play soccer "unto the Lord" and "with all our heart"? If not, a lot of our time is being spent in disobedience to God's will! I hope our faith is broad enough to see all of life as a gift from God to be lived as an act of worship. This is precisely where U2 comes in. Attending a concert is an appropriate way of taking part in the fullness of life as a Christian. However, though it may be worship*ful* music, it is part of life worship rather than worship music. The same is true of evangelism—it is part of our calling as Christians but doesn't necessarily belong in the worship service.

Our understanding of worship, though, shouldn't be primarily focused on how to separate life into tidy little boxes but rather on how all the facets of our life come together into a cohesive whole. The two arrows in the diagram below are the most important part of the diagram—and the most important part of any theology of worship. They show that life worship and the worship service flow back and forth in a symbiotic relationship. What we do in church spills out into our everyday lives and what we experience in our everyday lives flows back into worship.

This has huge implications for both the worship service and our life worship. When we come into a worship service, we may be tempted to, as the song says, "forget about ourselves, and concentrate on Him."[5] Instead we are invited to bring our daily struggles into worship with us to give to God. When we leave church on Sunday, we don't think of the rest of the week as a struggle to keep from being dragged down into the world. Instead we are given strength in worship to work for God's kingdom to come and for God's will to be done throughout the week.

Catholics have a good way of naming this relationship. They call the worship service the "source and summit" of the Christian life.[6] It is the *source* in that all good living is named and rehearsed in worship: we acknowledge that God is the only true authority in the world, we celebrate Jesus's full work on the cross, and we recognize that we are sinners saved by grace and called to serve in joy. It is the *summit* in that there is nothing we can experience in our "real" lives that is not discussed in Scripture and cannot be brought to God in worship. Further, we have a sympathetic advocate

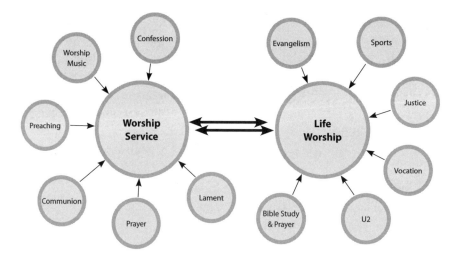

in Jesus Christ, who has fully experienced our human condition and now intercedes for us with the Father (Rom. 8:31–39). As the hymn says, "There is no place where earth's sorrows are more felt than up in heaven."[7]

This is good news for Christians! We don't have to hide our true selves in worship but rather can bring our full beings—warts and all—into God's presence. We are not thrown out of the doors of the church to face Monday unprepared, because worship provides a training ground for the Christian life. Indeed, God wants us to be fully Christian, fully human, and fully integrated. Worship is the key to this integration. The rhythms of worship and life flow back and forth like the beat of the heart, filling us with life.[8]

Gospel singer Mahalia Jackson boiled down the whole subject when she sang "I'm Going to Live the Life I Sing about in My Song." She knew that a holy song was worthless if not backed up by a holy life. God said it like this through the prophet Amos:

> Take away from me the noise of your songs;
> I will not listen to the melody of your harps.
> But let justice roll down like waters,
> and righteousness like an ever-flowing stream. (Amos 5:23–24)

Mahalia and Amos don't want us to stop singing: they want our song—and worship—to be completely integrated with our lives.

For Discussion

1. How did you define worship at the beginning of the chapter? In your definitions and practice, have you focused more on life worship, worship service, or worship music? Is there one you've ignored?

2. What changes in your thinking or practice could strengthen the connections between worship service and life worship? How would that make you a better worshiper? A better Christian?

3. The ancient way of stating the relationship between worship and life is *Lex Orandi, Lex Credendi, Lex Vivendi*. (As we worship, so we believe, so we live). Do you think it is true that worship shapes our beliefs and actions? Is it the only thing or just one of the things that shapes us?

2

What Is Biblical Worship?

Before you begin: Are candles in worship biblical?

You are the worship director at First Baptist and you have a problem. The youth of the church have begun a Wednesday night prayer meeting. You're excited that the young people of your church are inviting the whole church to pray more often and more intentionally. The problem is that recently they've been trying to create a more prayerful atmosphere by lowering the lights and placing candles around the sanctuary. Some of the older folks have complained that it "doesn't seem biblical." Is it?

Use Scripture to defend a position for or against the use of candles in worship.

Who wouldn't want their worship to be biblical? That's something we can all agree on, right?

While it seems so simple, the fact is that Christians have used the same Bible to defend snake handling, serving grape juice instead of wine at communion, banning musical instruments, and a host of other worship practices that are at odds with one another. So while we all agree that we want our worship to be biblical, we may be using the same Bible in very different ways to form our worship practices.

At a very basic level, when we state that our worship is *biblical*, we mean to say that it's *not heretical*. That is certainly a good starting point. Of course, heresy is not something most people set out to accomplish. They might label their own worship theology as liberal, relevant, or nontraditional, but they probably won't say it's heretical or unbiblical. Generally speaking, the word *heretical* is only used when speaking about *someone else's* worship! Let's take a look at some ways various people or traditions have used the Bible to form their worship practices.

Four Approaches

The first approach might be called *direct revelation*. This is the belief that God will reveal the truth of Scripture through the direct inspiration of the Holy Spirit, without the aid of a denomination, tradition, or seminary degree. This approach tends to be found in the Free Church, evangelical, and Pentecostal traditions. This confidence in God's ability to speak directly to the Christian is quite wonderful. What was the Reformation all about if not putting Scriptures directly in people's hands and giving them responsibility for their own faith?

At its best, those who expect direct revelation will search Scripture faithfully to discern their worship practices. At its worst, it unravels into proof-texting—searching Scriptures to find a verse confirming what we'd like to believe. As a pastor friend used to say, "Tell me what you'd like to believe and I'll find a passage to support it!" We need to be careful. We can't quote David dancing before the ark in his ephod, "I'll become even more undignified!" (see 2 Sam. 6:22) while ignoring the many places in the Old Testament where God ordained a solemn ritual. We can't condone handling poisonous snakes in worship based on Mark 16:14–18 but not consider whether this is a command for worship or simply a metaphor for God's protection for his children. Simply using Scripture doesn't ensure right practice. After all, in Matthew 4:1–11 the devil quoted Scripture when tempting Jesus in the wilderness!

The second approach is the *regulative principle*. Born of Zwingli and Calvin's branch of the Reformation, the regulative principle states that worship practice must be based solely on worship practices explicitly seen in

Scripture. If it's not in the Bible, we aren't allowed to do it. So, for example, Calvin didn't allow instruments in worship because they don't appear in New Testament worship. Zwingli went so far as to prohibit singing entirely because the New Testament says to sing and make music "in your hearts" (Eph. 5:19), as opposed to *with your mouths*. Churches from this tradition have melted organ pipes, burned icons, and stripped away centuries of religious art and culture. While this iconoclasm is extreme, they have a point: Isn't our worship most biblical when it's based on examples of worship from the Bible?

Certainly this is the safest way to arrive at a biblical worship practice, but at times it seems unnecessarily restrictive. For example, why should instruments be prohibited based on New Testament practice when they were clearly commended in the Old Testament (1 Chron. 25; Ps. 150)? Why should Christians restrict their singing to only using the Word of God (i.e., the psalms in Calvinist churches) when Ephesians 5:19 and Colossians 3:16 tell us to broaden our singing to "psalms, hymns, and spiritual songs"?

Luther was more lenient. He ascribed to the *normative principle*— anything in worship that is not prohibited by Scripture is left to our best judgment. Because this approach isn't focused on black and white prohibitions, it tends to search the Bible for patterns and norms of biblical worship. It focuses on what you *should* do in worship rather than what you *shouldn't*. Luther didn't feel the need to break with every Roman Catholic worship tradition that wasn't explicitly mandated in Scripture. In fact, he kept significant continuity with Roman Catholic practices, only rejecting those things he felt were in clear error. For example, he retained the basic structure of the Latin mass but encouraged the use of German instead of Latin and let the congregation take part in communion.

The normative principle could be seen as a slippery slope—a short step away from everyone doing what is "right in their own eyes" (Judg. 17:6). Certainly that is a danger, yet the normative principle is tethered to scriptural witness strongly enough to be considered a healthy approach to biblical worship.

Roman Catholics go one step further, understanding the scriptural witness within the context of the church's tradition and authority. This is often called the *three-legged stool* of Scripture, tradition, and church authority.[1] For example, when the pope met with bishops in the 1960s for the Second Vatican Council, they amended the church's Latin-only tradition to include Scripture and music in indigenous languages, a move they felt was closer to biblical practice. This type of top-down decision is foreign to the Protestant mindset. But before Protestants condemn this as an unbiblical approach to worship, let's be honest: we all have our traditions and authorities. How Protestants ended up with grape juice and crackers at communion certainly has more to do with the Wesleyan Holiness movement and American Prohibition than it does with the biblical witness! On the other hand, there is certainly the danger that centuries of human tradition can build up until the biblical witness is no longer recognizable. As the internet meme says: "Tradition: just because you've always done it doesn't mean it's not incredibly stupid."

> "Christian worship at its best is thoroughly biblical–guided by the Bible's instructions, shaped by its patterns, rooted in its truth, saturated with its language, following its narrative contours, and focusing on Jesus Christ."
>
> —RON RIENSTRA[2]

What can we learn from such a wide array of approaches to biblical worship? It should be obvious that there is no single, perfect way to worship. We all want our worship to be faithful to the Bible but we all arrive at different worship practices. That doesn't mean the Bible has no bearing on our worship practices; it just means we're all trying to interpret the Bible faithfully within our worship context. While we will never achieve perfect worship this side of heaven, we can certainly use Christian wisdom to arrive at better and best.

Biblical Principles

Perhaps we can synthesize these historic traditions into a flexible, big-picture approach to crafting biblical worship practice. First, *let the Bible speak on its own terms*. There are those who build detailed theories of congregational song based on the biblical phrase "decently and in order" (1 Cor. 14:40). It is clear that Paul's admonition was about congregational life and worship, not a rule about harmonic structures! There's no harm in inferring a music principle from this passage, but using it to mandate a specific worship practice is a load it was not created to bear. Let the Bible speak as it will. Don't twist it to say things it didn't intend.

Second, *understand the larger biblical witness.* Before diving into specific biblical passages about worship, it's important to remember the big picture. The Old Testament reflects a theocracy—God personally mandated what should be done in worship and civic life. Does this require us to adorn each of our sanctuaries with gold cherubim two and a half cubits long? No, but it does show that God took great care as a "worship planner." The psalms, while also the inspired Word of God, are poetry and song rather than a rulebook for worship. They shape our vocabulary, assuring us that biblical worship can express joy, trust, sadness, and rage to God. Unfortunately, some leaders extract verses from Psalms and apply them as mandates: "shout to God with *loud songs* of joy" (Ps. 47:1, emphasis added) was not intended as instruction for a church sound system's decibel level! The New Testament, while the closest thing we have to a guidebook for Christian worship, can seem frustratingly incomplete. It appears that the epistles mainly addressed aspects of worship that needed correction. Still, some derive a whole theology of congregational song based only on the phrase "psalms and hymns and spiritual songs" (Eph. 5:19; Col. 3:16).

Third, *consider the context of each Scripture.* Though the whole of the Bible is the Spirit-inspired Word of God, each Scripture addresses a unique context. For example, as Christians we are no longer required to observe many of the mandates of Old Testament law (Acts 15:1–21). The same God who said, "Vengeance is mine" (Deut. 32:35; Rom. 12:19) is surely not instructing us to kill our enemies' babies (Ps. 137:9). Knowing that the New Testament is silent on some areas of worship because the first Christians assumed many Jewish practices gives us a broader context for applying New Testament worship to today's context.[3] Understanding the Word in context deepens our hearing of what the Spirit is saying to us about worship.

Fourth, *improvise wisely.* Once we have filled ourselves with God's Word, we are ready to live it. Biblical scholar N. T. Wright gives the illustration of finding an incomplete play by Shakespeare. Who would be best suited to complete it? Perhaps Shakespearean actors who have steeped themselves in the bard's stories and styles would be able to improvise the remaining story. Wright suggests that the Christian's relationship to Scripture is like that. we steep ourselves in God's story and then improvise our lives the best we can as a continuation of that story.[4] Worship is the same way. We attempt to form a trajectory from the biblical witness through the early church to today.

Regardless of your approach to using the Bible to arrive at your worship theology, we should all be able to agree on using the Bible itself in worship. Sadly, some of the churches that pride themselves on being biblical literalists hardly use any Scripture in worship at all! This is a shame. Biblical literacy is at an all-time low and we can no longer expect people in our churches to know Scriptures well.[5] More importantly, we know that the Spirit works through Scripture, and that God promises his Word "shall not return to me empty" (Isa. 55:11). Our services should include the Word preached, sung, and prayed. The psalms should be the backbone of our worship language. Our services should be filled with the whole biblical witness, with regular readings from both the Old and New Testaments. The robust use of the Word of God in worship will be a huge step toward achieving "biblical worship."

For Discussion

1. Which of the historic models (direct revelation, regulative principle, normative principle, or three-legged stool) is closest to your approach? After reflecting on this chapter, are there any ways you could strengthen your approach?

2. Look at last week's service: How many Scripture passages were used throughout the service? If a child grew up in your church and only encountered the Bible in worship, would they have a good introduction to the whole Bible by the time they left for college? (Be honest!)

3. Having read this chapter on biblical worship, would you change your original answer about the candles?

3

Who Is the Audience of Worship?

Before you begin: Who is talking to whom?

Take out a bulletin, service order, or whatever your church uses to list the parts of the worship service. Next to each element, draw an up arrow when the people talk to God, a down arrow when God talks to the people, and a sideways arrow when the people talk to each other. For example, Scripture would have a down arrow, intercessory prayer would have an up arrow, and announcements would have a sideways arrow.[1]

There are no right or wrong answers.

If someone asked you what worship is about, or who it is for, you'd naturally answer "God." Many people have affirmed, with songwriter Matt Redman, "I'm coming back to the heart of worship, and it's all about you."[2] While this may be true, on a practical level there are large stretches of worship that are not directed to God at all. For example, does God really need to hear a sermon? More practically, anyone who has spent significant time in ministry will tell you that despite our stated intentions, many of our week-to-week decisions have nothing to do with God at all but focus instead on what people need (or think they need).

So who is *really* the audience of worship?

Three Models

One model positions the *congregation* as the audience. Few of us would claim this model as our own, but many of our churches follow this model in our week-to-week worship practices. It may start by asking what kind of worship is relevant to our culture or by targeting a particular demographic with a specific music style. We may try to reach non-Christians with worship that has none of the trappings of religion, or we may feel like we can't stray too far from what the charter members of the church intended. None of these are bad in themselves, but they can present a deeper problem: they quietly turn our attention away from God and focus our attention on the desires of the congregation. We treat the congregation like consumers, a role they know well and are happy to play. They choose a church based on music style, church demographics, and sermon appeal. We understand that they'll remain loyal to the church as long as those things remain intact. In the end, worship is compromised by an environment that drives people deeper into their cultural identities rather than calling them to a new identity in Christ.

A second model positions *God* as the audience, with the people as performers of God's praise. Certainly this God-centered model is an improvement over the first model. It has a number of proponents—most notably Søren Kierkegaard[3]—and is perhaps the default ideology of most worship leaders. (The phrase "Audience of One" is this model in slogan form.) However, there are some subtle problems inherent in this way of approaching worship. For one thing, it assumes that we have something beneficial to give to God. Think about it: in a concert setting the performer is the reason for the event. If we are performing for God, does it unintentionally put us and our praise at the center of worship?[4] Further, what could we give God that would be a worthy offering? We have nothing to offer except what has been given to us: Jesus Christ, the perfect offering. This may seem abstract, but the practical result of a God-as-audience worship paradigm is that church musicians feel pressure to offer a pure gift of worship. They beat themselves up when they are distracted, have sins and sorrows weighing them down, or make musical mistakes. They are aiming for a perfection that is not achievable and worrying that God won't accept what they've given. Finally, this model connotes that God is somehow incomplete without our praises. These lyrics by Waterdeep express this line of thinking:

> And with a thankful heart I bring my offering
> And my sacrifice is not what You can give
> But what I alone can give to you.[5]

Does God really need our praise? Is God somehow incomplete until I offer, "what I alone can give"? It may be true that we were created for worship, but perhaps we're overstating God's need of our praise when we describe him as the audience of our worship.

© 2016 Matt Plescher

A third model puts the *Trinity* at the center of worship. Any attempt to understand God's nature and the essence of worship must begin with the Trinitarian character of God. Too often we view God as a majestic being waiting to be appeased with our offerings, or we concentrate on Jesus as a friend (or even lover) who longs for intimacy with us. But at the heart of God's character is Trinitarian community: Father, Son, and Holy Spirit.

Christians often approach the Trinity as a problem to be solved. How could God be both Three and One? Is the Trinity like water in three forms: ice, liquid, and gas? Who is the "boss"? Who should we pray to, and who does the work of answering prayers? These are all valid questions, but they represent what could be called "triangular thinking." That is, three static corners that remain forever in tension.

While the Trinity is surely an incomprehensible mystery, James B. Torrance and others present a way of thinking about the Trinity that celebrates three-in-oneness as a key to unveiling the nature of God.[6] This could be called "circular thinking." Imagine the Trinity as an interlocking circle, a dynamic, unbroken ring. In fact, some have portrayed this circular Trinitarian theology as a dance.[7] This is not just some fresh way of diagramming the Trinity but rather reveals that at the core of the Godhead is community.

> Come, join the dance of Trinity,
> before all worlds begun—the
> interweaving of the Three:
> the Father, Spirit, Son.
> The universe of space and time
> did not arise by chance,
> but as the Three, in love and hope,
> made room within their dance.
>
> —Richard Leach[8]

So much love existed within this eternal, self-sufficient, all-glorifying God that it couldn't be contained. Like a loving husband and wife who want to expand the borders of their relationship by bearing or adopting children, the love of the Trinity flowed beyond itself in the form of creation: boundless galaxies, fertile earth, and humanity in their image. When humanity broke communion with the Godhead by sinning, the Trinity called us back through the sacrifice of Jesus Christ on the cross, making a way for the relationship to be restored. Through Jesus Christ we are invited into the very life and love of the Godhead!

Implications of Trinitarian Worship

This is not some abstract theology but a truth that has important consequences for our worship. In worship we are invited into communion with the Trinity. Worship is not a matter of us doing something or something being done for us. It's a matter of simply accepting God's hospitable offer: "Listen! I am standing at the door, knocking; if you hear my voice and open the door, I will come in to you and eat with you, and you with me" (Rev. 3:20). We experience this communion with the Trinity throughout worship, but perhaps it is most visible at the communion table. Here we feast on the very life of Christ, a foretaste of the eternal banquet we'll share as God's family in heaven.

Trinitarian worship is not something we humans have to manufacture. The Trinity existed before time itself, complete and full of glory. This glory continues today as the Son glorifies the Father (John 17:1–5), the Father commends the Son (Matt. 3:16–17), and the Spirit declares Christ's glory to the world (John 16:13–15). This glory resounds in an endless chorus of the saints in heaven (Rev. 5:11–12) and on earth (7:9–10). Even creation

Ancient Christians had a great image for describing this relationship of Jesus Christ and God the Father and the Holy Spirit. They said the relationship between the Three was like a big dance. The technical word was *perichoresis*. Like a lot of useful words, it's a combination of two other words: *peri* meaning around and *choresis* meaning dance. We know these words: think *periscope* as something that allows you to look around and *choresis* as related to choreography. With respect to the Trinity, think of the three Persons as involved in a circle dance, moving so gracefully, so quickly, and so eternally that they seem as one although they are also three distinct partners.

And we get invited into this dance. It's not like one of those movie scenes about a prom where some guy goes in, taps another guy on the shoulder, and takes over dancing with the partner while the original guy heads to the sidelines. No, it's more like what used to happen to me as a kid with my dad. When it came time to dance, he would have me climb up on his feet and hold his hands. And he would start to dance around the room. My job wasn't to initiate the dance. My job was to stay attached to him, feet firmly on his, hands firmly in his, and be attentive to his movements so I could join in with him. And we would dance around the room. When we were dancing, was it his movement or mine? Was it his energy or mine? Was it his liturgy or mine? Yes.

And so by the Holy Spirit we have been joined to Jesus Christ, we have climbed onto his nail-scarred feet and held on to his nail-pierced hands and, joined to him, have been invited into the eternal circle dance of Father, Son, and Spirit. While we're dancing with him, is it Jesus's movement or ours on Sunday morning? Is it his energy or ours on Sunday morning? Is it his liturgy or ours on Sunday morning? Is it his worship of God the Father or ours on Sunday morning? Yes. Our job is not to initiate but to stay close to him, attentive to his movement and eager to follow his every sway. And that's the perspective that leads to liberation.

Lester Ruth[9]

itself proclaims the glory of God (Ps. 19). When our lungs fill with air on a Sunday morning, our praise is not something we create from scratch—we are simply joining the eternal chorus of praise that began in the Trinity itself and now reverberates throughout all of heaven and earth.

How do we bring this cosmic vision of worship into the week-to-week worship of a local congregation? That will vary from church to church, but certainly worship services should reflect the character of God. Like the architectural maxim "form follows function," our worship should flow from the very nature of the Trinity: communal, hospitable, and full of glory. We can't expect a worship service that is run like a lecture hall or variety show to adequately convey the deep truths of God. Of course, the deep truths of God are found in the Word of God, so our services must be rooted in the Bible and filled with Scripture.

Trinitarian worship is led by Christ. The priesthood of all believers is a result of the work of Jesus Christ, the Great High Priest. No longer do we have to worry about being sufficient "lead worshipers," guiding the people to the throne room, but instead we rely on the perfect sacrifice of Jesus Christ as our perfect offering. The Holy Spirit enables our worship, Jesus perfects it, and God accepts it. This is the emancipation of worship leaders! We no longer bear the spiritual burden for our church's worship but are instead freed to simply be musicians assisting the people's song.

Another result of embracing a Trinitarian worship model is that we'll understand that worship is for the people of God. That is not to say that people are the audience of worship. No, we are not passive observers but rather active participants. This goes beyond mere relevance and demographics and instead meets people in their deepest needs: community, forgiveness, and love. After all, God delights in our worship but doesn't need it—we do. God already enjoys the fullness of Trinitarian life. Worship is God's invitation to us to participate fully in that abundant life.

For Discussion

1. Do you find the Trinitarian model of worship convincing?

2. Lester Ruth questions whether contemporary worship moves away from a traditional understanding of worship—we worship God through Christ in the power of the Holy Spirit—to a model where we worship Jesus in the power of music.[10] Do you think your church could be accused of this?

3. Are any members of the Trinity—Father, Son, or Spirit—relatively elevated or diminished in your worship?

4. If form does indeed follow function, what parts of your worship could be changed to be more Trinitarian? Think of some specific examples

of parts in your services that either support or undermine a healthy understanding of God's nature. (For example, singing together could be seen as a way that God's people bind themselves into Trinitarian-shaped community. A stage could display a congregation-as-audience model.)

4

What Does Worship Do?

Before you begin: What do you expect from worship?

We've probably all taken part in post-church critique sessions—the sermon was too long, the singers were out of tune, we sing that song every week. Let's set aside the quality of the service for a moment and focus on this simple question: What do you expect from worship? If worship were perfect, week after week, what would the outcome be? Please be honest. Sunday school answers like "God would be glorified" don't count.

We have explored the question, "What is worship?" Now we turn our attention to "What does worship do?" The answers to this question tend to lead in two different directions: information and experience.

Head and Heart

Fifty years ago, someone walking out of church might have said, "That was a good service," and what they probably meant was, "That was a good sermon." Until relatively recently, all other worship elements were dwarfed by the sermon. Some even referred to the two-part service as "the preliminaries and the preaching." It was clear from the lecture-style format of the service that the goal of worship was information dissemination. This goal went hand in hand with the rational approach of the modern era, which valued knowledge, science, and philosophy above emotional and physical ways of understanding the world and God. Even the singing reflected this goal, with multiple-verse hymns that expounded on a theme one verse at a time.

An intellectual approach to worship is not restricted to a particular era. It can be favored by a particular kind of person too—what we might call a "head" person. Head people are not necessarily smarter than "heart" people; they simply favor a rational approach to life, relationships, and worship. Head people are not better or worse than other people; they just have a certain God-given disposition. Even cultures can lean toward the head or the heart as their primary mode. The positive thing about a rational approach to worship is that it seeks the truth and is not swayed by fickle feelings. On the other hand, in its most extreme form it can ignore the body and emotions to such a degree that it feels like, as Jamie Smith says, we have churches full of "brains on sticks."

> "Christian worship was no longer a full-orbed exercise that recruited the body and touched all of the senses. Instead, Protestants designed worship as if believers were little more than brains-on-a-stick. The primary target was the mind; the primary means was a lecture-like sermon; and the primary goal was to deposit the right doctrines and beliefs into our heads so that we could then go out into the world to carry out the mission of God."
>
> —JAMES K. A. SMITH[1]

More recently, someone walking out of church might have said, "That was a good service," and what they probably meant was, "The worship music was good." Beginning with the explosion of contemporary praise music in the 90s, churches began to put more and more weight on the experience of worship. Music sets became longer and more emotional. Worshipers valued expressing themselves to God with singing that was passionate and intimate. Less emphasis was put on the preaching and other spoken elements while people began to use language like "breaking through" and "entering the holy place" to describe that moment of emotional overflow they experienced in worship.

This shift in worship reflected a shift in the broader culture that minimized the rational modes of modernism in favor of the experiential modes of post-modernism. This approach is not confined to post-modernism, however. This "heart" mode can be the favored approach of individuals, churches, and cultures. The advantage of this mode is that it engages the affections in worship. For too long our emotions have been treated like the "weaker member" of our beings (1 Cor. 12:21–23), so it is a blessing that worship is finally engaging more than the mind. However, there are also dangers to an experiential approach to worship. For one, we can spend so much energy expressing ourselves to God that we overlook the ways God may want to express himself to us. The emotional goals of heart-oriented worship can also lead us to chase after emotional highs like a drug addict chasing after the next hit.

Neither the head nor the heart should be seen as good or bad in and of itself. Information and experience are both valuable but are incomplete by themselves. It is important to understand that different people and churches tend to favor one of these approaches over the other. Knowing this helps us communicate better with Christians who are different from us. It also helps us understand possible blind spots in our own worship.

Even though most people come to worship with a disposition toward the head or the heart, could there be an approach to worship that would gather both information and experience into a cohesive, unified whole?

Worship as Nourishment

We're all aware that our physical health is not determined by one meal but rather by the cumulative effect of all we eat over time. A dinner of fried chicken, soft drinks, and ice cream doesn't immediately plummet us into obesity and heart disease, but a little too much of foods like these every day will. As running guru Jason Fitzgerald says, "it's more important what you do *most* of the time than what you do *some* of the time."[2] What if we took the same approach with our worship diet?

If worship services are indeed sustenance for lives of worship, we could approach them

> **Further Reading**
>
> James K. A. Smith, *Desiring the Kingdom: Worship, Worldview, and Cultural Formation* (Grand Rapids: Baker Academic, 2009).
>
> James K. A. Smith, *Imagining the Kingdom: How Worship Works* (Grand Rapids: Baker Academic, 2013).

in the same way we do with the meals that maintain our physical health. We wouldn't fall into the trap of the head mode, which is all vegetables and no dessert. And we wouldn't fall into the trap of the heart mode, which chases after anything sweet and memorable. Instead, we would be careful about our long-term worship diet. Are there some things we focus on to the exclusion of other things? (All praise and no lament, for example.) Is there enough Scripture to fill our services with the right "nutrients"? Do we sing about all facets of the faith? Do we pray for the needs of the whole world? Do we enjoy a balanced diet of Word and Table and celebrate the work of the Father, Son, and the Holy Spirit?

If we approached worship like nourishment, it would quickly change our services for the better. First, it would make us more intentional about the things we do when we assemble for worship. We can't guarantee that our services will fully equip each worshiper for the Christian life, much less that people will live it, but we can at least try. If our preaching is all law and no grace, it's likely our people will live under a weight of failure and shame. If our services don't include confession, it's unlikely they will have the vocabulary to practice this discipline on their own. Our job as worship directors is to open doors of possibility for worshipers.

Second, approaching worship like nourishment would help mitigate some of the arguments that center on personal taste. Each worshiper has their personal preferences but the worship meal is planned for the whole community and with an eye to the long-term health of all. There will always be something we like but not everything will be our favorite. Individual and community tastes are always taken into consideration but ultimately worship directors may have to use the time-honored parenting phrase, "No dessert until you eat your broccoli!"

This list of Vertical Habits on the next page, developed by the Calvin Institute of Christian Worship, is a series of simple relational words that help us identify a variety of worship expressions. This is a good starting place for understanding a healthy worship diet—and a healthy Christian life (more at http://worship.calvin.edu/resources/resource-library/showcase-vertical-habits-worship-and-our-faith-vocabulary/).

Finally, thinking of worship as diet keeps us from putting too much weight on one meal. The fact is that we don't always get it right. We may not strike the proper balance in a particular service, or we may simply choose to focus more heavily on one "food group" on a given Sunday. This is okay. Rather than worrying about the lack of something in a particular service, we keep an eye on the balance of elements over the course of a month or a year. Further, our worship services don't always go as smoothly as we'd like. We can probably expect at least one disaster per year! But if we're focused on the congregation's larger diet, we don't have to beat ourselves up for these periodic failures. If a child refuses to eat a meal, she won't starve. She'll just be hungry. In the same way, a congregation that endures a poorly executed service won't die of malnutrition; they may get a bit hungry but will rely on all the healthy worship they've enjoyed in the months and years leading up to that service.

The ultimate goal is for our worship to reorient us to the kingdom of God. Worship engages our minds, hearts, and bodies, but it doesn't stop there. Over time, the things we learn, feel, and do in worship begin to shape who we are at our core. Through repetition we develop habits of thanking, confessing, forgiving, and sharing that we practice in our everyday life. Worship aligns our deepest instincts with God's character, growing in us holy reflexes for faithful living.

"Love You"
Praise

"I'm Sorry"
Confession

"Why?"
Lament

"I'm Listening"
Illumination

"Help"
Petition

"Thank You"
Thanksgiving

"What Can I Do?"
Service

"Bless You"
Blessing

"Creed"
Commitment

Images courtesy of Cardiphonia and Matt Hale. Reprinted by permission.

For Discussion

1. Are you more of a head or heart person? Are you in a head or heart church? Does your culture lean more toward head or heart? What can you learn from those in the other mode? What can they learn from you?

2. How would approaching worship as nourishment change your thinking and practice? How would it change your discussions of worship?

3. Look at the list of Vertical Habits on page 51. Which ones are done the best, or most, during worship in your church? Which are done poorly or least? Are there any habits you would add to the list?

PART 2

PAST

5

Learning from the Past

Solomon declared, "there is nothing new under the sun" (Eccles. 1:9).[1] Indeed. While we may think we're unfettered from the past and free to craft our own worship, even a brief look at worship history shows us we are reliving patterns, questions, and controversies as old as the Bible itself. To better understand where our worship comes from and what forces compel us today, we need to understand what precedes us.

Worship in Ancient Israel

Burning bush, tabernacle, temple: the Old Testament is a fascinating account of the way humans met with God. Many books have been written about Old Testament worship, but we'll focus on some major themes. First, Judaism was unique in having one God. All the surrounding cultures were polytheistic (multiple gods, one for everything from rain to fertility). They sought to gain their gods' favor by making offerings to idols. Jews were not only monotheistic but claimed that God was a living God above all other gods and that this one true God had entered into a covenant with them, his chosen people. This plays out throughout all the Old Testament writings. For example, neighboring nations had water gods—gods of chaos who needed to be appeased to grant safety. When Genesis starts by saying "God moved over the chaos of the water" it is making the audacious claim, "Our God is bigger than yours." This theme is reinforced throughout the Old Testament. At the same time, while Israel positioned itself as unique from surrounding religions, there is good evidence Israel simultaneously borrowed culturally from their neighbors—poetic forms, literary genres, and musical instruments.[2] So while some Christians may rankle at secular music styles making their way into the sanctuary, it seems there is precedent in the earliest biblical witness for sanctifying worship material that came from many—and even pagan—sources.

Second, the place of worship is a recurring theme in Judaism. During the formation of Judaism, interactions between God and the chosen people were miraculous encounters like Moses and the burning bush (Exod. 3:1–4:17) and the appearance to Abraham (Gen. 18:1–15). Next, God's presence was seen in the pillar of fire or smoke, then found in the ark of the

Further Reading on the History of Worship and Music

Tim Dowley, *Christian Music: A Global History* (Minneapolis: Fortress Press, 2011).

Donald P. Hustad, *Jubilate II: Church Music in Worship and Renewal* (Carol Stream, IL: Hope Publishing Company, 1993).

Elmer L. Towns and Vernon M. Whaley, *Worship Through the Ages: How the Great Awakenings Shape Evangelical Worship* (Nashville: B&H Academic, 2012).

Paul Westermeyer, *Te Deum: The Church and Music* (Minneapolis: Fortress Press, 1998).

James F. White, *A Brief History of Christian Worship* (Nashville: Abingdon Press, 1993).

covenant and the portable tabernacle that traveled with the Jews on their journey through the wilderness. When they arrived in the promised land, the place of worship transitioned from tabernacle to temple. The temple was the location of worship and the center of Jewish life and identity. The ensuing years saw the temple destroyed and rebuilt, and the Jews scattered throughout neighboring countries. During this period a synagogue system was instituted, so far-flung Jews could learn Torah in their own communities. However, the temple still remained central to Jewish worship, even when they couldn't assemble there.

We see this focus on the location of worship in Jesus's conversation with the woman at the well. She, a Samaritan, said:

> "Our ancestors worshiped on this mountain, but you say that the place where people must worship is in Jerusalem." Jesus said to her, "Woman, believe me, the hour is coming when you will worship the Father neither on this mountain nor in Jerusalem. You worship what you do not know; we worship what we know, for salvation is from the Jews. But the hour is coming, and is now here, when the true worshipers will worship the Father in spirit and truth, for the Father seeks such as these to worship him. God is spirit, and those who worship him must worship in spirit and truth." The woman said to him, "I know that Messiah is coming" (who is called Christ). "When he comes, he will proclaim all things to us." Jesus said to her, "I am he, the one who is speaking to you." (John 4:20–26)

This passage, and Jesus's claim while cleansing the temple, "Destroy this temple, and in three days I will raise it up" (2:19), make it clear that Jesus intended to relocate the center of worship in himself. While this is true, we shouldn't be too quick to dismiss the examples of worship location in the Old Testament: miraculous encounters, an abiding presence, a specific assembly, and learning centers are all important facets of our worship life—and all find completion in Jesus himself.

Early Christian Worship

One of the overriding themes of the New Testament is that Jesus completes the requirements of Jewish law, including the many requirements surrounding worship. The book of Hebrews portrays Jesus as the unblem-ished sacrifice, the Word, and the High Priest. While this is immensely freeing from a theological perspective, practical advice in the New Testament about worship is thin. There is no rule book for worship. Instead, we are only given a few lists of elements included in New Testament worship and some corrective admonitions (such as 1 Cor. 14:26). Some people have taken this as license to say that, beginning with the New Testament, forms of worship don't matter. Others allow only what the New Testament mentions. It may be instructive to fill in a little context.

Early Christianity was a branch of Judaism. The earliest converts were Jews; later, Gentile converts struggled to figure out the role that circumcision and other Jewish laws played in their faith (Acts 15:1–21). There is strong evidence that Christians adopted many Jewish customs as the foundation for their new worship life.[3] Worship service forms, Scripture readings, and baptism were reinterpreted for a Christian worship context. Importantly, when the New Testament describes early worship, it is not meant as a complete manual for worship. Instead, it is an echo of their full practice, filling in details when things were going wrong, as they were in the Corinthian church during communion (1 Cor. 11:17–34). It is frustrating that we are not given more complete instructions on worship, but we can fill in what the New Testament tells us with historical eyewitness accounts and writings such as the *Didache*, a first-century document with instructions about Christianity. The evidence shows us that the early church's worship was not the free-form hippie fest that some people would like it to be. It followed regular patterns and displayed great continuity with the Jewish faith; for example, singing the psalms, adopting and adapting some Jewish feast days, and reading and teaching Scripture.

However, Christian worship was also unique in many ways. On Pentecost, the miracle of the gospel being heard in numerous languages established a precedent: Christianity was a global religion. Unlike Judaism, which has a specific ethnic identity, or Islam, which requires adherents to read the Koran in Arabic, Christianity has always been a religion that plants itself uniquely in local soil. The church in Damascus was different from the church in Rome which was different from the church in Alexandria. Persecution fueled the spread of Christianity throughout the world. By the end of the New Testament writings, we see the gospel reaching people from Rome, the Middle East, and Ethiopia. Some even say that Thomas took the gospel to India as early as AD 52.

A short history like this can't follow all the threads in this global tapestry, so we will focus primarily on major movements of the Western church. With the conversion of Roman Emperor Constantine in AD 313, Christianity was no longer a persecuted underdog but rather became, in essence, a state religion. This served to institutionalize worship. As the church moved into the medieval period, the variety of worship forms that had been developing organically within various local bodies became centralized and codified. Pope Gregory standardized the church's music repertoire in the form of Gregorian chant. The Desert Fathers (such as Benedict) began the monastic tradition of communities set apart for prayer and study, which would serve as the church's intellectual centers for years to come. The mass—the structure of worship—was established throughout the church, and became considerably more complex than the basic worship patterns of the early church. In the Great Schism of 1054, the Eastern and Western branches of Christianity split, with Constantinople serving as the center of Eastern Christianity and Rome serving as the center of Western Christianity as well as forming the backbone of Western culture.

The Reformation

By the time Martin Luther nailed his 95 Theses to the door of Wittenberg Church on October 31, 1517, the Roman Catholic Church had become deeply entangled with political powers and its worship was so encrusted with complexity that professional musicians and priests performed it while the people watched in silence. Luther and other Reformers sought to return worship to the people, with Scriptures read in local languages, the restoration of preaching, participation in communion, and congregational singing. It is difficult to summarize all the forms the Reformation took under the influence of different Reformers in different locations, but certain traits were shared: people were expected to take personal responsibility for their faith. The printing press made it possible for common people to read and understand the Scriptures in their own language. There was also a flourishing of congregational song, both hymnody and psalmody.

The next four centuries saw the Protestant Church grow throughout Europe. The branches of the Protestant Church—Lutheran, Reformed, Anglican, and Anabaptist—produced numerous highlights in worship, including *The Genevan Psalter*, *The Book of Common Prayer*, J. S. Bach, Isaac Watts, and Charles Wesley, among others. In the larger Western culture, developments in science and transportation led to an Age of Discovery. It also led to a dark period in the history of the West: a period of conquest and colonization. While there were certainly many Christians who sincerely wanted to bring the good news of Jesus Christ to newly discovered lands, many were motivated by expanding their kingdoms and plundering resources. By the end of this era, European supremacy was seen as divine right (sometimes called the "doctrine of discovery"), non-Europeans were seen as savages, and slaves were traded like spices. This period also cemented the idea that Christianity was a "white" religion—an irony given the Jewish ethnicity of Christ and the multicultural message of Pentecost (Acts 2).

Great Awakenings

Protestant Europe quickly fell to the same ills as the Roman Catholic Church: politics and religion became inseparable, and the Christian faith became so institutionalized that the original spark of the Reformation dwindled to smoldering embers. Beginning in the 1700s, two "Great Awakenings" aimed to restore the fire of faith. Preachers such as George Whitefield, Jonathan Edwards, John Wesley, and Charles Finney held open-air sermons and camp meetings that led to waves of revival throughout America and England. By the end of the Great Awakenings a number of worship innovations were introduced: display of emotion, bodily/vocal expression, minimization of Calvinism, outdoor meetings, multiethnic gatherings, and folk music used in worship.[4]

This set the stage for what is sometimes called the Third Great Awakening, a movement that birthed modern worship. In the late nineteenth century, various parachurch organizations sprouted up in America and England: the YMCA, Salvation Army, and Sunday School movements. Also popular during this era were revival meetings, most notably those held by Dwight Moody and Ira Sankey. Sankey's singing set up Moody's evangelistic sermons. More specifically, Sankey used tunes in a contemporary style, music that would draw nonbelievers in and warm them up to hear the message. This method proved to be incredibly successful.

Moody and Sankey's revival meetings set the template for evangelical worship for years to come.[5] This songs/sermon sequence quickly became the de facto "liturgy" of evangelical worship. The use of popular music styles has also been replicated throughout the history of evangelicalism. William Booth, a contemporary of Moody and Sankey and founder of the Salvation Army, is reported to have said, "Why should the devil have all the good tunes?" Indeed, since this time, music has been adopted for its popular appeal rather than its aesthetic value or worship function. Also established during this period was the idea that music and worship perform an evangelistic role. As these revivals blossomed and moved into established churches, these worship innovations became the new norm. Likewise, as missionaries left these churches to share the gospel with unreached people, a revivalist model of worship spread throughout the world.

While the revival movement focused on salvation, the Holiness Movement in late-nineteenth-century America focused on the "second blessing" of entire sanctification. Based on Wesley's teachings, followers believed that a life devoted to God could achieve an intention of devotion that bore the fruit of the Spirit. Adherents were quick to point out that the second blessing didn't mean they were sinless but rather on the path of sanctification. However, they generally agreed on a set of outward standards that reflected inner sanctification: dressing modestly, abstaining from worldly entertainment, and prohibiting alcohol, tobacco, and gambling. (Or as they used to say when I was a kid: "Don't drink, swear, chew, or go with girls that do!")

Pentecostalism

The Holiness Movement set the stage for a group who sought the "third blessing," that is, the outpouring of the Spirit with signs and wonders as seen in Acts 2. Indeed, Agnes Ozman, a student at Bethel Bible School in Topeka, Kansas, spoke in tongues on the first day of the twentieth century, setting the stage for a worship movement that would become a dominant branch of Christianity by the end of the century. Pentecostalism, as it came to be known, exploded into the public arena in 1906 with the Azusa Street revivals, and quickly spread throughout the United States and beyond.

Pentecostal worship introduced (or reintroduced) a number of worship practices. Pentecostals are proudly spontaneous, rejecting repeated worship patterns in favor of following the Holy Spirit in the moment. Pentecostal worship is exuberant, reviving biblical practices such as clapping, dancing, and raising hands. More than expressing mere human exuberance, Pentecostals aim to be Spirit-filled. They are best known for manifestations of the Spirit such as speaking in tongues, miraculous healings, and being "slain in the Spirit" (falling down when overwhelmed by the Spirit's power). Pentecostal worship is music-intensive. Whereas evangelical music might be merely functional, Pentecostal music is essential. Many church services have more than a half-hour of uninterrupted music and singing. The Pentecostal experience is personal. While they gather in groups like every other church, in Pentecostal worship there is an expectation that the Spirit will meet each person in a unique and powerful way. Finally, Pentecostal worship is much more racially mixed than most denominations. This may come from the movement's Azusa Street history, where a mixed crowd was led by an African American, William Seymour, and a Caucasian, Charles Parham. As one observer put it, "The color line is washed away by the blood of Jesus Christ!" Or it may be that the validation of the Spirit, as evidenced by speaking in tongues, trumps race, class, and gender.

From Azusa Street, Pentecostalism made its way to Main Street. In the 1960s Pentecostal traits emerged in mainline denominations in the form of the Charismatic Movement. These worshipers remained in their own churches but explored gifts of the Spirit and new worship styles. In the late 1960s, the Jesus People married hippie culture to evangelical belief with a Pentecostal-leaning worship style. This soon birthed the contemporary praise genre, reconnecting with Pentecostalism most clearly in the Vineyard movement.

Whereas traditional Pentecostalism focused on exuberance and spiritual gifts, this new Vineyard-inspired Pentecostalism focused on expression and intimacy. The latter proved to be much more marketable. Indeed, a new generation of praise and worship songs exploded beyond the boundaries of the local church and quickly became a global phenomenon. In the same way that hymns and gospel songs traveled throughout the world with the missionaries, praise music traveled via CD and radio to all ends of the earth. The commercialization of worship music has fundamentally changed how churches engage with songs. Instead of using hymnals or denominational sources for new music, they began learning repertoire through popular media. In fact, the contemporary worship industry soon looked very much like its secular music industry counterparts, with a Top 40 list (CCLI), a stable of stars, and thriving scenes in Nashville, England, and Australia.

Pentecostalism has been growing by leaps and bounds since the early twentieth century through the efforts of post-Azusa missionaries, Pentecost-flavored worship music, and more recently the influence of Spirit-filled megachurches like Australia's Hillsong. Some have identified Pentecostalism's orality as one of its appeals in pre-literate cultures.[6] Perhaps Pentecostalism's spontaneity and exuberance are key reasons it has connected so strongly with the more communal, expressive cultures outside of the Western world (and in the West as well). Scholars like Philip Jenkins have documented a broad shift in Christianity: it is shrinking in the West and is now centered in the Global South, a shift that has been fueled in large part by Pentecostalism. The evidence is all around: half of the world's missionaries come from the Global South, the Rwandan Anglican church has taken a number of conservative Episcopal churches under its wing, and the Catholic church has lost millions of worshipers to local, charismatic congregations. Christianity is no longer a white and Western religion.

Ancient-Future Worship

While the summary of worship in the twentieth century could be "the Pentecostalization of worship," in recent years the pendulum has begun to swing back. Led by the late Robert Webber and others, there has been a growing move toward "Ancient-Future" worship—worship that reclaims pre-Reformation worship patterns, mysticism, and spiritual disciplines. In reaction to simple, repeated Pentecostal praise choruses, there has been a trend toward more substantial lyrics, whether in the form of newly written hymns, historic hymns with new tunes, or the rediscovery of gems from previous centuries. Some worshipers have become fatigued with spontaneity, preferring worship that has regular weekly patterns rather than neverending innovation. There have even been accounts of Vineyard churches converting en masse to Orthodoxy![7] Rarely are these trends exclusive. The postmodern mindset is much more willing than previous generations to blur lines of genre and denomination, mixing elements from various eras, denominational branches, and artistic traditions into new combinations.

Lessons Learned

So many centuries of worship in so many places with so many different perspectives. What can a local worship director learn from it all?

There is, indeed, nothing new under the sun. Every church—every new worship movement—has a history. Each seeming revolution grows out of the soil of a previous movement. Each tradition has been informed and changed by other traditions. It's not really a question of whether or not we're drawing on the past but rather how thoughtfully we're drawing on it.

It is striking that all historic worship movements are some mix of sacred and secular. That is, they inherit some of their worship materials from a previous generation of worshipers, and some they draw from the vernacular—the culture around them. The Israelites separated themselves theologically from neighboring kingdoms while using some of their art forms. Luther drew on sacred folk songs of his time when crafting new congregational songs. William Booth and Ira Sankey used the "devil's tunes" as a way of enticing people to hear the gospel.

Once again, it is not a question of whether or not we're mixing sacred traditions with vernacular styles—it's how effectively we're doing it. Are the secular styles overwhelming the gospel message? Is our adherence to tradition disconnecting us from those to whom we're called to minister?

Tradition and innovation are not the only polarities worship communities balance. There are multiple pendulums that swing back and forth between extremes: stability and revival, script and spontaneity, head and heart, community and individuality. A wise observer of worship history will realize that reacting too strongly against a previous pole will create a weakness in your congregation's worship.

History also shows us how God works in spite of us and our situations. One would think persecution would be the death knell of a church, but instead God has used that very thing to spread the gospel and grow the church. When Christians have clearly sinned—conquests of Latin America and enslavement of Africans, for example—God has worked to redeem the wrong we've done. This in no way condones atrocities carried out upon or by Christians, but it shows that even in the worst circumstances we and others can claim with Joseph, "Even though you intended to do harm to me, God intended it for good, in order to preserve a numerous people, as he is doing today" (Gen. 50:20). Further, God uses Christians to call one another back from our wandering. The Reformers attempted to purify the medieval Catholic church; centuries later Protestants were strengthened by Vatican II renewals. Nineteenth-century missionaries carried the gospel to the non-Western world; the Global South is now sending missionaries to the West.

Finally, worship history teaches us that we are all a work in progress. History shouldn't be seen as a series of cautionary tales (bad Catholics went astray and daring Reformers set it right) but as a plethora of possibilities, some of which may be helpful correctives for our own worship. God has moved throughout the years and the world, and we would be wise to welcome this cloud of witnesses when we consider our own worship.

For Discussion

1. Can you trace some of your church's roots in this sketch of worship history?

2. Which period do you, personally, relate to best?

3. If all worship is a mix of sacred and secular, can you identify some elements in your worship that stem from either the sacred (the worship traditions of the church) or the secular (popular entertainment or other nonreligious sources)?

4. How would you summarize the lessons of worship history? Worship keeps getting better each century? There is no "right" way to worship? Every era sees the pendulum moving in a different direction? Something else? Explain your answer.

5. What do you think is coming next in Christian worship?

6

Liturgy

A Four-Letter Word?

Before you begin: What's your plan?

How would you describe your church's worship: Free? Liturgical? Spirit-led? Try not to think of music style so much as the service order. Are your services mostly spontaneous or mostly planned? If planned, how far in advance and how precisely planned? If spontaneous, are there any elements that appear regularly in a certain order? Do you have any nagging doubts about your approach? Perhaps your spontaneous church does lots of singing but rarely prays, or your planned-in-advance services leave little flexibility for congregational responses. Write down any of these deficiencies you would like to address in coming years. Be honest. No church is perfect.

For the first fifteen hundred years of the church's history, worship was exclusively liturgical. Sunday worship was called *mass* and followed a specific pattern each week.[1] Even after the Reformation, these patterns remained intact in Lutheran, Anglican, Orthodox, and Roman Catholic churches. In fact, it wasn't until late in the nineteenth century that nonliturgical revival meeting worship models became the norm in evangelical and Pentecostal churches and liturgy became, for some, a dirty word. In the 1960s some Protestants began rediscovering the early church roots of liturgy and attempted to reclaim these historic worship patterns in modern worship. Truth be told, they didn't make much headway in the broader evangelical church. Many Protestants had, and still have, a knee-jerk reaction against anything that seems "too Catholic." This aversion to liturgy is a shame. Though it is unlikely that most evangelical churches will decide to "convert" to liturgy, perhaps there is something in the patterns and themes that liturgical churches have addressed through the centuries that will enrich our own church's worship.

Before digging into the details of liturgical worship, we need to ask the basic question: Why would we want to repeat patterns of worship over and over again? Doesn't that constitute the "vain repetitions" Jesus warned us against?[2] There are a number of good reasons worshipers may want to submit themselves to repeating cycles of worship.

First, though there is no commandment that says, "Thou shalt order your worship services this way," numerous biblical examples indicate that God orders time and that God's followers have shaped their time and worship in repeated cycles to good effect. Creation itself is ordered into cycles of the sun and moon, day and night (Gen. 1:1–19). One of the first things God did after creating the earth was to establish the seventh day as a Sabbath, a day of rest (2:1–3). Similarly, God established a schedule of festivals for the Israelites to follow: Passover (Exod. 12), Festival of Harvest (later known as Pentecost; Exod. 23:16), and the Year of Jubilee (Lev. 25:8–55). Early Christians adapted many of these into their worship life. The early church also added the "Lord's Day"—the day of resurrection (Acts 20:7)—after the Sabbath—the day of rest—to the weekly worship cycle. Further, early Christians continued the Jewish practice of daily prayer times. It is no accident that the Spirit descended on the apostles at the "third hour," or 9:00 a.m., and that a vision came to Peter praying on the roof at noon (Acts 2:15; 10:9). These were established times of prayer for both Jews and Christians. Of course, following daily cycles of prayer doesn't guarantee we'll receive miraculous signs from the Holy Spirit. But perhaps setting aside specific times of prayer and worship creates space and availability for the Spirit to work.[3]

A second compelling reason to follow yearly, weekly, and daily worship cycles is that the "cloud of witnesses" has followed them for centuries before us. It is only in the last two hundred years that we've left these practices behind. Have modern Christians really found a better path than the one walked by Benedict, Luther, and Wesley? Are we so strong in our faith that we no longer need external forms to shape our faith? The burden of proof rests with those of us who have left an established practice behind. This, of course, is not a matter of salvation, but it should certainly be a matter of earnest reflection.

Third, though worship cycles of human making are extraneous to the core of the faith, they may aid us in experiencing the fullness of the gospel. The yearly church calendar allows us to walk with Christ each year—birth, ministry, death, resurrection, ascension, and hope of his return. Without these external patterns we can very quickly fall into the trap of focusing on some aspects of Christ to the exclusion of others. We may spend more time on the crucifixion than the resurrection, for example, or come to know Christ as a brilliant teacher but ignore his ongoing ministry of intercession. It also creates accountability for preachers. All preachers have their favorite themes, such as salvation, personal integrity, or social justice. Taking part in external cycles of preaching topics encourages pastors to preach the whole biblical witness.

Fourth, repeated cycles of worship help us experience time in a way that builds hope. We've all heard the saying, "Those who cannot remember the past are condemned to repeat it."[4] The positive corollary is also true: those who remember the past have a context for understanding the future. Because we worship a loving and omnipotent God, that future is always full of hope. The Israelites understood this well. Passover was not just some yearly party; it was a reenactment of God's past deliverance that worked its way deep into the memory and gave a basis of hope for future deliverance. This kind of memory is called *anamnesis*, a word used most often in describing the Lord's Supper. "Do this in remembrance of me" (1 Cor. 11:23–26) is not referring to the kind of memory we use when taking a test. It is the deep-in-the-bones memory that places our lives in the context of God's timeline; it makes God's activity in the past a present and powerful reality.

It is perhaps easier to understand anamnesis in a simpler context: birthdays. A birthday isn't only a day to receive gifts; it's a day to celebrate a person's life. On my sons' birthdays we tell the story of how newly born Simon looked at Amy, his mother, like he had known her forever and how Theo was the biggest baby the Orange City, Iowa, hospital had seen in years (10 lb. 12 oz.). We take out photo albums to remind us of milestones. The boys love hearing these stories because it places them in a larger context: a family that has always loved them, a flow of years and accomplishments, and the hope of good things to come. The same could be said of anniversaries and a host of other special days. The ritual of celebrating these occasions not only honors the past but builds hope for the future. The black gospel song says it well:

> We've come this far by faith
> Leaning on the Lord
> Trusting in His holy Word
> He's never failed us yet
> Oh we can't turn back
> We've come this far by faith[5]

Do we need rituals of remembrance to sustain a healthy faith? Probably not. We could, in fact, live productive lives without celebrating birthdays, anniversaries, or Easter. But our lives would be poorer for it. Without the shape that special days give our lives and our worship, we experience time as a series of unconnected events—a relentless stream of days that threatens to overwhelm us.

In the end, even the most antiliturgical of us will still find that our time is shaped by something. One of the advantages of adopting the church's established yearly, weekly, and daily worship cycles is that it keeps us from being shaped by "Walmart time." If we don't celebrate Advent and Christmas, our people will simply experience what the rest of the world does: Halloween, Thanksgiving, and Christmas. Even though these have religious roots, today they are all fully secular rituals celebrating ghouls, over-consumption, and consumerism. Our culture's calendar conforms us "to the patterns of this world" whereas the church calendar encourages us to "be transformed by the renewing of our minds" (Rom. 12:2). Churches that forego Lent and Easter as unbiblical rituals often end up celebrating "Hallmark" holidays like Mothers' Day and civic celebrations like Independence Day. These are not bad in and of themselves, but we have plenty of opportunities to celebrate them elsewhere, whereas religious events such as Good Friday can only take place within a worship setting.

Liturgical worship is not a biblical imperative. However, we should all understand the basic patterns of worship and at least consider adapting some elements for our own churches.

For Discussion

1. Do you consider liturgy biblical? Why or why not?
2. If your church is not liturgical, how would it benefit from adopting intentional repeated patterns as described above? What would be lost?

7

The Church Year

Before you begin: Mark your calendar.

Does your church have annual worship services such as a Christmas Eve service? What about items such as Youth Sunday, elder commissioning, or Mother's Day that occur yearly within worship services? Make a calendar of all worship services and events that take place at your church every year. Double-check it with some church friends to make sure you remembered everything.

The church follows multiple cycles that could be thought of as a liturgical "orbit." The *church year*, also called the *liturgical calendar*, is an annual rotation of seasons (Christmas, Easter, and so forth). This yearly cycle of seasons is grouped into a three-year cycle of Bible readings called the *lectionary*. Each Sunday of the church year is a weekly pattern of gathering, hearing the Word, taking communion, and being sent out to serve.[1]

The church year unfolds in two broad sweeps. The first half of the cycle (from Advent to Easter) follows the life of Christ, and the second half (from Pentecost to Advent) follows the life of the church.

Whereas the civic calendar begins a new cycle on January 1, the liturgical calendar begins with the first Sunday in Advent. *Advent* ("coming") is

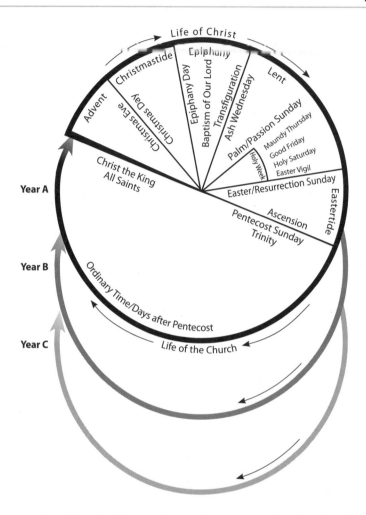

a season of waiting for Christ's incarnation. It starts four Sundays before Christmas and is often celebrated with Advent candles, Advent wreaths, and Jesse trees. Advent is not only a time to remember how Israel waited for the Messiah but also a season during which we wait for Christ's return. (Liturgical anamnesis in action!) Christmas was originally intended to be a season rather than just a day. *Christmastide* is the "Twelve Days of Christmas" during which we rejoice over the birth of our Lord.

Beginning January 6, *Epiphany* ("manifestation" or "to reveal") follows Christ through his earthly ministry, including his baptism, the visit of the

Magi, and his miracles. The stretch of time between Advent and Epiphany reminds us every year that we worship Emmanuel—God with us. Jesus, this God in flesh, grew in his mother's womb, learned a trade from his father, and walked the earth astounding people with his teaching and miracles. Epiphany concludes with *Transfiguration Sunday*, a glimpse of Christ's glory before his suffering.

Lent is a season of penance and preparation beginning forty days before Easter (not including Sundays). The season begins with *Ash Wednesday*, a reminder of our mortality, and then continues walking with Jesus through his forty days of temptation and the close of his earthly ministry. *Holy Week*, the last week of Christ's life, starts with *Palm Sunday*, also called Passion Sunday. Highly liturgical churches celebrate each day of Holy Week, but most observe only *Maundy Thursday*, a service of the upper room, and/ or *Good Friday*, which remembers Christ's crucifixion. Lent allows us to walk in the footsteps of Christ—in temptation, suffering, and the cross. It reminds us that we have an Advocate who was tempted like us (Heb. 4:14–16), that we share in Christ's suffering (Phil. 3:10; 1 Pet. 4:13), and that we daily take up our cross to follow Jesus (Luke 14:27).

The forty days of following Christ to the cross during Lent prepare us to more richly experience the season of *Eastertide*, a fifty-day season that begins with *Easter Sunday*. This is the crux of the church year and of Christianity. We share in Christ's sufferings and glory in Christ's cross but we live in the power of the resurrection. Eastertide concludes with *Ascension Sunday*, when Christ ascends to the Father in his humanity to intercede for us.

The conclusion of Christ's earthly work at the Ascension signals the beginning of the Holy Spirit's work among us. *Pentecost Sunday* celebrates the coming of the Holy Spirit and the foundation of the church. This initiates the second half of the church year, which follows the Spirit's work among God's people. Many liturgical churches call the Sundays between Pentecost Sunday and Advent *Ordinary Time*. Others give it the accurate but also uninspiring name *Days after Pentecost*. This section of the year doesn't enjoy the festive highlights of the first part of the year but rather allows us to settle into being God's people. At its heart, this is what the whole church year attempts to do: shape us over and over again into a church that looks more like Christ. Like clay on a potter's wheel, we are brought a little closer to the form of our Savior with each rotation of the wheel.

A further tool for shaping the church's annual calendar and expanding the use of Scripture in worship is the *lectionary*. There are a few variations of the lectionary; Lutherans, Roman Catholics, and Anglicans each have their own, while denominations that don't have a mandated lectionary mostly use the Revised Common Lectionary.[2] The lectionary is a three-year cycle of Scripture readings; each week has four Scripture readings (Old Testament, Psalm, Epistle, and Gospel) and each year leads worshipers through different parts of the Bible. For example, Year A focuses on the Gospel of Matthew, while Year B focuses on the Gospel of Mark and Year C on the Gospel of Luke. Likewise, the Old Testament readings cycle through the patriarchs, kings, and prophets. This allows worshipers to experience each year through a different scriptural lens, providing a richer experience of the church year and a robust cross section of Scripture.

One distinct advantage of using the lectionary is that numerous worship resources have been developed to go with the readings. These lectionary aids range from Scripture commentary to hymn suggestions. *Call to Worship*, for example, is an annual publication that includes suggestions for each week's service: prayers, congregational songs in a variety of styles, choral anthems, and organ preludes.[3] Similar aids can be found online. *The Text This Week* is a wealth of resources mapped out to the lectionary readings for each week.[4] Included are songs, artwork, and Bible commentary. The Center for Excellence in Preaching has "sermon starters" for each passage of the week's lectionary readings.[5] Since so many resources have been created for use with the lectionary, even worship planners who are not tied to the lectionary may find the resources useful. Look up a Scripture in a "reverse lectionary" (a Scripture index that shows which weeks in the lectionary use that Scripture) to find a wealth of resources based on that Scripture passage.[6]

It is important to remember the lectionary is only a tool. It serves us rather than the other way around. In fact, the three-year list of readings doesn't include the whole Bible. But while it is an imperfect tool, it is useful in disciplining our use of Scripture in worship. There are other tools; for example, preaching straight through a particular book of the Bible (*lectio continua).* Whatever system or approach each church takes, it should include substantial portions of Scripture from the entire Bible week after week, so the congregation hears the full witness of Scripture.

Churches from nonliturgical traditions may be attracted to traditional resources like the church year and the lectionary but don't know how to introduce them into their churches. The easiest way to begin is with what your church already knows. Most churches already celebrate Christmas and Easter day. Try introducing the seasons that anticipate these festive days: Advent before Christmas and Lent before Easter. Once a congregation has experienced the fullness of these seasons of preparation, they will likely be more receptive to the spiritual rhythms of the larger church year.

For Discussion

1. Compare your church's annual worship calendar to the church calendar described above. What are the similarities? Differences?

2. As you read about the church year and the lectionary, does it strike you that any biblical themes are missing from your own church's worship?

3. Whether your church uses the lectionary, *lectio continua,* or sermon series, is there a good balance of Scripture represented over time? Old Testament as well as New Testament? Epistles and prophets? Well-loved as well as perplexing passages?

8

The Fourfold Worship Order

Before you begin: Identify your church's liturgy.

Admit it. Your church has a liturgy. Even the most spontaneous churches inevitably fall into patterns that they repeat each week or each year. Write down your church's patterns in as much detail as you can. (It may be helpful to consult a bulletin, projection, or cue sheet from some previous services.) What is your basic worship order? Do some items remain absolutely consistent? Are some more flexible from week to week? Do certain items (communion, baptism) get inserted into the service only periodically? Write down each worship element in your church's services and then either share it in a group discussion or have a few members from your church check it for accuracy.

Just as two millennia of Christian worshipers have found the rhythms of the church calendar and lectionary to be helpful in shaping their faith, Christians since the early church have patterned their worship services according to what Robert Webber called the fourfold worship order: Gathering, Word, Table, and Sending.

The earliest believers were Jews. Even after their conversion they continued to attend synagogue on the Sabbath (Saturday)

Gathering

Word

Table

Sending

to study God's Word. They supplemented this with worship services on Sunday that celebrated Christ's resurrection with the Lord's Supper. When the beliefs of these early Christians put them at odds with local Jewish authorities, Christian believers combined these two basic gestures—Word and Table—into one service on Sundays. By the third century the Christian church had added Gathering and Sending elements to the Word and Table to establish the basic fourfold worship service still used today. The pendulum has swung throughout the history of the church, with the Table overshadowing all other elements in the medieval Roman Catholic Church and the Word taking precedence in many Protestant traditions, but overall Christian worship continues to center on Gathering, Word, Table, and Sending.

While this four-part structure is not biblically mandated, it developed throughout the church's history as a weekly rhythm that presents a balanced spiritual diet, nourishing a healthy Christian faith. If worship and life flow back and forth like blood through the body, then a fourfold service is the steady pumping of the heart of worship.

Gathering

The heartbeat begins with the Gathering. The most fundamental gesture of the Gathering is that God calls us to worship and we answer. You may protest, "Isn't all of life worship?" Yes, but in the worship service we are called by God from our scattered, individual lives into worship together as the body of Christ in one place. This is a concentrated, heightened experience of God's presence. It is not easy to move from our hectic everyday lives—worrying about money, trying to get the kids' hair combed, loading the family into the car—to sitting in a sanctuary ready to listen to the "still, small voice" of the Spirit.

Gathering

Prelude/Welcome

Call to Worship

Song

Confession/Forgiveness

The Gathering begins with elements to facilitate this transition: prelude, welcome, announcements, and gathering songs. They signal the start of the service, call people together, and shift our minds into attentiveness. Some of these are practical rather than liturgical elements. For example, a welcome or an-

nouncements are community build-
ers rather than formal parts of a worship service. This is not necessarily
bad. We need to be attentive to the
needs of worshipers (a new family
may never enter into worship if they
don't know where the nursery is), but
we also need to be careful that these
practical details don't overshadow
the rest of the service. We want to
be moving toward a profound, life-
changing encounter with the living,
Triune God.

The next step in this profound
encounter is the Call to Worship.

> ## First Words
>
> The Ship of Fools website has a
> series of reports from "church
> spies." Each report includes the
> answer to this question: What
> were the first words spoken in
> the service? While this may seem
> nitpicky, it says a lot about what a
> church hopes worship to be. What
> tone is set by, "Good morning!
> How's everyone doing today?"
> as opposed to, "The Lord be with
> you!" What are the first words in
> your church most Sundays?[1]

Though a human being pronounces these words, it is actually God who
calls us to worship. For this reason, it is most often taken from Scripture.
A classic Call to Worship is, "This is the day that the LORD has made; let
us rejoice and be glad in it" (Ps. 118:24). Different traditions have variations on this basic call-and-response pattern. For example, in the Reformed
tradition, the Call to Worship is followed by God's Greeting: "The grace
of the Lord Jesus Christ, the love of God, and the communion of the Holy
Spirit be with all of you" (2 Cor. 13:13). A Call to Worship not only establishes worship as an act of the Triune God but also sets up an important
rhythm of worship: call and response. We need to remember right from
the outset that it is God who motivates worship, not us. Worship is nothing we could do on our own. Like Samuel, when God calls our name all
we can do is say, "Speak, for your servant is listening" (1 Sam. 3:10). We
may respond by singing a song of praise, answering the leader's words, or
simply saying "Amen."

Having been called into God's very presence, we have a similar reaction
to Isaiah, who, in his vision of the Lord, exclaimed, "Woe is me! I am lost,
for I am a man of unclean lips, and I live among a people of unclean lips"
(Isaiah 6:5). In worship, this is called the Confession. We gaze on the holy
beauty of God and immediately understand the depth of our sinfulness.

Many see this exchange in Isaiah 6:1–8 as establishing the basic outline of worship: we encounter God, we confess our sin, our sins are forgiven, and we are sent out to do God's work in the world.

In the year that King Uzziah died, I saw the Lord sitting on a throne, high and lofty; and the hem of his robe filled the temple. Seraphs were in attendance above him; each had six wings: with two they covered their faces, and with two they covered their feet, and with two they flew. And one called to another and said:

"Holy, holy, holy is the Lord of hosts;
the whole earth is full of his glory."

The pivots on the thresholds shook at the voices of those who called, and the house filled with smoke. And I said: "Woe is me! I am lost, for I am a man of unclean lips, and I live among a people of unclean lips; yet my eyes have seen the King, the Lord of hosts!"

Then one of the seraphs flew to me, holding a live coal that had been taken from the altar with a pair of tongs. The seraph touched my mouth with it and said: "Now that this has touched your lips, your guilt has departed and your sin is blotted out." Then I heard the voice of the Lord saying, "Whom shall I send, and who will go for us?" And I said, "Here am I; send me!"

This is our opportunity to remind ourselves of the fundamental truth of the Christian faith: Christ's death and resurrection have accomplished what we ourselves could never do. We can't be holy on our own. We can't approach God on our own. But thanks be to God, Jesus Christ has become our righteousness. The Confession, then, is not a time for us to beat ourselves up for the ways we've failed God and neighbor throughout the previous week. Instead it is an opportunity for us to recalibrate ourselves to the truth: though we are sinners, God is gracious and has forgiven us—and will continue to forgive us—in Jesus Christ. We reaffirm that God is God and we are not.

A full Confession sequence has four elements: Call to Confession, Confession (Penitence), Assurance of Pardon (Absolution, Words of Forgiveness), and Gloria (either a *Gloria in Excelsis Deo* from the mass or a more general song of thanksgiving for the work of Christ). If your denomination recommends specific words or forms for the confession sequence, that's great, but it is also fine to simply improvise on this basic pattern. The style and form are not as important as giving our congregations a vocabulary for getting right with God. Our people come to church with heavy burdens. Church services that are always upbeat and happy give them the impression that they need to get their act together before coming to God. This is poisonous to the life of faith. Instead, we want to remind our people they serve a merciful God. In worship and in life, we need to take responsibility for our actions, say we're sorry (and mean it!), be grateful for forgiveness, and commit to changing our ways.

Word

Having been called into God's presence and having reminded ourselves of our complete dependence on the work of Christ and the power of the Holy Spirit, we are ready to hear from the life-giving Word of God. In many churches this is simply a sermon. Let me gently suggest that if you're getting only a sermon, you're having a meal without the appetizers or dessert! The historic pattern for the Service of the Word fills in the sermon with a more robust experience of preparing, hearing, and responding to the Word.

We begin with a Prayer for Illumination. This may be as simple as the pastor praying or reciting Scripture before preaching. A classic pastoral Prayer of Illumination comes from Psalm 19:14: "Let the words of my mouth and the meditation of my heart be acceptable to you, O Lord, my rock and my redeemer." Other churches may want to sing or speak it together: "Lord, to whom can we go? You have the words of eternal life" (John 6:68) or "Your word is a lamp to my feet and a light to my path" (Psalm 119:105). No matter what format you use for the Prayer of Illumination, it serves the important function of asking the Spirit to give us ears to hear the Word. This is no small thing. Too often we approach the Word of God as a textbook to be studied like any other, or a mysterious tome that only the pastor can decipher. No, the Bible is the very Word of God meant for all of us. The Spirit grants the preacher special gifts of teaching and grants the rest of the congregation special gifts of hearing. That's what

Word
Prayer for Illumination
Scripture Reading
Sermon
Sermon Response (song, prayer)
Affirmation of Faith
Intercessory Prayers

the Prayer of Illumination does—it places our trust entirely in the Spirit's work when preaching and hearing the Word.

The Scripture reading follows. In a highly liturgical church, this can include as many as four readings: Old Testament, Psalm, Epistle, and Gospel, with songs and prayers interspersed. Other churches may have one reading (the sermon Scripture) or the preacher might simply weave the Scripture throughout the sermon. Whatever method is used, we should attempt to give weight and dignity to the reading of Scripture. Read each passage clearly and with great love. We don't add anything to God's Word by overemoting, but we can certainly convey a contagious sense of awe and attention as God speaks to us. Always err on the side of using more rather than less Scripture in worship. Maybe your church isn't ready for four readings every Sunday, but certainly a sermon from the New Testament would benefit by a related Old Testament passage or Psalm. It is a shame that in many churches sermons have gotten longer while Scripture reading has gotten shorter. The sermon should serve the Scripture rather than the other way around. (For a more in-depth discussion about reading Scripture well in worship, see chapter 13, "The Gospel Enacted: Drama and Wordsmithing.")

> If you're not quite sure how to get started with Prayers for Illumination and other parts of the service, you will find a treasure trove of prayers and readings in *The Worship Sourcebook, 2nd ed.* (Grand Rapids: Faith Alive Christian Resources, 2013).

The subject of preaching is beyond the scope of this book. However, the sermon is an important part of worship, so we'll look at it in that context. One of the liabilities of the sermon-dominated service structure that has developed over the last century is it places incredible pressure on the sermon and preacher. When a sermon is three or four times as long as the rest of the worship service, the clear message conveyed is that the sermon is where the real spiritual work is done, and the rest of worship is simply warm up and cool down. This is a great loss for everyone. The preacher takes on the whole burden of the congregation's spiritual formation while other possible avenues are minimized. Further, a sermon-dominated service concentrates on only one mode of experiencing God's presence. The mind is an important part of our spiritual formation, but we need to support it with physical, emotional, communal, and intuitive ways of knowing God.

We should always strive for better balance and deeper connections. Could the pastor rely more on Scripture readings, hymns, and other worship elements to "preach"? Are visual learners or physical processors left out by the predominantly verbal modes of the sermon? While this may sound like an attempt to minimize the Word in worship, it is actually advocating the exact opposite. The Word needs to speak in every part of the service. This will not only strengthen the message throughout the service but also provide a richer context for the preaching.

Finally, the sermon needs to preach the Word. People can find no end of good life advice on TV and in magazines. Sometimes the words of Scripture contain good marital or financial advice, but more often they're perplexing and difficult, calling us to "enter through the narrow gate . . . that leads to life" (Matt. 7:13–14). John Calvin believed that when preachers stepped into the pulpit, they took on a prophetic voice that, in a sense, became the living Word of God. You may not see preaching in quite such bright light as Calvin, but certainly we should expect sermons to be profoundly biblical.

Following the sermon, there are a number of appropriate forms of sermon response: a Prayer of Application, a moment of Silent Reflection, or

---

Recommended Books on Preaching

St. Augustine, *On Christian Doctrine* (Pickerington, OH: Beloved Publishing, 2014).

Frederick Buechner, *Telling the Truth* (New York: Harper & Row, 1977).

Fred Craddock, *Preaching* (Nashville: Abingdon Press, 2010).

Scott Hoezee, *Actuality: Real Life Stories for Sermons That Matter* (Nashville: Abingdon Press, 2014).

Peter Jonker, *Preaching in Pictures: Using Images for Sermons that Connect* (Nashville: Abingdon Press, 2015).

D. Martyn Lloyd-Jones, *Preaching and Preachers* (Grand Rapids: Zondervan, 2011).

Thomas Long, *The Witness of Preaching* (Louisville, KY: Westminster John Knox Press, 2005).

Michael Quicke, *Preaching as Worship* (Grand Rapids: Baker, 2011).

John Stott, *Between Two Worlds: The Art of Preaching in the Twentieth Century* (Grand Rapids: Eerdmans, 1994).

Barbara Brown Taylor, *The Preaching Life* (Lanham, MD: Rowman & Littlefield Publishers, Inc. 1993).

Frank Thomas, *They Like to Never Quit Praisin' God* (Cleveland, OH: Pilgrim Press, 2013).

Paul Scott Wilson, *Preaching as Poetry: Beauty, Goodness, and Truth in Every Sermon* (Nashville: Abingdon Press, 2014).

a Song of Response or Reflection all allow the Word to settle into hearers' hearts. Although It's not a traditional part of the fourfold worship pattern, an Altar Call or similar means of letting people commit to live the words they've just heard is entirely reasonable.

Filling out the Service of the Word is an Affirmation of Faith (Creed) and the Intercessory (pastoral, congregational) Prayer. While a congregational Affirmation of Faith may seem like too much of a good thing after the sermon, it serves to summarize the gospel. That is, we've heard the Word preached to this specific congregation in the sermon, and now we finish by summarizing what the church universal has believed throughout the ages. It serves as a powerful antidote to the "me and Jesus" mentality that so quickly creeps in at the local church level; it reminds us we're part of a larger communion and share the faith with others throughout the world and the ages.

The Intercessory Prayer has traditionally been placed after the sermon because our prayers are, fundamentally, a response to the Word of God in our lives. We pray that God would give us the faith to live according to the Word we've heard. We pray to a God who has responded to believers in the past and trust that God will hear our prayers too. Knowing that the God of Scripture is merciful, we pray for healing, peace, and wisdom. Because of the scriptural witness, we don't narrow our prayers to those within our church walls but also pray for those who God has put in authority over us (1 Tim. 2:1–2) and pray for our enemies (Matt. 5:44). This is our opportunity to take part in God's work in our lives and the whole world. Pray confidently and expansively!

Whether or not your church observes all the "official" post-sermon sections of worship, it is important that people are allowed to respond to the Word. The difference between a sermon and a common public lecture is

> ## Further Reading on Public Prayer
>
> Timothy J. Mulder, *So You've Been Asked to . . . Lead in Prayer* (Grand Rapids: Faith Alive, 1996).
>
> Hughes Oliphant Old, *Leading in Prayer: A Workbook for Worship* (Grand Rapids: Eerdmans, 1995).
>
> John Pritchard, *Intercessions Handbook,* reissued ed. (London: SPCK, 2011).
>
> Laurence Hull Stookey, *Let the Whole Church Say Amen!: A Guide for Those Who Pray in Public* (Nashville: Abingdon Press, 2001).

that in the sermon God is speaking to us directly. A lecture doesn't obligate us to respond, but the Word of God does.

Table

The Service of the Table section of the fourfold liturgy will be most foreign to nonliturgical churches, so it will be helpful to begin by explaining why some churches have found weekly communion to be a vital part of their faith. Broadly speaking, churches that observe communion once a month or less come from the memorial tradition (Baptist, Pentecostal, evangelical), and those that celebrate it on a weekly basis come from liturgical or "sacramental" traditions (Catholic, Orthodox, and some mainline Protestants).[2] The memorial tradition generally calls the event communion (sometimes "the Lord's Supper") and sees the communion elements as no more than symbols of Christ's sacrifice. It is an ordinance,

Table
Invitation to the Table
Preparation of the Table
Great Prayer of Thanksgiving
Passing of the Peace
Preparing the Elements
Invitation to the Table
Distribution of the Elements (Communion)
Prayer after Communion

or something worshipers do because it is commanded. ("Do this in remembrance.") The liturgical tradition names it the Eucharist or "the Table (of the Lord)," understanding it as spiritual sustenance. It is a sacrament; a physical sign that does a work of a spiritual grace.[3]

Instead of trying to explain two thousand years of contentious communion theology, it may be more helpful to describe my own journey from a monthly memorialist to someone who finds weekly communion an important part of my faith.

My formative years were spent in an independent Pentecostal church. When I was young, I didn't think much about communion—it was just something we did at church periodically. I certainly didn't think about the theology of communion. (As my church saw it, "theology" was something people did when they no longer believed the Bible!) We were suspicious of any tradition other than our own: Baptists would probably get to heaven (though not with the fullness of the Spirit we enjoyed), but we didn't expect

A Range of Communion Practices

Memorial			Sacrament
Baptist, Pentecostal, Evangelical	Reformed/Mainline	Lutheran, Catholic, Orthodox	
Communion	Lord's Supper	Table of the Lord	Eucharist
Quarterly/Monthly			Weekly/Daily
Grape Juice			Wine

to meet many Catholics, Episcopalians, or Presbyterians in eternity. (Forgive me. My world was very small.)

Given my history, I had more reasons to be wary of a sacramental view of communion than to be drawn to it. However, as time went on, communion left me with more questions than answers. Communion was a somber experience, with subdued organ music playing while men in dark suits quietly handed out little plastic cups of grape juice and bread cubes. A good deal of emphasis was placed on examining our hearts to make sure we weren't taking communion in an unworthy manner (1 Cor. 11:27–32). If our hearts were not right, we would be eating and drinking damnation, as the King James Version puts it. Of course I wanted my heart to be right, but I still didn't know what role communion played in that process. My discomfort came to a head one day when I visited a church that passed out bread wafers the size and shape of pills and plastic cups of grape juice vacuum sealed with a foil top.[4] The person passing out the elements waited as each person took communion, looking away modestly like a nurse waiting for a urine sample. *There must be something more to this!* I thought.

While there is biblical support for searching one's heart and other aspects of this approach to communion, later reflection revealed some fundamental tensions in what I had experienced. The funereal atmosphere emphasized—perhaps unintentionally—the crucifixion of Christ over the resurrection. Yes, Christ died for my sins, but he now lives and reigns in resurrection power. It is in that resurrection power that I live. In the words of the beloved Easter hymn, "I serve a risen Savior."[5] Of course, the crucifixion and resurrection need to be kept in balance. But I found the balance tipping backward toward death rather than forward toward life. A ritual that focused primarily on Christ's death and my role in it made me dredge up my sins each month. Romans 6:10 says that Jesus died "once for all," but I found myself recrucifying Christ each month in order to feel the full weight of the pain I caused him on the cross. I became exhausted trying to make the memorial meaningful through my self-examination and remorse. Of course, my spiritual fatigue makes sense: Christ has completed the work of salvation, and there's nothing we can add to it with our spiritual fervor and nothing we can take away from it with a lack of focus. While I'm sure many have had satisfying experiences in a memorial communion context, I was longing for something more life-giving.

I found it in the Eucharist. *Eucharist* may sound like some highfalutin' mumbo jumbo, but the word simply means "communion" in liturgical churches. More specifically, it comes from the Greek word for *thanksgiving* as found in 1 Corinthians: "For I received from the Lord what I also handed on to you, that the Lord Jesus on the night when he was betrayed took a loaf of bread, and when he had *given thanks*, he broke it and said, 'This is my body that is for you. Do this in remembrance of me'" (11:23–24, emphasis added). The root meaning of the word *Eucharist* gets at the heart of the difference that I felt when experiencing this form of communion: it was full of thanksgiving rather than remorse. It was full of joy rather than mourning. It was full of life.

> For another person's journey into liturgical worship and a sacramental understanding of communion, read Glenn Packiam's *Discover the Mystery of Faith: How Worship Shapes Believing* (Colorado Springs: David C. Cook, 2013).

What made the Eucharist feel so full of life for me? For one thing, the words, songs, and spirit of the Eucharist joyfully celebrated Christ's resurrection rather than somberly observing Christ's death. Though Christ's crucifixion will always be part of the narrative, the story ends well. This makes the Eucharist a celebration of new life in Christ; a service of thanksgiving for God's mercy. The focus is not on the past but on how Christ feeds us for the journey ahead.

My personal experience, however, won't resolve thorny theological questions. Christ giving himself as spiritual food is one of the sticking points of the Eucharist for many memorialists. How can we eat Christ's body? Isn't that crucifying Christ all over again at best—or cannibalism at worst?

After all, a memorialist would point out, at the first Lord's Supper, Jesus said, "Do this in remembrance of me" (Luke 22:19). Yes, but he also said, "Take, eat; this is my body" (Matt. 26:26). Elsewhere Jesus said, "Very truly, I tell you, unless you eat the flesh of the Son of Man and drink his blood, you have no life in you" (John 6:53). These are difficult words. It wasn't long after this that "many of his disciples turned back" (v. 66).

There is biblical precedent for both views; hence, the unsettled controversy over the centuries. Too often, memorialists misunderstand those who believe in Christ's "real presence" in the elements. They think that they all adhere to transubstantiation, which is the traditional Catholic belief that the consecrated bread and wine actually become the body and blood of Jesus Christ. However, there is a wide range of views among those who subscribe to real presence. The Lutherans believe in consubstantiation, that Jesus is present in, with, and under the elements. Calvinists believe the elements *spiritually* become the body and blood of Christ. These beliefs transcend logic. The theology of the real presence, like the Trinity, is perhaps better approached as a mystery of faith rather than a problem to be solved.

Where all real presence approaches agree is that Jesus Christ is present (in some form) in the communion, offering himself as spiritual food. That is, the Eucharist is something *Christ does*, rather than something *we do*. That is what sealed the deal for me. I was worn out trying to put meaning into the symbols of communion and was ready to rest myself entirely in the finished work of Christ. Christ died for me and rose again for me, and until he comes again for me to bring me into his eternal presence, he offers me a weekly feast in which he is both host and meal. This has nourished my faith in a way that a memorial communion never did.

Is it farfetched to believe that a simple chunk of bread can be true spiritual food for the Christian life? Yes. But is it any less farfetched that the eternal Son of God could become a man who died and came back to life?

In the end, those who believe in a memorial and those who believe in real presence have something important in common: faith. Ultimately, faith is what tipped me into the real presence camp. Christians believe some pretty mysterious things by faith. But I discovered that some Christians wanted to eliminate anything mysterious from worship itself. I find it helpful, week after week, to experience something in worship I can't fully understand or

Further Reading on the Theology and Practice of Communion

Baptism, Eucharist, and Ministry (Geneva: World Council of Churches, 1982).

Gary Macy, *The Banquet's Wisdom: A Short History of the Theologies of the Lord's Supper* (Ashland City, TN: OSL Publications, 1992).

Alexander Schmemann, *For the Life of the World* (Crestwood, NY: St. Vladimir's Seminary Press, 1963).

Gordon T. Smith, *A Holy Meal: The Lord's Supper in the Life of the Church* (Grand Rapids, Baker Academic, 2005).

Lawrence Hull Stookey, *Eucharist* (Nashville: Abingdon Press, 1993).

Leonard J. Vander Zee, *Christ, Baptism and the Lord's Supper: Recovering the Sacraments for Evangelical Worship*, (Downers Grove, IL: InterVarsity Press, 2004).

John D. Witvliet, "Covenant Theology in Ecumenical Discussions of the Lord's Supper," *Worship Seeking Understanding: Windows into Christian Practices* (Grand Rapids: Baker Academic, 2003).

N. T. Wright, "N. T. Wright on Word and Sacraments: The Eucharist," *Reformed Worship*, March 2009, http://reformedworship.org/article/march-2009/nt-wright-word-and -sacraments-eucharist).

control. Christ stands at the door and knocks. My only work is to answer the door. Mysteriously and wonderfully, Christ invites me to eat with him (Rev. 3:20).

As a worship director, I have found that weekly celebration of the Eucharist helps bring healthy balance to worship services. Weekly Eucharist requires a balance of Word and Table that restores the heart of the historic fourfold pattern and begins to even out the sections of worship that are head-dominated and those that are heart-dominated. Further, I found that as worshipers begin to trust the mysterious riches of the Table, they also begin to place more weight on every other part of the service. Intercessory prayer isn't just a list of well-wishes but actually us taking part in God's work on the earth. The benediction isn't just a nice way to end a service but a palpable blessing from God. This has brought a profound sense of importance to every moment of the service.

I don't expect readers to convert from their current communion practice based on my story. However, we can all benefit from understanding the broader spectrum of communion theology and practice. A Eucharistic approach to communion has been the practice of the church from as early as the second century.[6] It warrants a closer look.

While there are nearly as many variations as there are churches, most Eucharistic communion orders follow these general contours. First, communion begins with an invitation to, and preparation of, the table. The *Invitation to the Table* is often based on 1 Corinthians 11:23–26:

> For I received from the Lord what I also handed on to you, that the Lord Jesus on the night when he was betrayed took a loaf of bread, and when he had given thanks, he broke it and said, "This is my body that is for you. Do this in remembrance of me." In the same way he took the cup also, after supper, saying, "This cup is the new covenant in my blood. Do this, as often as you drink it, in remembrance of me." For as often as you eat this bread and drink the cup, you proclaim the Lord's death until he comes.

This serves both as an introduction to this section of the service and as a biblical foundation for the sacrament itself. Other churches may provide a similar invitation but in the form of a litany or a more free-form style. In a sense, the invitation functions similarly to the call to worship at the beginning of the service. It makes it clear that God calls us to the table, and that our only contribution is our joyous participation.

While some congregations assemble the bread and wine on the communion table before the service starts, many make this a part of the service itself. The Preparation of the Table may include a procession to the table with the elements as well as a prayer and a hymn. Interestingly, in the early church the Giving of Tithes and Offerings was combined with the preparation of the communion elements. People's gifts were brought forward, used in communion, and distributed to the needy shortly thereafter. This is a beautiful intermingling of God's gifts and our gifts, God's work and our work, God's mercy shown to us and shared with others. We lose a wonderful opportunity for responding to God's love when the offering is removed from worship or relegated to automatic bank withdrawals.

The Great Prayer of Thanksgiving is an extended prayer that prepares communion. It is one of the oldest and most beautiful prayers of

---

The Sursum Corda

The Lord be with you.
And also with you.
Lift up your hearts.
We lift them up to the Lord.
Let us give thanks to the Lord
   our God.
**It is right for us to give
   thanks and praise.**

the church, with a heartfelt call and response of Trinitarian thanksgiving shared between the pastor (or priest or liturgist) and congregation. It begins with the *Sursum Corda*, so named for the phrase, "Lift up your hearts." The Great Prayer continues with a section of thanksgiving for God's great deeds. Then the congregation responds with the *Sanctus*, a song that echoes the angel's song in Isaiah 6:3, "Holy, holy, holy is the LORD." Next, the

> ## The Sanctus
>
> Holy, holy, holy Lord,
> God of power and might,
> heaven and earth are full of
>   your glory.
> Hosanna in the highest.
> Blessed is he who comes in the
>   name of the Lord.
> Hosanna in the highest.

pastor gives thanks for Christ's redemptive work. If not included earlier, this includes the Words of Institution ("On the night he was betrayed. . . . Do this in remembrance of me"). The people respond with the Memorial Acclamation: "Christ has died, Christ is risen, Christ will come again," a succinct creed if there ever was one. The Great Prayer ends with thanksgiving for the Holy Spirit's work, focusing especially on the Spirit's work in the mystery of sacrament. This is called the Prayer of Consecration. This robust three-part prayer ends with the quintessential Lord's Prayer.

After this extended vertical prayer between God and the people, the service takes a decidedly horizontal turn: the Passing of the Peace. This is not just a time to greet visitors or catch up with friends but part of our spiritual work as worshipers. Just as God has made peace with us through Jesus Christ, we share that peace with one another. God's peace is never only personal: the two phrases of the angel's song in Luke always belong together: "Glory to God in the highest heaven, and on earth peace among those whom he favors!" (Luke 2:14). The horizontal and vertical dimensions of God's peace are always present but are especially vivid within the Eucharist, in which we remember the great cost of reconciliation in Jesus Christ. Typically, people turn to one another and exchange words such as "The peace of the Lord be with you," "And also with you." This exchange reflects themes of reconciliation and unity of the body of Christ that are important during communion (Matt. 5:23–24). Worship traditions that don't have a substantial confession section earlier in the service may have a more extended time of confession here or elsewhere in the communion liturgy so that participants may examine their hearts for sins against God or neighbor.

Especially in traditions that believe in the real presence, Preparing the Elements is the apex of the communion liturgy. In fact, in the medieval Catholic church, a bell was rung as the bread was broken, signaling the moment of transubstantiation. This is followed by singing the *Agnus Dei*: "Lamb of God, who takes away the sins of the world, have mercy on us." After the pastor breaks the bread and pours the wine, the only thing remaining is to invite people to come. This is called the Invitation to the Table. In some churches this is as short as, "All things are ready. The gifts of God for the people of God." Others make a point of "fencing the table." That is, if we can eat and drink judgment against ourselves by taking communion unworthily (1 Cor. 11:27–32), we should be clear about who should and should not be taking part. Fencing the table draws a clear border that focuses on who should stay away; most churches today prefer an invitation that focuses on who is welcome (any member of our denomination, all Christians, and so forth).

> ## Preparing the Elements
>
> [breaking the bread] The bread that we break is our sharing in the body of Christ.
> **We who are many are one body, for we all share the same loaf.**
> [pouring the cup] The cup for which we give thanks is our sharing in the blood of Christ.
> **The cup that we drink is our participation in the blood of Christ.**

With that the Distribution of the Elements begins. There is no end to the variations in distributing the bread and the cup. In some churches the people walk forward to take communion. This emphasizes our response and participation in the sacrament. Worshipers may kneel at an altar rail while the pastor gives them the elements directly—highlighting our humility before God's gifts. They may pass the elements to the person beside them, focusing on the fellowship we share with our brothers and sisters in Christ. Worshipers may remain in their seats and pass the elements down the row, waiting until everyone is served. This reflects our unity in Christ but also provides opportunity for personal reflection.

The elements themselves may be any "fruit of the vine" but tend to be either red wine or grape juice. Sometimes the wine is mixed with water, reminding us of the water and blood that flowed from the side of our Lord at his crucifixion and also indicating the Spirit's role in the sacrament. Decisions tend to be based on pastoral concerns (the presence of children and recovering alcoholics) or church tradition (Holiness churches are tee-totalers) rather than on biblical command.

Bread options are less contentious but just as varied: matzos or other crackers reflect the "unleavened bread" that Jesus would have used at the Last Supper (though saltines would not have been an option in Jesus's time). Pulling a piece from a loaf provides a more visceral experience of the communion bread and connects the commonness of eating to the mystery of the sacrament. Some churches place efficiency and hygiene before spiritual symbolism, using cubed bread, wafers, or vacuum-sealed packets of juice and wafer.

There is no right or wrong way to lead this ritual, but we should remember that the physicality of eating and drinking with our brothers and sisters is part of what Jesus intended for communion. This, it seems, was one of the major points of the Last Supper. By using everyday food, Jesus was reminding his disciples, "I am the bread of life" (John 6:48). By instituting the sacrament among his gathered disciples, Jesus showed us that we are one body. This sense of unity and community can be emphasized by simple words spoken to fellow worshipers as we share the elements: "Greg, the body of Christ given for you."

After everyone has participated in both bread and cup, we do what any guest does who has experienced a rich feast: we thank the host. The Prayer after Communion is our thanksgiving for God's gift to us in Jesus Christ that we have just experienced in the sacrament. This may be a responsive prayer, it may be a psalm such as the oft-used Psalm 103:1: "Bless the LORD, O my soul; and all that is within me, bless his holy name," or it may simply be a hymn of praise.

Prayer after Communion

Eternal God, you have graciously accepted us as living members of your Son, our Savior, Jesus Christ, and you have fed us with spiritual food in the sacrament of his body and blood. Send us now into the world in peace, and grant us strength and courage to love and serve you with gladness and single-ness of heart, through Christ, our Lord. **Amen.**

We shouldn't feel burdened by this complex Eucharistic liturgy. We are neither more complete Christians if we use it in its entirety nor second-class worshipers if we don't. Instead, try to understand the spirit at its heart. This basic form has served the church well for thousands of years; certainly there is something here that could enrich our own church's worship! Do we assemble the worship elements in a way that creates a reverent environment? Are the words we speak before communion a winsome invitation into Trinitarian community at the table? Do we offer opportunity for worshipers to celebrate the reconciling peace of God with each other? Do we make it clear who is invited to participate in the sacrament? Do the actions we take and elements we use during communion communicate what we intend?

Too often when churches hold communion it feels tacked on to the "real" service and driven by a sense of somber obligation. Is it any wonder our people don't look forward to communion Sunday? Whatever choices we make about the logistics of communion, it should convey a sense of mystery, delight, and spiritual immanence. As one priest said to a friend, "In the Eucharist the separation between heaven and earth is wafer thin!"

Sending

The final section of the fourfold liturgy, the Sending, is also the shortest. We've gathered as the people of God, we've fed on the Word in sermon and sacrament, and now we are sent out to be the body of Christ in the world. The Sending can be thought of as the bookend to the Gathering. Just as God called us together in the Gathering, God sends us out in the Sending. That is, our worship service and our worship in life both begin with God's action rather than our own.

Sending

The Charge
Song of Sending/Blessing
Benediction

The Sending begins with the Charge, also known as the Call to Service or Commissioning. It can be as simple as "Go in peace to love and serve the Lord" or as complex as an extended scriptural exhortation such as the Great Commission (Matt. 28:19–20). The gist of this charge is always "Go!" God has made it clear throughout the scriptural witness that our faith is not for ourselves. The love we receive from God is always "paid forward" to others, whether through evangelism (Acts 1:8; "to the ends of the earth"), justice (Mic. 6:8; "do justice, love kindness, walk humbly"), or the day-to-day fruit of faith (James 2:26; "faith without works is dead"). Often the congregation responds with a Song of Dedication, which is their way of saying, "Yes, we'll go!"

Finally, the pastor sends the people out with the Benediction (blessing, "God's good word"). This mirrors the Call to Worship at the beginning of the service. Like the Call to Worship, the Benediction is most often trinitarian, reminding us once more of the nature of the God who sends us out, and taken from Scripture, making it clear that the pastor is speaking God's blessing rather than his or her own. The congregation may respond with "Amen" or "Thanks be to God," but their real response to God's blessing is to live faithfully for God throughout the coming week.

> ### Benediction
>
> The grace of the Lord Jesus Christ, the love of God, and the communion of the Holy Spirit be with all of you (2 Cor. 13:13).

Called by God. Sent by God. The heart of the Christian faith—worship—beats again and again, sustaining and strengthening the people of God.

For Discussion

1. Does your church follow this fourfold worship pattern? If not, what could you learn from this historic norm? Make a list of all the worship elements in this chapter that are not included in your church's worship. Are there any that would enrich your worship if you added them to your worship order?

2. Discuss: "The liturgy serves us rather than us serving the liturgy."

3. Readers will generally fall into one of two camps: those who believe we are enriched by following historical worship patterns like those described above, and those who want local churches to have the freedom to do what suits their context. Choose a side and defend it: How does your side make you a better worshiper? How does it make you a better follower of Christ?

4. Play "Survivor: Liturgical Edition." Which of the following worship elements would you eliminate first? Announcements, confession, creed, Lord's Supper, prayer, prelude, and sermon. Continue eliminating elements until only one remains.

9

The Psalms in Worship

Before you begin: How are the psalms used in your church?

Did your church sing, read, or recite a psalm last Sunday? (Not a phrase of a psalm or something psalm-like, but a whole psalm or a substantial portion of one.) How often have you used the psalms in worship in the last month or year? In what form (song, responsive reading, sermon topic) does your church use them?

In the broader life of the Christian church, asking the question "Do the psalms still have a place in worship?" would be nonsensical. Throughout the church's history, psalms have formed the backbone of congregational singing, and many churches have adhered exclusively to psalm-singing. These churches would have asked an entirely different question: Do hymns and praise songs have a place in worship? While there are still traditions that regularly make use of the psalms in worship, it is clear that the tide has turned; many modern worshipers would be hard-pressed to name one song they sing in church that is based on a psalm.

Is this just a simple matter of musical styles changing over the years? Psalms replaced by hymns replaced by gospel songs replaced by praise songs? Yes and no. It is natural that church music will change over the years. Certainly worship has been enriched by new song styles. Protestants (the source of most of these popular new hymns and songs) are known for their singing, and it is due to a strong tradition of singable tunes carrying rich texts. In fact, Thomas Day, himself a Catholic, commends Protestant hymnody in his provocative book *Why Catholics Can't Sing* for being "good, wholesome, plain, homely music."[1] Whether the hymns of Wesley in the eighteenth century, the gospel songs of Crosby in the nineteenth century, or the praise anthems of Tomlin in the twentieth century, these simple songs have provided us a way to express ourselves to God in our musical heart language. But have we lost our connection to the psalms as the wellspring of worship song?

Why Sing the Psalms?

You may wonder why we would want to sing the psalms in worship when we have so many hymns that have stood the test of time and praise songs that have gone platinum. Why trade something we know and love for something foreign and difficult?

First, the psalms give us a vocabulary of faith. Our faith is profoundly difficult to express. We enter into our new life like babies, having no experience and no words to articulate what we encounter. Like babies, we need to grow beyond self-centered screaming toward mature communication. But how do we do that unless we are taught how to express ourselves? Like a child hearing his or her parents communicate, we are given a chance through the psalms to listen in on our elders' conversations with God. Here we find what is appropriate to say to God. (It turns out few emotions are off-limits!) We discover words for questions we haven't quite been able to articulate. We build a repertoire of responses for what we experience in a robust life of faith.

In his book, *Through the Language Glass: How Words Colour Your World*, linguist Guy Deutscher shows how language can affect the way we perceive our world. He tells the story of the Guugu Yimithirr language of Australia, which has no words for left, right, front, or back, but instead orients all directional language to the compass. "Look out for that careening bus from the south!" seems unwieldy to me, but speakers of this language certainly are more aware of their relational location than I ever will be. In a *New York Times* article, Deutscher puts it this way:

> When your language routinely obliges you to specify certain types of information, it forces you to be attentive to certain details in the world and to certain aspects of experience that speakers of other languages may not be required to think about all the time. And since such habits of speech are cultivated from the earliest age, it is only natural that they can settle into habits of *mind* that go beyond language itself, affecting your experiences, perceptions, associations, feelings, memories and orientation in the world.[2]

Doesn't this sound like what Christians hope to cultivate when called to be "filled with the knowledge of God's will in all spiritual wisdom and understanding" (Col. 1:9) or compared to "trees planted by streams of water, which yield their fruit in its season, and their leaves do not wither" (Ps. 1:3)? The more we immerse ourselves in the psalms, the more vocabulary we have to engage in God's reality on God's terms.

However, the vocabulary of faith that the psalms offer is different than our everyday vocabulary. It is no accident that the psalms are songs. The arts have always allowed us to explore the deeper things of life that reason can't quite reach. Just as a great book or painting allows us to explore the depths of our own souls or put ourselves in someone else's shoes, the psalms open up new pathways for our own spiritual awareness. We wonder how the psalmist knew about our homesickness when sitting "by the Babylonian rivers." We are given permission and language to question God: "How long, O LORD? How long?" We may even be exposed to emotions that are completely new to us: rage, contrition, or complete rest.

We can think of the psalms as the whole of the Bible distilled into poetry. They are the emotional echo of Scripture—a theology of the heart. Certainly the New Testament writers saw it this way, quoting copiously from the psalms. They immersed themselves in the psalms to the point that psalm language flowed from them as they wrote. Even Jesus communicated through the psalms. When he cries, "My God, my God, why have you forsaken me?" from the cross, he is clearly invoking Psalm 22. Given that in Jesus's time psalms were known by their opening lines rather than numbers, it is very likely Jesus quoted that first line of Psalm 22 intending hearers to consider the whole psalm. Very striking, when you consider that Psalm 22 ends with these words:

> To him, indeed, shall all who sleep in the earth bow down;
>> before him shall bow all who go down to the dust,
>> and I shall live for him.
> Posterity will serve him;
>> future generations will be told about the Lord,
> and proclaim his deliverance to a people yet unborn,
>> saying that he has done it. (vv. 29–31)

Second, the psalms disconnect us from our own cultural and personal perspectives. Every culture suffers from myopia. We see some things clearly but can't perceive other things at all. Some aspects of our culture are wonderfully redeemed and other parts are dreadfully sinful. Though the psalms, too, come from a particular culture, they are the inspired Word of God. We can trust that immersing ourselves in the psalms introduces us to God's perspective, which transcends culture. Using the psalms in their entirety forces us to grapple with biblical perspectives that may not come naturally

---

Do the psalms still speak today? Ask Shane, who wandered the streets of Seattle, looking for his next high, until God rescued him. Shane now claims Psalm 107 for his own:

> Has the Lord redeemed you? Then speak out!
>> Tell others he has redeemed you from your enemies.
> For he has gathered the exiles from many lands,
>> from east and west,
>> from north and south.
>
> Some wandered in the wilderness,
>> lost and homeless.
> Hungry and thirsty,
>> they nearly died.
> "Lord, help!" they cried in their trouble,
>> and he rescued them from their distress.
> He led them straight to safety,
>> to a city where they could live. (Ps. 107:2–7 NLT)

to us. For example, American culture knows little of suffering and tries its best to separate itself from death and pain in every form. The Psalms of Lament help modern Americans verbalize our fears and struggles in a way that our culture doesn't allow. Even when we ourselves are not suffering, the psalms tune our ears to those who are.

Every person, too, has a unique way of seeing the world. Our differences make us who we are but still must be submitted to biblical reality. For example, it is easy for me to recognize the hand of God in creation: "The heavens are telling the glory of God" (Ps. 19:1). But when I read further in that psalm, "The law of the LORD is perfect . . . more to be desired . . . than gold . . . sweeter also than honey"(vv. 7, 10), it sits less comfortably. By immersing myself in the psalms I transcend what comes easily to me and discover that God's creation and law both reveal God's nature and are both beautiful. While adopting the language and thought patterns of the psalms might appear unnatural or impersonal, it can actually be freeing: we are no longer trapped by our personal vocabulary but are welcomed into an ever richer, deeper way of expressing ourselves.

No matter what our unique perspective or place in life, the psalms speak to us. Old Testament scholar Walter Brueggeman categorizes the psalms into three types: orientation, disorientation, and reorientation.[3] In psalms of orientation, everything is at peace. In psalms of disorientation, something disturbs that balance: sin, sickness, doubt, or persecution. In psalms of reorientation, the psalmist has finished complaining to God and now returns with deeper faith and trust. Brueggeman also shows that the psalmist often cycles through all three perspectives in one psalm. This is much like our lives—a continuous cycle of surety, doubt, and renewed faith that leads us deeper and deeper into God's love. The psalms accompany us on this journey.

Finally, the psalms connect us to the historic and global church. They have been a foundation of Judeo-Christian piety for millennia, and there is no reason to believe this should change in a new millennium. They have nourished Christians of every nation in both times of peace and times of persecution. The psalms are the universal hymnal of the church universal. We would do well to join the "cloud of witnesses" in singing God's song. This is an invitation to join our voices to the universal church in a concrete way—a rehearsal for heaven. No command compels us to sing the psalms, but it is clear that they are the norm for Christian worshipers. The burden of proof rests on the church that *doesn't* sing the psalms.

Why *sing* the psalms rather than just read, preach, and study them like any other Scripture? The most obvious answer is that the psalms are songs, and songs are meant to be sung. While we don't know what the music of the psalms sounded like or how they were used in worship, we do know they were the congregational songs of the Jews.[4] Since singing was the original context of the psalms, it makes sense for us to experience them in that same context. Further, while all Scripture can be studied and preached, certain genres of Scripture lend themselves well to certain forms of engagement. The drama of Genesis, for example, comes alive when heard as a story. When we sing the psalms, we engage with them on the level that they were written. This allows the words of the psalms to dig deep into our hearts, impacting our emotions and affections the way only songs can. The psalms are God singing to us—how can we keep from singing along?

But if we don't know what the music of the psalms sounded like, how can we sing them? What follows is an answer to that question. It can't be a definitive answer, because each church must work out the details in their own context. However, there are thousands of years of psalm-singing Christians who inform the way we approach singing psalms in today's churches. Though we'll be drawing on the rich tradition of psalmody (psalm singing) throughout the ages, we shouldn't feel beholden to any particular tradition of psalm singing. Instead, we seek to be informed by the past so we can be more creative in the present.

How Do We Sing the Psalms?

First, let's begin by considering ways that words and music can be combined in worship. Catholic priest and composer Joseph Gelineau has done much of the work for us in his chapter "Music and Singing in the Liturgy."[5] As seen in the chart below,[6] Gelineau shows word and music combinations ranging from ordinary speech on one end to speechless music on the other end.[7] Ordinary speech is self-explanatory. From there we move toward forms of heightened speech: proclamation and meditation. In each of these forms, the tone or rhythm of ordinary speech is heightened somewhat, such as the steady rhythm of a congregation reciting the Lord's Prayer or an African-American preacher who begins to intone the sermon as it comes to a climax. In all three examples on the left side of the chart—ordinary speech, proclamation, and meditation—the requirements of speech trump musical considerations. That is, though there are musical aspects to these forms, they are still, at their core, speech.

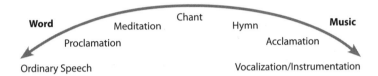

In the middle of Gelineau's chart is chant. Gelineau points out that in chant (plainchant, Gregorian chant) the requirements of word and music are perfectly balanced. (This doesn't make it better, just balanced.)

As we move to the right side of Gelineau's chart, the balance tips more and more toward musical considerations. For example, in the hymn, the melodic contour, poetic meter, and rhyme scheme force words out of natural speech patterns in order to fit the music. It's important to recognize that most Protestant music centers on Gelineau's definition of a hymn, whether traditional hymns or modern praise songs. This leaves us a lot of other territory to explore! As we move right toward acclamation and vocalization/instrumental, we experience meditative choruses, extended "hallelujahs," and singing in the Spirit—less verbal information and more focus on the music.

Gelineau's model may seem like a lot of unnecessary detail, but defining congregational music by *function* rather than *genre* allows us to think more expansively about the types of music we use in worship. For example, historically the heightened speech on the left side of Gelineau's chart may have been chant, but there's no reason in a modern context it couldn't be rap. Understanding our history doesn't lock us into endlessly aping the past; instead, it frees us to think creatively about what could be done in our own context. In this same spirit of historically informed creative exploration, let's apply Gelineau's model to psalmody.

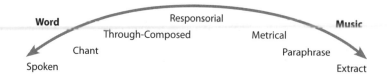

Spoken, of course, has no music at all. Many churches use the psalms this way on a regular basis. A leader may read a psalm as one of the Scripture readings. The people may do a responsive reading (leader/people) or antiphonal reading (different sides of the congregation trading verses, back and forth). A spoken rendition could even include creative methods such as a choral reading (a group reading that distributes verses of the psalm throughout the ensemble) or a dramatic presentation of the psalm text. As noted previously, the main disadvantage of simply reading the psalms in worship is that worshipers miss out on the "songness" of the psalms. Further, responsive and antiphonal readings have a tendency to flatten the original psalm's inherent structures. However, certain genres of psalms lend themselves well to speech. For example, the rhythmic phrases of Psalm 19:7–10 lend themselves beautifully to antiphonal reading.

Chant can range from simple intoned speech (sometimes called *cantillation*) to bona fide chant, with flowing melodies that heighten the natural pitches and rhythms of the spoken word. It is likely that the psalms were chanted in Old Testament times, and it is quite possible that some traits of this Jewish cantillation carried over into New Testament chant and then into medieval plainchant, more commonly known as Gregorian chant.[8] Plainchant is the backbone of church music and, indeed, Western classical music. Legend has it that Pope Gregory I (c. 540–604) received plainchant directly from the Spirit, often depicted as a dove singing into his ear; history indicates that he likely began the process of collecting and standardizing the chants and Latin texts of the mass. These are still in use today, and can be found in the *Liber Usualis,* a modern collection of plainchant compiled by the monks of Solesmes.

When psalms are chanted, it is done using "psalm tones," a sequence of pitches with a "reciting tone" on which the bulk of the text is intoned. This simple formula can be used to sing long Scripture passages, heightening the text beyond what normal speech could provide. While few of us will sing plainchant in Latin, there are a number of modern traditions of chanting the psalms. Anglicans and others use "Pointed Psalms," similar to the Gregorian psalm tone system except that it is in four-part harmony and tone changes are indicated by dots above the psalm text. In the 1950s Joseph Gelineau created a psalm translation for chanting the psalms in French that followed the rhythms of the Hebrew text. Gelineau used a type of "sprung rhythm" in which a basic pulse remained constant but the number of syllables within each pulse varied. Gelineau's system follows the natural emphasis of spoken text while allow-

Psalm 19:7–10

The law of the LORD is perfect,
reviving the soul;
the decrees of the LORD are sure,
making wise the simple;
the precepts of the LORD are right,
rejoicing the heart;
the commandment of the LORD is clear,
enlightening the eyes;
the fear of the LORD is pure,
enduring forever;
the ordinances of the LORD are true
and righteous altogether.
More to be desired are they than gold,
even much fine gold;
sweeter also than honey,
and drippings of the honeycomb.

ing it to be sung using a psalm tone melody. The *Grail Psalter*, an English translation of the psalms based on Gelineau's work, was released a decade later. An updated edition of the *Grail Psalter* is still in use today and is the mandated version of psalmody for English-speaking Roman Catholics.

Many churches will never sing a psalm in one of these historic chant styles, but there is still much to learn from the basic idea of chant as heightened speech. For example, churches that regularly speak the psalms in worship may find that the Grail translation works well for them, because its singability will translate into easy readability. Chant-like music forms such as rap, spoken word, or the half-spoken, half-sung style that is often used in pop songs may be a good modern substitute for chant.[9] African-American churches, especially, can draw on the black preaching tradition of moving fluidly from speech to tones to song. Too often we draw boundaries between speech and song in worship; we would benefit from chant-like forms that bridge the two—forms that allow longer, more informational portions of psalms to be used in worship without the dulling effect of unadorned speech or the monotony that would come from singing a twelve-verse metrical psalm.

Through-composed psalm settings follow the psalm text from start to finish rather than adhering to a repeated musical form such as strophes (multiple verses) or verse/chorus. Because of this, they are not well suited to congregational singing. However, there are many stellar examples of through-composed psalm compositions that could be sung by choirs or soloists, such as Franck's *Psalm 150*, Purcell's *I Was Glad*, and Bernstein's *Chichester Psalms*. There is also a tradition of Scripture songs that set verbatim psalm texts to music. While helpful as a memorization aid, they rarely sing well in a congregational setting.

Responsorial psalmody shares some traits with chant in that it uses psalm tones for long, chanted verses. However, responsorial psalmody breaks up these verses with a short congregational response (called a *refrain* or *chorus*). This leader/people responsive approach to psalmody has precedent in the psalms themselves; for example, Psalm 118 repeats "His steadfast love endures forever." This kind of volley back and forth between a leader and the congregation has been a staple of worship throughout the ages—and for good reason. It allows a gifted and prepared leader to read or sing the bulk of the text while an unrehearsed congregation can quickly join in with a repeated response. In the West, we often assume everyone can read from a hymnal or screen, but in many worship settings a majority of the people can't read or the churches don't have access to hymnals or projection systems that would allow everyone to take part. Also, we need to remember that even in highly educated worship settings there will always be children, people with poor eyesight, and immigrants new to the language who will benefit from simple structures like responsorial psalmody.

Much of the plainchant repertoire that developed in the early years of the church is responsorial psalmody. A leader chants the psalm text and the people interject a response every three to five verses. Sometimes the response is extracted from the psalm itself; in other cases the response is another Scripture that complements the psalm. For example, the responsorial psalm prescribed for the foot washing ceremony of the Maundy Thursday service in the Catholic church is Psalm 133, which begins: "How very good and pleasant it is when kindred live together in unity!" The congregation responds by singing Jesus's words from the upper room: "I give you a new commandment, that you love one another" (John 13:34). What a rich pairing of Scriptures!

This responsorial psalmody tradition is alive and well today. In fact, if you're Catholic, it might be the only way you can imagine singing the psalms. However, Lutherans, Episcopalians, and Presbyterians sing responsorial psalms as well. Because so many churches use this form of psalmody— some of their denominations mandate that particular psalms be used on particular days—a significant repertoire has grown in a wide variety of musical styles. The Gelineau Psalms continue to be widely used. Other composers follow suit with traditional style responsorial psalmody: Michel Guimont, Hal Hopson, Chabanel Psalms, or even plainchant in Latin. An outpouring of responsorial psalmody in modern music styles followed in the wake of Vatican II. Many of these were in a "liturgical folk" style that has become ubiquitous in today's Catholic churches, including composers Marty Haugen, David Haas, John Foley, Bernadette Farrell, and Steven Warner. There has also been a flowering of ethnic and global psalmody: *Psalms from the Soul, Lead Me, Guide Me*, the work of Roy James Stewart and Rawn Harbor (African-American); *The Living Church Acclaims* (jazz influenced); Thánh Ca Dân Chúa (Vietnamese), AILM (Asian Institute of Liturgy & Music); and *Oramos Cantando/We Pray in Song*, the music of Pedro Rubalcava, Tony Alonso, and Ronald Krisman (Hispanic and bilingual); to name a few.

While there is much to commend in responsorial psalmody, there are also drawbacks. The verse/response musical form beautifully complements some psalms but undermines the inherent form of others. Responsorial psalms function well in the context of worship, but they tend not to be the most memorable melodies. A steady diet might get wearisome. On the other hand, they are an important psalm-singing tool to have available. Perhaps some churches will benefit most by adapting the general idea of responsorial psalmody. They might speak psalm verses over a simple musical accompaniment and invite the congregation to respond by singing a well-known Scripture chorus.[10] New songs could be written that capitalize on the benefits of the verse/response structure of traditional responsorial psalmody. Chris Tomlin takes this approach in his song on Psalm 136, "Forever," as did Townend and Keyes in "My Soul Finds Rest"

(Ps. 62). This is fertile territory to be explored by imaginative church musicians.

Metrical psalms are essentially "psalm hymns." Like hymns, they are *strophic*—multiple verses of text set to the same melody. Unlike hymns, the lyrics are not the author's invention but a rendition of a psalm. The goal of metrical psalmody is to stay as close to the original psalm as possible, simply "translating" the psalm into poetic meter and rhyme scheme. The first metrical psalter emerged in John Calvin's Geneva. Calvin wanted the people to sing the psalms for themselves, as opposed to the Catholic tradition of trained musicians singing for them. Inspired by psalm versifications such as those of Luther, he began to assemble people with the skills to create a whole metrical psalter. *The Genevan Psalter*, with all 150 psalms set to music, appeared in 1562, under the musical supervision of Louis Bourgeois and with text contributions from Clément Marot and Theodore de Beza.

From these Calvinist beginnings, metrical psalms have tended to travel in Reformed circles. Within a few decades of *The Genevan Psalter*, metrical psalters appeared in Dutch, German, and English. Later psalters include Sternhold and Hopkins' "old version," *The Scottish Psalter*, Tate and Brady's *A New Version of the Psalms of David* (the "new version"), and the first book published in America, *The Bay Psalm Book*. A number of songs introduced in these psalters continue to be used today. A few denominations still sing metrical psalms exclusively, but most congregations experience only a few of the most popular ones. Prominent modern metrical psalm writers include Michael Morgan, Martin Leckebusch, Ruth Duck, and Carl Daw. The work of these contemporary writers and updated versions of historical metrical psalms can be found in a number of Reformed hymnals: *The Psalter Hymnal* (Christian Reformed, 1987), *Cantus Christi* (Christ Church, 2002), *Glory to God* (Presbyterian, 2013), and *Lift Up Your Hearts* (Reformed/Christian Reformed, 2013).

One of the reasons the metrical psalms have worked so well over the years is that, like hymns, they have sturdy, singable tunes. As we move farther right on our graph of psalmody, the music becomes more prominent and the words become less identical to the original psalm text. That makes for memorable melodies but can result in lyrics that are forced. Further, the strophic nature of metrical psalmody complements the poetic form of some psalms perfectly but undermines others.[11] But for any weaknesses, there are hundreds of excellent metrical psalm settings waiting to be utilized. Some may need to have language updated, others could use new arrangements[12] or even freshly written tunes,[13] but they all represent an opportunity to introduce congregations to whole psalms in a format that is familiar and tuneful.

When singing metrical psalmody, the congregation may not be aware that they're singing a psalm. It is helpful for worship planners to get in the habit of noting the Scripture reference of the psalms they use in worship. This will increase the congregation's awareness of the psalms, help them make connections between the psalms they sing and the psalms they read, and allow them to build a mental map of the psalms' themes.

A *psalm paraphrase* is similar to a metrical psalm in that it is a strophic setting of a psalm. However, unlike the metrical psalms' intention of "translating" each word and phrase of the original psalm, the goal of the paraphrase is to versify the basic ideas of the psalm. Paraphrases usually address the whole psalm, or at least substantial portions of it, but are less literal. They tend to be shorter than metrical psalms and often summarize lengthy passages into a single song verse. They may also take liberties in leaving out difficult sections of the original psalm text or updating images to a contemporary context.

While Martin Luther was an inspiration behind Calvin's Genevan psalms, Luther's psalm versifications were considerably less literal than Calvin's. Notice below in Luther's well-known psalm paraphrase, "A Mighty Fortress Is Our God," that he strays quite far from the original psalm, whereas the metrical version from *The Scottish Psalter* stays close to the psalm, phrase by phrase. Isaac Watts is known as the father of English hymnody, but he also wrote 138 psalm paraphrases. A unique aspect of Watts's psalm paraphrases is that he often "Christianized" the psalm texts. For example, the prophesied king of Psalm 72 is named in Watts's versification, "Jesus Shall Reign." Charles Wesley, also known primarily as a hymn writer, paraphrased a number of psalms, including "Praise the Lord Who Reigns Above (Ps. 150)." While many post-Vatican II songwriters continued in the Catholic tradition of responsorial psalmody, some also wrote psalm

Psalm 46

Martin Luther, 1529 (paraphrase)

1 A mighty fortress is our God,
a bulwark never failing;
our helper he, amid the flood
of mortal ills prevailing.
For still our ancient foe
does seek to work us woe;
his craft and power are great,
and armed with cruel hate,
on earth is not his equal.

2 Did we in our own strength confide,
our striving would be losing,
were not the right Man on our side,
the Man of God's own choosing.
You ask who that may be?
Christ Jesus, it is he;
Lord Sabaoth his name,
from age to age the same;
and he must win the battle.

3 And though this world, with devils filled,
should threaten to undo us,
we will not fear, for God has willed
his truth to triumph through us.
The prince of darkness grim,
we tremble not for him;
his rage we can endure,
for lo! his doom is sure;
one little word shall fell him.

4 That Word above all earthly powers
no thanks to them abideth;
the Spirit and the gifts are ours
through him who with us sideth.
Let goods and kindred go,
this mortal life also;
the body they may kill:
God's truth abideth still;
his kingdom is forever!

Scottish Psalter, 1650 (metrical)

1 God is our refuge and our strength,
in straits a present aid;
Therefore, although the earth remove,
we will not be afraid:
Though hills amidst the seas be cast;
Though waters roaring make,
And troubled be; yea, though the hills,
by swelling seas do shake.

2 A river is, whose streams do glad
the city of our God;
The holy place, wherein the Lord
most high hath his abode.
God in the midst of her doth dwell;
nothing shall her remove:
The Lord to her an helper will,
and that right early, prove.

3 The heathen rag'd tumultuously,
the kingdoms moved were:
The Lord God uttered his voice,
the earth did melt for fear.
The Lord of hosts upon our side
doth constantly remain:
The God of Jacob's our refuge,
us safely to maintain.

4 Come, and behold what wondrous works
have by the Lord been wrought;
Come, see what desolations
he on the earth hath brought.
Unto the ends of all the earth
wars into peace he turns:
The bow he breaks, the spear he cuts,
in fire the chariot burns.

5 Be still, and know that I am God;
among the heathen I
Will be exalted; I on earth
will be exalted high.
Our God, who is the Lord of hosts,
is still upon our side;
The God of Jacob our refuge
for ever will abide.

Psalm 46 (NRSV)

[1]God is our refuge and strength,
a very present help in trouble.
[2]Therefore we will not fear,
though the earth should change,
though the mountains shake in the heart of the sea;
[3]though its waters roar and foam,
though the mountains tremble with its tumult. Selah

[4]There is a river whose streams make glad the city of God,
the holy habitation of the Most High.
[5]God is in the midst of the city; it shall not be moved;
God will help it when the morning dawns.
[6]The nations are in an uproar, the kingdoms totter;
he utters his voice, the earth melts.
[7]The LORD of hosts is with us;
the God of Jacob is our refuge. Selah

[8]Come, behold the works of the LORD;
see what desolations he has brought on the earth.
[9]He makes wars cease to the end of the earth;
he breaks the bow, and shatters the spear;
he burns the shields with fire.
[10]"Be still, and know that I am God!
I am exalted among the nations,
I am exalted in the earth."
[11]The LORD of hosts is with us;
the God of Jacob is our refuge. Selah

paraphrases such as "Shepherd Me, O God" (Ps. 23, Marty Haugen) and "Sing a New Song unto the Lord" (Ps. 98, Dan Schutte).[14] John Bell, best known for his work with the Iona community and global hymnody, has written many psalm paraphrases. Hundreds of other modern songwriters have contributed psalm paraphrases to the ongoing psalm repertoire of the church, among them Stuart Townend, Bob Kauflin, and Tommy Walker.

Though some might complain that many psalm paraphrases stray far from the original psalm texts—and they would be right—they are also one of the most winsome ways of introducing the psalms to congregations. They are as tuneful as hymns and contemporary praise songs, but the lyrics don't have as many of the awkward phrases and forced rhymes of metrical psalmody. Though they are not literal renderings of the psalms, it could be argued that these paraphrases faithfully translate the *essence* of the original Scriptures. That is, the Spirit gave the psalms within a particular culture, and it may be that a translation of the psalm's sense or essence renders the psalm more faithfully than a literal translation.[15] Singing "Happy shall they be who take your little ones and dash them against the rock!" (Ps. 137:9) may not be the best way for a congregation to internalize Scripture.

The advantages of the paraphrase approach can clearly be seen in the paraphrase of Psalm 137 by Ewald Bash. The author tracks closely to the first part of the psalm, but instead of rendering the violence of verse 9, he ends with the cross, the violence that Christ took upon himself in order to free us from tyranny and need for revenge.

A *psalm extract* is a song that is drawn from a short section or phrase of a psalm.[16] These songs often focus on a central image. For example, Marty Nystrom's "As the Deer" uses the image of the deer panting for water from Psalm 42:1. They are often short, meditative songs, repeating a number of times, such as Peter Sanchez's "I Exalt Thee." When psalm paraphrases have multiple verses, they don't follow the rest of the psalm like metrical or paraphrased psalms but instead use the psalm as a launching point for verses on other themes. Such is the case with the anonymously authored "Be Still and Know." Its first verse comes from Psalm 46:10 but then it veers into "I am the Lord that healeth thee" and "In thee, O Lord, I put my trust."

As you can see from these examples, the Scripture songs of the 1970s were frequently choruses extracted from the psalms. This trend continued in subsequent generations of praise songs with such songs as "I Lift My Eyes Up" (Ps. 121:1, Brian Doerksen) and "Better Is One Day" (Ps. 84:10,

Psalm 137

¹By the rivers of Babylon–
there we sat down and there we wept
when we remembered Zion.
²On the willows there
we hung up our harps.
³For there our captors
asked us for songs,
and our tormentors asked for mirth, saying,
"Sing us one of the songs of Zion!"

⁴How could we sing the LORD's song
in a foreign land?
⁵If I forget you, O Jerusalem,
let my right hand wither!
⁶Let my tongue cling to the roof of my mouth,
if I do not remember you,
if I do not set Jerusalem
above my highest joy.

⁷Remember, O LORD, against the Edomites
the day of Jerusalem's fall,
how they said, "Tear it down! Tear it down!
Down to its foundations!"
⁸O daughter Babylon, you devastator!
Happy shall they be who pay you back
what you have done to us!
⁹Happy shall they be who take your little ones
and dash them against the rock!

Psalm 137 NRSV

1 By the Babylonian rivers
we sat down in grief and wept;
hung our harps upon a willow,
mourned for Zion while we slept.

2 There our captors, in derision,
did require of us a song;
so we sat with staring vision
and the days were hard and long.

3 How shall we sing the Lord's song
in a strange and bitter land;
can our voices veil the sorrow?
Lord God, hear your lonely band.

4 Let your cross be benediction
for all bound in tyranny;
by the power of resurrection
loose them from captivity.

Ewald Bash, "By the Babylonian Rivers,"
© 1964 American Lutheran Church,
admin. Augsburg Fortress.
Reprinted by permission.

Matt Redman). Psalm extracts are not only within the purview of the praise and worship genre. They are found anywhere short, meditative worship songs are used. For example, Jacques Berthier of the Taizé community has contributed dozens of psalm extracts, including "Bless the Lord, My Soul" (Ps. 103:1) and "The Lord Is My Light" (Ps. 27:1).

Some have criticized this style of psalm song for straying so far from the original text. Indeed, some of these songs skim over the surface of the psalm, touching down only at the most comforting images and phrases. How much more powerful would Nystrom's "As the Deer" have been if he had stayed with the original themes of Psalms 42 and 43 ("Why are you cast down, O my soul?") instead of the rhapsody of images he chose (strength, shield, gold or silver, apple of my eye)? But for all the potential pitfalls of psalm paraphrases, they can also be very powerful.

In fact, the church has a long history of approaching the Scriptures in short, meditative sections. The Benedictines have practiced *lectio divina*, or "divine reading," for centuries. This approach encourages a quiet reading of Scripture until a phrase or image rises to the top, at which point the reading turns to meditative prayer based on that short passage. The idea is that the same Spirit that breathed life into the words of the Scriptures when they were first penned will reveal to attentive readers what they need to internalize from those words.

Psalm extracts are a valid and valuable approach to psalmody. We just need to make sure we use them as a way to drill deeper into a specific section of a psalm rather than as a way of avoiding the difficult themes of the psalms.

Perhaps we can see a theme emerging. There is no right or wrong way to sing the psalms—no one size fits all. Instead we need to match the most appropriate musical form to support the inherent form and message of the psalm itself. We can do this, in part, simply by knowing the psalms well and having a wide repertoire of psalm songs to draw on, picking the song that best supports a particular psalm. But since many psalms have multiple forms or voices, it may take more than one song to support the larger message of that psalm. This type of psalm calls for a hybrid of musical and spoken forms.

> **Excellent Psalm Commentaries**
>
> Robert Alter, *The Book of Psalms: A Translation with Commentary* (New York: Norton, 2007).
>
> J. P. Fokkelman, *Reading Biblical Poetry: An Introductory Guide* (Louisville: Westminster John Knox Press, 2001).
>
> John Goldingay, *Psalms*, vols. 1–3 (Grand Rapids, Baker Academic, 2006).
>
> James L. Mays, *Psalms: Interpretation: A Bible Commentary for Teaching and Preaching* (Louisville: Westminster John Knox Press, 1994).
>
> Samuel Terrien, *The Psalms: Strophic Structure and Theological Commentary* (Grand Rapids: Eerdmans, 2003).

Creating a hybrid psalm for worship begins with understanding the psalm itself. What are its basic sections? What poetic forms are used? (Acrostics, mirrored sections, and parallelisms are frequent poetic devices used in the psalms.) Is it a wisdom psalm? History? Lament? What voices are used? First person speaking to God? Third person? God speaking to us? The voice of a priest/leader? When does the voice or tone of the psalm change? Some of this will become clear with a careful reading of the psalm, but we can usually arrive at deeper insights with the help of some good Bible commentaries.

We don't need to make this overly complicated. The goal is to help our congregation engage with the psalms more deeply, not create more work for ourselves. This could be as simple as assigning parts appropriately in a responsive reading rather than the standard practice of alternating between leader and people every line. For example, look at the simple rendering of Psalm 95 below. All it requires beyond a typical responsive reading is one song, a half-hour of psalm study, and perhaps a bit of rehearsal to make sure the reader and musicians can lead the transitions smoothly.

Some publishers and songwriters have experimented with hybrid mixes in their psalm settings. Each psalm in *Psalms for All Seasons* has options for either speaking or chanting the psalm text, often interspersed with an appropriate song of response. A few settings in that collection go further. In Andrew Donaldson's setting of Psalm 73, "Why Do the Powerful Have It So Good?" we journey with the psalmist through the age-old question: Why do good things happen to bad people? The verses feel like beatnik poetry over a musical vamp; a short refrain subtly changes throughout the song to reflect the psalmist's journey from envy of the powerful to trust in God. My own setting of Psalm 5 in the same collection reflects the psalm's structure with two readers and a shift in musical accompaniment that help worshipers hear the change in voice that occurs in the psalm.

Psalm hybrids can also be more extensive compositions in which the psalm text is supported with multiple songs, prayers, and other acts of worship. These "psalm sequences" provide a way to move from a generic set of praise music toward a Scripture-saturated worship experience. Below is an example. The text of Psalm 27 is interspersed with songs and prayers inspired by the psalm itself. This is just one suggestion of how this particular psalm could be used as the backbone of worship. Each worship planner should adapt it to his or her local context.

Ephesians and Colossians encourage us to sing psalms, hymns, and spiritual songs. In recent years, most churches have sung far more hymns and spiritual songs than psalms. To be sure, the psalms themselves tell us we need to "sing to the LORD a new song" (Ps. 96:1; 98:1; 149:1). But perhaps we also need to sing anew the song of the Lord. That is, we first

Psalm 95

(leader's part; **people's part**)	Notes
¹ O come, let us sing to the LORD; let us make a joyful noise to the rock of our salvation! ² Let us come into his presence with thanksgiving; let us make a joyful noise to him with songs of praise!	*The leader pronounces this as a call to worship.*
	Since the leader has said, "Come, let us sing!" it makes sense for the congregation to respond by singing. Perhaps a song on the theme "Come, let us sing" or "Come let us worship and bow down" could be used.
³ For the LORD is a great God, **and a great King above all gods.** ⁴ In his hand are the depths of the earth; **the heights of the mountains are his also.** ⁵ The sea is his, for he made it, **and the dry land, which his hands have formed.**	*Alternating between the leader and the people highlights the parallelism of this part of the psalm.*
⁶ O come, let us worship and bow down, let us kneel before the LORD, our Maker! ⁷ **For he is our God, and we are the people of his pasture, and the sheep of his hand.**	*Longer responses in this section create a pastoral exhortation ("O come!") and a congregational affirmation ("He is our God/we are his people").*
	Optional: repeat the song that was sung earlier.
O that today you would listen to his voice! ⁸ Do not harden your hearts, as at Meribah, as on the day at Massah in the wilderness, ⁹ when your ancestors tested me, and put me to the proof, though they had seen my work. ¹⁰ For forty years I loathed that generation and said, "They are a people whose hearts go astray, and they do not regard my ways." ¹¹ Therefore in my anger I swore, "They shall not enter my rest."	*This is the most difficult part of the psalm, but it is also essential: if God is a king above all other gods and we are God's people, it requires the trust and obedience described in verses 8–11. In this section, God is speaking directly to the people, reminding them of the pain their hard hearts had caused. It makes sense for this to be spoken to the people so they can listen to God's warning in the same way the Israelites would have listened to a priest speak these words.*
	The psalm ends on such a harsh note that it may be pastorally wise to soften the blow. This could be achieved by speaking the verses 6–7 once again, summarizing the theme of the psalm and reaffirming, "You are our God and we won't harden our hearts," or by singing the song that was used earlier.

learn the songs God has given us, and once we have internalized them we begin to craft new songs for our day and age. This is what Mary did when she praised God for choosing her to be the mother of the Messiah (Luke 1:46–55). She improvised a new song based on the song of another miraculous mother, Hannah (1 Sam. 2:1–10). Hannah, in turn, drew upon sections of Psalm 113.

A Psalm Sequence on Psalm 27

Psalm 27 (leader's part; **people's part**)	Worship Instructions
	Opening songs: begin with gathering praise and move into "light and salvation" themed songs.
The Lord is my light and my salvation; whom shall I fear? The Lord is the stronghold of my life; of whom shall I be afraid? When evildoers assail me to devour my flesh— my adversaries and foes— they shall stumble and fall. Though an army encamp against me, my heart shall not fear; though war rise up against me, yet I will be confident. **One thing I asked of the Lord,** **that will I seek after:** **to live in the house of the Lord** **all the days of my life,** **to behold the beauty of the Lord,** **and to inquire in his temple.**	
	Sing a "one thing" song.
For he will hide me in his shelter in the day of trouble; he will conceal me under the cover of his tent; he will set me high on a rock. Now my head is lifted up above my enemies all around me, and I will offer in his tent sacrifices with shouts of joy; I will sing and make melody to the Lord.	
	Sing "one thing" song, as above.
Hear, O Lord, when I cry aloud, be gracious to me and answer me! **"Come," my heart says, "seek his face!"** **Your face, Lord, do I seek.**	
	Sing "Wait for the Lord" (Taizé) or other waiting song.
Do not hide your face from me. Do not turn your servant away in anger, you who have been my help. **Do not cast me off, do not forsake me,** **O God of my salvation!** **If my father and mother forsake me,** **the Lord will take me up.**	

Psalm 27
(leader's part; **people's part**)

Worship Instructions

Psalm 27	Worship Instructions
	Prayers of confession and assurance.
	Sing "Wait for the Lord" (Taizé), as above.
Teach me your way, O LORD, and lead me on a level path because of my enemies. **Do not give me up to the will of my adversaries, for false witnesses have risen against me, and they are breathing out violence.**	
	Prayers for guidance.
	"Wait for the Lord."
I believe that I shall see the goodness of the LORD in the land of the living. Wait for the LORD; be strong, and let your heart take courage; wait for the LORD!	
	Sing concluding song about trusting in God's goodness.

Finding new ways to sing the psalms allows us to take part in the song of God's people, from everlasting to everlasting.

For Discussion

1. Do you think your church should sing more psalms? How would your congregation react to the change? Create a strategy for slowly introducing more psalm songs over the next three to five years.
2. Do you ever go through periods of orientation, disorientation, and reorientation? What sustains you during those times?
3. How would your worship change if you committed to singing at least one psalm in each worship service? How would your worship planning change if the first song you chose were a psalm to complement the service's themes?
4. When your church sings psalms, what types of songs are they (metrical, responsorial, and so forth)? Are there particular types of psalmody that you're especially eager to explore?

PART 3

PRACTICE

Music in Worship

It is no accident that this book begins with *principles* and explores the *past* before moving on to crafting our own worship *practice*. Just as in Jesus's parable, we want to build our worship practices on solid rock (Matt. 7:24–27) rather than the shifting sand of current fashion and popular opinion.

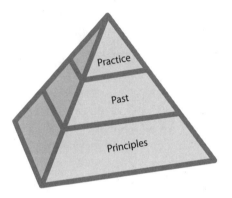

The bedrock of our foundation is God's Word. We search Scripture to understand how God wants us to worship. What does God command? What is left to our own wisdom? What biblical examples are given? As we saw earlier, faithful Christians have interpreted Scripture differently on many points. Nonetheless, with Spirit-filled Scripture study, reading widely on worship, and guidance from our own church tradition, we can establish a strong foundation on the most important worship principles.

On top of the solid rock of God's Word, we build our foundation further on the example of faithful Christians who have gone before us. Billions have worshiped God in the past and we should learn all we can from them. What are common themes and areas of consensus? What are recurring problems? What factors have precipitated seasons of revival, renewal, or decline? How did different communities' worship beliefs affect their practice, for good or ill? Having a good understanding of the history of worship means we don't have to make everything up from scratch. Instead, we have numerous templates to draw on for our own worship. A keen insight into worship history also means we won't need to repeat the mistakes of the past!

10

The Senses, the Arts, and Worship

Before you begin: Go beyond words.

Describe a time when you experienced something in worship that transcended words. It might have been moving music, ashes on your forehead on Ash Wednesday, or the Spirit moving your heart. Take some time to consider the events and emotions of that experience.

The *Shema* was given to the Israelites directly after the Ten Commandments. Many Jews still recite it daily: "Hear, O Israel: The LORD is our God, the LORD alone. You shall love the LORD your God with all your heart, and with all your soul, and with all your might."[1] Jesus quoted it centuries later when asked to name the greatest commandment: "You shall love the Lord your God with all your heart, and with all your soul, and with all your mind" (Matt. 22:37). Though Jesus worded it a little differently, the meaning in both is clear: love God with your whole being.

We Christians often excel at loving God with our minds but are not quite sure what to do with our hearts (emotions), souls (inner beings), or might (bodies). Especially in worship, we are uncomfortable engaging the nonrational parts of our humanity. This is a shame. If God knit us together in the womb (Ps. 139:13) and commands us to worship with our

Our Senses	
The Five Main Senses	**Other Senses Include**
Sight	Balance
Hearing	Temperature
Taste	Kinesthetic
Smell	Sense
Touch	Pain
	Perception of
	Time
	Interoception

whole being, we should make a point of knowing God through all the paths given to us.

Some of the ways God has given us to know him are called *the five senses*: sight, hearing, taste, smell, and touch. Evidently, God thought it was so important for us to have many ways of perceiving, knowing, and worshiping that he attached most of the gear directly to our heads! We are not disembodied minds but whole human beings with eyes, ears, tongues, noses, and hands with which we can interact with God. Isn't it interesting? God could have attached wires directly to our brains to facilitate divine communication but instead has chosen to speak with us through the everyday stuff of life. This is part of what it means that God is *incarnational*. Our God is not an ethereal, hands-off God but one who meets us *in the flesh*. Of course, the ultimate example of God's incarnational impulse is Jesus Christ. Eugene Peterson phrases this beautifully:

> The Word became flesh and blood,
> and moved into the neighborhood.
> We saw the glory with our own eyes,
> the one-of-a-kind glory,
> like Father, like Son,
> Generous inside and out,
> true from start to finish. (John 1:14 Message)

Historically, Western Christians have had an uneasy relationship with our senses. Consider the "sense" words we use: we admire things that are "sensible" and people who are "sensitive," but we want to avoid being overwhelmed by "sensory overload," worry that reason will be trumped by "sensationalism," and fear that "sensual" things will lure us away from God. Certainly "the desire of the flesh [and] the desire of the eyes" (1 John 2:16) can lead us astray. On the other hand, the senses are God-given and have great potential to deepen our love of our Maker. Can we find a way to give our whole beings to God—heart, soul, and mind? Can we utilize all of our senses as beneficial ways of communicating with God? Can we embrace the arts as a way of engaging our senses and whole being in worship?

Two Schools of Thought and a Third Way

There are two main schools of thought about the arts in worship. The *utilitarian approach* views worship arts simply as a way to deliver words. Augustine eloquently lays out the dilemma in his *Confessions*:

> I admit that I still find some enjoyment in the music of hymns. . . . But I ought not allow my mind to be paralyzed by the gratification of my senses, which often leads it astray. For the senses are not content to take second place. Simply because I allow them their due, as adjuncts to reason, they attempt to take precedence and forge ahead of it, with the result that I sometimes sin in this way but am not aware of it until later. . . . I am inclined to approve of the custom of singing in the church in order that by indulging the ears, weaker spirits may be inspired with feelings of devotion.[2]

Augustine and others in his wake have been suspicious of the arts in worship, fearing they would lead to idolatry. Those who subscribe to this thinking today are content to use the arts to draw people to church, to sweeten the message with colors and tones, or to confirm the church's social status ("the sophisticated congregation with the forty-rank organ" or "the hip, young church with the cool praise band"), but they don't see the arts as having anything but a utilitarian value.

In contrast, the *aesthetic approach* views the arts as having intrinsic value that should be honored regardless of how it contributes (or doesn't contribute) to the worship context or to Christian formation—since the arts are part of God's good creation, they deserve a place in worship. While this seems reasonable on the surface, it can lead to problems. Too often, an exquisitely performed Bach fugue can turn a worship service into a concert; visual art or dance can lead us to ponder the creation rather than the Creator, bringing us back to Augustine's fear. In modern worship contexts,

> "Art is a lie that tells the truth."
> —Pablo Picasso

the music is often given such a prominent position that we end up moving away from a traditional understanding of worship—worshiping God through Christ in the power of the Holy Spirit—to a model in which we worship Jesus in the power of music.[3]

Perhaps there is a third way: the worship arts as *metaphor*. Talking about the image of the Good Shepherd, Old Testament scholar James L. Mays says:

> A metaphor used for theological purposes is very serious business. It conveys more, and it speaks more powerfully than is possible to do in discursive speech. A metaphor is not as precise and limited as discursive speech. It draws on varied experience and evokes imagination. It is therefore plastic in meaning, capable of polysemy.[4]

This third way would recognize the power of the arts' nonrational voice to speak clearly in worship.

Many Christians would be uncomfortable with the idea of communicating truth nonverbally. We are, after all, people of the Word. Does it not follow that *words* are the best—or only—way of communicating the Word? Harold Best, for example, states in his book *Music Through the Eyes of Faith*:

> I take the position that, with certain exceptions, art and especially music are morally relative and inherently incapable of articulating, for want of a better term, truth speech. They are essentially neutral in their ability to express belief, creed, moral and ethical exactitudes, or even worldview. I also assume that, no matter how passionately artists may believe what they believe or try to show these beliefs in what they imagine and craft, their art remains purposefully "dumb."[5]

It is not only disturbing that Best—himself a musician—seems to be claiming that music is meaningless, he also seems to be claiming that only words can transmit truth.

Certainly St. Francis didn't believe in the primacy of verbal communication when he admonished us to "Preach the Gospel at all times. Use words if necessary." If verbal messages were the only necessary tool to communicate truth, think how easy parenting would be—we would simply tell our children all the right things to do and their education would be complete! But we all know this "Do as I say and not as I do" method doesn't work. Children are constantly picking up the nonverbal messages we give them. We can tell them not to fight with their siblings but our peaceful way of talking to our spouse will speak with far more clarity. These powerful forms of nonverbal communication are what sociologists call "enculturation." These are the forces that shape us even more deeply than words. The Bible, too, indicates

> Hurry, copy down this dream
> Before the dawn steals it away
> Oh, my heart knows what it means
> Before it finds the words to say
> Like a snowflake on my tongue
> Don't let it melt away too soon
> Cause the place
> Where dreams come from
> Is nothing but the truth
>
> —Pierce Pettis[6]

that there are times when words fail us: "Likewise the Spirit helps us in our weakness; for we do not know how to pray as we ought, but that very Spirit intercedes with sighs too deep for words" (Rom. 8:26).

The Christian faith is not just a series of rational propositions to which we give intellectual assent but rather something we know and live in our whole being—heart, mind, and body. Words speak clearly to the mind, but what medium should we use to speak to the heart and body? The arts. Many aspects of the faith are intangible and mysterious (the Trinity, for example), and this is why we need the worship arts. They help our hearts and bodies know what our minds can't comprehend. We need to hear what Van Morrison called "the inarticulate speech of the heart." Perhaps being open to the powerful but ambiguous language of music and other arts trains us to hear the surprising, still, and small voice of the Spirit.

Of course, the arts shouldn't be set in opposition to word-based communication. They are commonly partners with words, to great effect. We would be wise to observe the way music can support or undermine a text. Consider for example Sylvia Dunstan's text "All Who Hunger."

> All who hunger, gather gladly, holy manna is our bread.
> Come from wilderness and wandering. Here in truth, we will be fed.
> You that yearn for days of fullness, all around us is our food.
> Taste and see the grace eternal. Taste and see that God is good.[7]

This text is commonly paired with two different tunes, Holy Manna and All Who Hunger. The American revival tune Holy Manna is a wonderfully robust melody that invigorates its most common text, "Brethren, We Have Come to Worship." Though it has in its favor a history as a gathering song and a tune title that relates to the communion theme of the text of "All Who Gather," this melody doesn't allow us to settle into the deeper messages of the text. On the other hand, Bob Moore's tune All Who Hunger slows down the pace of the song and lets us hear the deep comfort that is offered in the text and in communion itself.

> So, if I get carried away
> Like I'm not in my right mind
> Still, my heart is in the right place
> Though it may not seem so at the time
> I know this stuff can come off odd
> A little vague, a little rude
> But I swear
> So help me. God
> It is nothing but the truth
> —Pierce Pettis[8]

This is only one example. We can all think of moments in which the worship arts supported the verbal message, whether it was skillful oration, clear graphic design, or appropriate music. And we have all attended worship services in which a video or melody has trivialized the profound message of the gospel. The challenge for churches is to find ways to preach the gospel with words *and* the arts in a way that forms us in Christ's likeness—mind, heart, and body.

Creating a Context for the Arts in Worship

If you are a worship artist, you most certainly already affirm the important role of the arts in worship. But how do we put these ideas into practice in a climate that is often suspicious of the arts?

The first step in implementing the arts as a theology of the heart in local churches is to redefine the "frame" in our worship services. All art has a frame. In the visual arts it is often a literal frame, but every art form has a frame, whether it is the actors' stage, the edges of a movie screen, or the quiet page of poetry. Too often we simply adopt the frame of an art form such as music and import it into the sanctuary, replicating the context of a classical recital hall or a rock concert. But worship needs a new frame that breaks the paradigm of performer and audience. Once the people in the pews understand that worship is their work rather than a specialized musician's role, they will move from adulation or critique of the worship arts and will understand them as their own form of sacred communication.

One of the primary ways of redefining the frame in worship is to give more weight to the sacraments. Worship services that consist of a music set followed by preaching inevitably feel like a mini-concert followed by a lecture. Emphasizing the sacraments not only focuses on Christ's work rather than our feelings but also creates more opportunities for worshipers to take responsibility for worship rather than leaving it to professionals.

Because the people who plan and lead worship are usually trained artists, they often bring the assumptions of their discipline into the worship context, including the assumption of performer and audience. While there is much good to be gained by skilled arts leadership, we need to be more intentional about cultivating *communal* arts in our churches. Traditions such as *Sacred Harp* singing may be too rough around the edges for the concert hall but are exciting examples of how every person in a sanctuary becomes part of the music making and worship leading.

Another way trained artists need to adapt when applying our skills to worship is in our pursuit of quality. We should always strive for excellence, but we shouldn't confuse excellence with perfection. Excellence is our best offering in response to God's love. Perfection is the impossible taskmaster of those who are trying to win God's love and people's affection. It's also important to remember that no matter how good our drama ministry is or how lovely our sanctuary looks, it isn't (or shouldn't be) the reason people come to our church. Let them be consumers of art on Saturday night, but on Sunday morning let them feel God's presence with God's people.

Keeping Our Priorities Straight

Indeed, our modern culture offers us many temptations to lure our worship away from its intended purpose. How can we stand firm on a strong foundation?

First, we need to resist the tyranny of novelty. The worship industry, influential churches, and popular worship leaders all focus on things that are new: new songs, new musical equipment, and new worship movements.

Creative new ideas and resources are not bad in and of themselves, but they are also not good in and of themselves. If we are not careful, the pressure to keep up with every new trend can overwhelm us. We will be convinced that the latest technology will solve all our problems, the latest worship model will bring new people to our church, and the latest song will bring our people into God's throne room. We begin to fear that if we don't keep up with the latest trends, we will be left behind, irrelevant to our culture.

While new technologies and ideas can often be beneficial, they can just as easily become an exhausting merry-go-round of novelty—what King Solomon would have called "a chasing after wind" (Eccles. 1:14). G. K. Chesterton put it this way: "Tradition means giving votes to the most obscure of all classes, our ancestors. It is the democracy of the dead. Tradition refuses to submit to the small and arrogant oligarchy of those who merely happen to be walking about."[9] You may be worried this focus on tradition will leave us living in the past, unable to deal with the needs of the modern church. Hardly! If there is truly "nothing new under the sun" (v. 9), an understanding of our history is the very thing that will prepare us for any twist or turn the future brings us.

Second, we need to rethink what it means to be contemporary. Unfortunately, many modern church gurus have proposed that current popular music and media styles are the only way to remain relevant to the world around us. They would lead us to believe that any connection to tradition will make us inaccessible to today's worshipers. (And worse, make us appear old-fashioned!)

> "Really, that's what tradition is all about—connecting the past with the present while imagining a better future."
>
> —BANNING EYRE[10]

By definition anyone reading this book is "contemporary," that is, currently alive. But being modern or current doesn't mean having no relationship with the past. We are part of a continuum. Genetically this includes grandparents, parents, children, and grandchildren. Intellectually we inherit our place from authors long dead and childhood teachers; we'll pass on what we've learned to our children, students, and those who read our books. We carry the torch, but we didn't light it.

On the other hand, those who favor anything old as inherently better are in danger of becoming lost in the "good old days." As Jaroslov Pelikan so pithily stated, "Tradition is the living faith of the dead, traditionalism is the dead faith of the living."[11] Ideally, worship directors will serve as bridges between the past and present, grounding ourselves in the best of what has gone on before and gleaning the most promising of exciting new worship movements. The more steeped we are in what has come before us, the more freedom and confidence we have to improvise creatively. The deeper our roots grow in the soil of the past, the higher our branches can grow into the future.

Rooted in the past, growing into the future. This is a tall order! What might that look like in the worship arts in your church? Those of us who are responsible for worship should be intentional about the way we use music, arts, and technology. While we can't guarantee that singing songs of thanksgiving will form our congregants into grateful Christians, we can certainly shape services in a way that allows thankful hearts to pour out their praise, like water filling the shape of a glass. We can't guarantee that grieving members will rely on God for their comfort, but we can shape our worship in such a way that their grief can be expressed. Like the architectural axiom "form follows function," our shaping of the arts in worship should encourage the character traits we hope are growing in the lives of our church members.

Too often we focus on everything *but* the desired spiritual outcome. We want to make sure the band sounds good, the lighting is impressive, and the production is smooth. What if we instead focused on using the arts in worship to form our congregations spiritually? If our worship services were "Jesus disciple factories," what kind of machinery would we set up to have fully formed Jesus disciples at the end of the production line? Will the fruit of self-control thrive better in services that are flashy or modest? Will generosity grow more in services that understand the offering to be an act of worship or those that have collection boxes at the exits? Will patience be fostered more in worship services that have space for silence or in those that are paced like talk shows?

Of course, it isn't as simple as this. As Jamie Smith points out, "secular liturgies" are constantly competing for our affections.[12] That is, the mall, the arena, and the media are bombarding our members 24/7 with their own brand of theology. We can't expect one hour in church a week to produce fully formed disciples of Jesus Christ. However, worship directors have a responsibility to do what we can. The reality is that many people in our congregations will spend no more time on their faith than the hour they spend in church on Sunday. If they come to our church fifty-two times a year for ten years, will they have been introduced to the basics of the Christian faith? The whole biblical witness? Will they have practiced thanksgiving and lament, confession and forgiveness? Will their time in worship have grown their capacity to hear the still, small voice of the Spirit in their daily lives?

The worship arts open doors of spiritual formation for our people through rooted creativity. Worship is not first about innovation and self-expression. Instead, we creatively adapt age-old worship concepts to our unique time and place. The Calvin Institute of Christian Worship's sixth of ten core convictions phrases it well: "Worship is enriched by artistic creativity in many genres and media, not as ends to themselves or as open-ended individual inspirations, but all disciplined by the nature of worship as a prophetic and priestly activity."[13] Even though we want our worship arts to be high quality and we take pride in the work we do, the arts in worship don't serve themselves and they certainly don't serve us. They serve the worship: they proclaim Scripture, they give voice to prayers, and they call us to repentance. For worship directors, keeping our priorities straight is half the battle.

For Discussion

1. Which best describes your church's approach to the arts: utilitarian, aesthetic, or metaphorical?

2. Do you believe truth can be communicated nonverbally? If yes, give some examples. If no, explain why not.

3. If the "frame" of a movie is a screen and of a concert is a stage, what is the "frame" of worship?

4. In what ways has your church fallen prey to the novelty of contemporary worship or the nostalgia of traditional worship?

5. If Chesterton is right that "tradition is the democracy of the dead," how could your church give the dead a vote in how you run your worship?

11

The Gospel Intoned

Music

Before you begin: What is your theology of music?

As you know, theology is the study of God and religious belief. It attempts to answer the questions: Who (or what) is God? How do we know God? What does God require of humans? Likewise, a theology of music would tackle questions such as: What is music? What is it capable of doing? How should it be used in worship? See if you can articulate a basic theology of music that you might want to share and discuss with your church's musicians.

Christianity is an incarnational faith. We see this most vividly in Jesus, the Word of God, who took on flesh and lived among us. In worship, the Word of God takes on flesh in part through the arts. It is the work of the worship director to shape artistic elements of the service in a way that makes the faith graspable by the senses. Let's consider the ways music, the arts, and technology proclaim the gospel in worship.

Music's Role in Worship

Music has undeniable power. David soothed Saul's spirit with his harp. The Greek philosophers saw music as the glue of the cosmos and social order.

"Music" by Anne Porter

When I was a child
I once sat sobbing on the floor
Beside my mother's piano
As she played and sang
For there was in her singing
A shy yet solemn glory
My smallness could not hold
And when I was asked
Why I was crying
I had no words for it
I only shook my head
And went on crying
Why is it that music
At its most beautiful
Opens a wound in us
An ache a desolation
Deep as a homesickness
For some far-off
And half-forgotten country
I've never understood
Why this is so
But there's an ancient legend
From the other side of the world
That gives away the secret

Of this mysterious sorrow
For centuries on centuries
We have been wandering
But we were made for Paradise
As deer for the forest
And when music comes to us
With its heavenly beauty
It brings us desolation
For when we hear it
We half remember
That lost native country
We dimly remember the fields
Their fragrant windswept clover
The birdsongs in the orchards
The wild white violets in the moss
By the transparent streams
And shining at the heart of it
Is the longed-for beauty
Of the One who waits for us
Who will always wait for us
In those radiant meadows
Yet also came to live with us
And wanders where we wander.[1]

No human culture has ever been found that lacks some form of music. It is exceedingly strange that mere vibrating columns of air tickling the tiny hairs of our inner ear could hold such sway over our souls, but there is no denying the power of song. Certainly each of us has been inexplicably moved by the sound of a voice or instrument, as Anne Porter describes in her poem "Music."

Music also plays a vital role in worship. Luther viewed music's place as second only to Scripture, calling music "the handmaiden of theology." Scripture itself includes a songbook—Psalms—and commands us to sing them as well as hymns and spiritual songs. While it is theoretically possible to have worship without music, it is rarely done.

Perhaps actors or dancers would balk at giving music a favored status among the worship arts—the self-serving view of a musician authoring a book on worship. However, the biblical witness and church history seem to support this music-centric worship philosophy. In the Old Testament, the Levites, Israel's priests, included in their number a guild of musicians who were exempt from other duties because they were ministering in the temple day and night (1 Chron. 9:33). The New Testament, while largely silent about worship, lists music among the recommended acts of worship, and is thought to include quotes from songs that circulated in the early church (for example, see Phil. 2:6–11). The Bible ends with all of the redeemed singing a new song (Rev. 5:9).

Certainly, in historical worship practice music dominates all other worship arts. Music is second only to preaching in terms of the amount of time dedicated to it in most worship services. In-

"Is it not strange that sheep's guts could hail souls out of men's bodies?" —William Shakespeare, *Much Ado About Nothing*

"All audible musical sound is given us for the sake of harmony, which has motions akin to the orbits in our soul, and which . . . is not to be used, as is commonly thought, to give irrational pleasure, but as a heaven-sent ally in reducing to order and harmony any disharmony in the revolutions within us. Rhythm, again, was given us from the same heavenly source to help us in the same way; for most of us lack measure and grace." —Plato, *Timaeus*

"The modes of music are never disturbed without unsettling of the most fundamental political and social conventions." —Plato, *Republic*

"From these considerations therefore it is plain that music has the power of producing a certain effect on the moral character of the soul, and if it has the power to do this, it is clear that the young must be directed to music and must be educated in it." —Aristotle, *Politics*

deed, since the rise of Pentecostalism in the twentieth century and the explosion of modern worship bands in the twenty-first century, many churches spend more time on music than preaching. Perhaps this is why some have questioned the way music has come to dwarf other arts in worship. Has it grown too big for its own britches? Perhaps.

There is no doubt that some modern worship styles have adopted the rock concert as the paradigm on which they build worship: massive sound systems, elevated stages with the band front and center, lights bathing the singer while the "congregation" sways to the music in a darkened hall.

Veteran praise songwriter Graham Kendrick wonders if the trappings of the rock concert may be in part responsible for the lack of singing in many of today's churches.[2] Some churches are so deep into this music performance paradigm that no one bats an eye when things clearly move beyond the scope of anything that could reasonably be considered worship. For example, a number of churches have recently been singing Pharrell Williams's song "Happy" in worship. Yes, it is an infectious, joyous song. No, there's nothing intrinsically evil about it. However, in the context of worship it is at best a frothy three-minute diversion and at worst a dilution of the gospel.[3] Most churches don't go this far, but too many are taking their cues from Saturday night rather than Sunday morning; that is, they cast their musicians as performers and their congregation as audience rather than considering the unique role music plays in a worship context. In worship, all the arts must submit themselves to the "frame" that worship itself provides. In worship, music is never its own art but supports the larger worship context.

This functional view of music in worship might go against the grain of those who are steeped in the context of the concert hall or recording studio. In those venues it is "music for music's sake"—and there is nothing wrong with that philosophy in those settings. But in worship, music plays a supportive role. Catholics call the music of worship "ritual music" because of the way it supports the ritual actions of worship. Germans use the word *gebrauchsmusik* ("music for use") to describe music that plays a functional role. Nicholas Wolterstorff speaks of the "fittingness" of a work of art for particular use. No matter what term we use, music intended for use in worship needs to be evaluated not on its own intrinsic merit but on how well it supports the work of worship.

What can we reasonably expect music to accomplish in worship? First, music plays a formative role. The most obvious way that music helps form us into Christlikeness is in the theology of the songs we sing. New Testament scholar Gordon Fee sees a church's music as something of a faith thermometer: "Show me a church's songs and I'll show you their theology."[4] His point is that our cumulative repertoire over the years works its way deep into our being, shaping our beliefs. If we sing numerous songs about social justice but no songs about personal righteousness, how likely is it that we'll understand the vision of Psalm 85:10: "righteousness and peace will kiss each other"? If we sing only of the crucifixion and never of the resurrection, will we intuitively understand the depth of our own sin more than the depth of God's forgiving love?

Certainly, a full-orbed gospel can be preached and read in the Scriptures. But something about music drives the message down deep into the soul. Music is the Trojan horse of the emotions. We sing about the inevitability of death in "O God, Our Help in Ages Past" by Isaac Watts with the words, "Time, like an ever-rolling stream, soon bears us all away; we fly forgotten, as a dream dies at the opening day." Yet sung to the sturdy tune of St. Anne, it doesn't sound hopeless. In fact, by the time we get to the final verse, "O God, our help in ages past, our hope for years to come, still be our guard while troubles last, and our eternal home!" we have a strong sense, guided along by the music, that the message of Psalm 90 is really true: even though we will die, we have a God who is strong enough to raise us to eternal life.

Music not only sweetens messages we may be otherwise unwilling to consider but also heightens our emotions and engages our bodies. Some Christians may be uncomfortable with the idea that we may need anything more than the cold, hard facts of the gospel, but God made humans with more than brains; we have hearts, souls, and bodies that need to know the gospel as well. Music is effective therapy for Alzheimer's, autism, Parkinson's, and depression, and has been shown to coordinate the brain and the body in unique ways. We all know firsthand how emotionally powerful music can be, whether by singing a beloved hymn at a funeral or listening to upbeat music before competing in a sporting event. True, we should be careful not to be emotionally manipulative with music. But the danger of abusing the power of music shouldn't keep us from tapping its potential to preach the gospel. After all, people in our congregation are constantly barraged with music that sweetens messages of rebellion, adultery, and even murder. Do we want to leave the musically receptive parts of their beings saturated with everything but the gospel?

Second, music helps us express ourselves. Though not a universal language, it is a language nonetheless, often speaking for us when words fail. We usually think of the arts as self-expression. While this is certainly true—the songwriter and the worshiper express themselves to God in a personal way—in the case of congregational song we are simultaneously expressing something larger than our own emotions. We sing the truths of the Bible, taking on the voice of the psalmist, for example. We sing with the voices of the saints who have gone before us when we sing hymns written before our time. We sing with Christians of other lands when we sing songs from outside our own culture. And sometimes we even sing of things we have not yet experienced or truths we may not yet understand.

That is the beauty of music. It can simultaneously express the individual and the community. Ethnomusicologists—those who study music in its cultural context—point out that music can powerfully express, define, and support culture. Each church is unique, and music is a strong fingerprint in establishing and maintaining its values and perspective. Without saying a word, a church's music can express whether it is made up of young hipsters, educated middle-class families, or a particular ethnic group. Music also expresses the values of the larger culture beyond the church walls. Values such as consumerism, nationalism, and individualism necessarily seep into church life and are expressed in a church's musical choices. For example, churches within cultures that are communal in their orientation tend to have music that allows for strong participation from all, whereas in more individualistic cultures an admonition to participate may elicit resistance: "Don't tell me to sing!" Of course, music also inevitably expresses ethnicity. Music styles and values are refined over centuries in different cultures, and often those from outside have no way of interpreting another culture's musical language. So a Southern gospel–loving worshiper doesn't even consider a hip-hop worship leader to be making music, and neither of them have any idea how to engage the beauty of a Chinese worshiper's unadorned melody.

Music's unique ability to express culture is important for worship directors because, whether we like it or not, the music we use in our churches is constantly sending messages. We may be saying, "All are welcome" with our mouths, but our music is saying, "You are *more* welcome if you are _____." While it is impossible to be all things to all people, musically speaking, we certainly don't want to be so narrow in our musical choices that it marks insiders from outsiders, excluding some from the communal expression. In fact, while music has the power to clearly mark dividing lines between different people, it also has the ability to unite people. The very act of singing in a group has been shown to bind people together.[5] For Christian communities, our music can be a powerful force to unite us and solidify our identity as a new people in Christ.

Third, music accompanies acts of worship. From the focusing tones of the prelude to the joyous burst of notes that send us out in the postlude, we are swept along in a current of music. Some of the musical accompaniment in worship is what would be called "underscore" in plays or movies. Like a movie soundtrack, music can establish the tone in various parts of worship. Yes, this can be overused or distracting, but like the best movie scores it can add emotional impact while never bringing attention to itself.[6] Some African-American churches are known for the interplay between preacher and musician, each punctuating the other's phrases in a way that blurs the lines between speech and singing. However, we don't have to be part of a tradition of improvised music to take advantage of the way music can smooth transitions, highlight certain actions, or focus the room to an important moment.

One of the things music does best is help worship's pacing, creating flow between elements and giving vitality to things that would seem tedious if unaccompanied or not sung. For example, my church's worship includes a confession every week, and it is normally just spoken. One week we sang a haunting Ghanaian *Kyrie* ("Lord, Have Mercy") before and after the confession. Between those musical bookends, a marimba lightly rumbled the song's chords underneath the spoken confession. Just this simple musical touch gave import to the confession, focused people's minds to the moment, and created a distinct section within the worship service.

Silence, too, is part of a service's musical accompaniment, punctuating worship with moments of reflection or quiet anticipation.

Fourth, music dignifies and beautifies worship. This is not to say that worship has no dignity or beauty on its own, but that we are often unreceptive to it. The majestic sound of a pipe organ or the heartfelt passion of a simple praise chorus are often the thing that convinces us of the reality of the Christian faith. How could such beauty exist if there were no loving God behind it? Further, music can be engaged at many different levels. One worshiper may simply enjoy the tune, another may be philosophically considering the text, while a third is remembering a past experience in which the song played a pivotal role. Music is a glue that allows us to engage in worship both as individuals and as a community.

Finally, congregational music blurs the line between our worship within the church walls and the sacrifice of worship we offer in our day-to-day lives. We find ourselves recalling a song at a seemingly random moment and it becomes a moment of devotion. We read a passage of Scripture in the morning and it brings to mind a song that accompanies us throughout the day, binding the scriptural truth to our hearts. Even as we approach death we have a treasury of faith to draw on through the songs we've learned throughout our lives. Many people have discovered that faltering loved ones, who can't communicate otherwise, suddenly begin singing every word of a favorite hymn.

God has given us a precious gift in music!

For Discussion

1. At the beginning of this chapter you were asked to explain your theology of music in worship. Try to guess how your congregation would answer the same question.

2. Do you agree that music seems to have an elevated position among the worship arts? Why or why not? Is this a good or a bad thing?

3. In worship, music plays a supportive role. Can you think of a time when music became too dominant in one of your worship services? (That is, it served itself rather than serving the worship service.)

4. Would you ever sing Pharrell Williams's song "Happy" in one of your services? What about an organ piece by Ralph Vaughan Williams? (They are not brothers, by the way.) Give your reasons for including or excluding either.

5. Read some of the books and articles on the benefits of group singing mentioned in the endnotes. Does music in your church contribute to the unity or disunity of the people?

12

A Balanced Congregational Song Repertoire

Before you begin: Analyze your repertoire.

Look at a list of all the songs you've sung in the last five years. How many are there? How many do you sing regularly? Do you notice any trends? (A lot of rejoicing but no lamenting, heavy rotation of particular music styles, or music used exclusively in certain parts of worship?) Do you feel stuck in a rut or overwhelmed by too many options? Discuss this with other music leaders in the church to see if they observe the same things.

Music has fallen on hard times. Though music is all around us every day, people rarely listen—really listen—to music anymore. It is harnessed for its ability to connect with a target demographic and sell chewing gum. Music has become the sonic wallpaper of our lives: always there but never noticed.

Music doesn't fare much better in the church. Music style is used to define a service's intended audience—choirs for the cultured members, banjos for the hipsters—but we rarely consider music's ability to do much more than get people to their seats and warm them up for the sermon.

Songwriters have responded with a slew of generic praise songs that are defined by tempo and mood rather than intrinsic value.

In contrast, if we open up a hymnal and browse the subject index, we find songs that address hundreds of topics: the Trinity, funerals, church unity, communion, and so forth. It is refreshing to see such a wide range of topics addressed. In this context, congregational songs are clearly trusted to share the theological work of worship. However, some hymn topics are so narrowly focused that they couldn't be used more than once every few years. Consider, for example, a 2008 hymn by Robert Bayley about pornography, "O God, Who Made Us in Your Image."[1] This is a topic that needs to be addressed by the church, but perhaps a song is not the best place to do it.

Surely there is a happy medium between generic and specific songs in worship. We start by acknowledging that every song—including a "generic" praise song—does something. It may serve a broad function like calling the congregation to worship (such as Redman's "10,000 Reasons") or a specific function like proclaiming Scripture (such as Purcell's verse anthem "Rejoice in the Lord Always" on Phil. 4:4–7), but every song plays a role in the act of worship. The key is to find the places in each service where music will function better than a spoken alternative, and then find the right song to fill that need. It would be ludicrous to replace the announcements with a congregational song, but singing a benediction or creed could be effective.

A song is never just a song. Worship songs let us pray, remember, or meditate. Almost anything that can be done in worship can be done in song. Certainly, songs establish mood and lead us to express particular emotions, but this is only a byproduct of worship music's primary, functional role. Too many worship directors choose music for the wrong reasons: "Everyone loves this song," or "We need three upbeat songs in the key of E, and then we'll do a few slower songs in G." Is it any wonder that many people in our congregations think of our services as having two distinct sections, the singing part and the spiritual part? We need to move toward an understanding of singing not as something separate but as something that is integrated into the larger work of worship, with songs woven into every aspect of what we do, from praise to proclamation.

Some pastors feel threatened by music encroaching into their territory. As one pastor told me, "You pick some upbeat praise songs, and I'll take care of the theology." But wise pastors will understand that music supports their work rather than undermining it. What pastor wouldn't want to follow a sermon with a song that allows the congregation to respond with all their hearts?

If we trust the songs in a worship service to be part of the actual work of worship, rather than simply window dressing, our song choices are very important indeed. We become even more focused as we realize there are a limited number of songs sung in each worship service. Songs are, in a sense, worship real estate. In the same way that a real estate agent wouldn't waste a waterfront property, the worship director can't waste three minutes of worship real estate with poorly chosen or shoddily written songs. Instead, we should aim to use each opportunity to feed our congregation a balanced diet of songs.

Many of us think of balance in worship songs simply as a balance between traditional and contemporary. While balancing traditional and contemporary music is certainly admirable, it is a very narrow slice of a very large pie. There are dozens of other things to consider. We'll look at three areas: sources of songs, the roles songs play in our church's worship, and the musical forms of congregational songs.

Source

In the Sermon on the Mount, Jesus tells us,

> No good tree bears bad fruit, nor again does a bad tree bear good fruit; for each tree is known by its own fruit. Figs are not gathered from thorns, nor are grapes picked from a bramble bush. The good person out of the good treasure of the heart produces good, and the evil person out of evil treasure produces evil; for it is out of the abundance of the heart that the mouth speaks. (Luke 6:43–45)

James addresses the same theme, posing the question, "Does a spring pour forth from the same opening both fresh and brackish water? Can a fig tree, my brothers and sisters, yield olives, or a grapevine figs? No more can salt water yield fresh" (James 3:11–12). It's clear that both Jesus and James see a direct connection between the inside and outside of a life—"garbage in, garbage out," as we say in modern parlance. While these passages are directed to individual believers, it's appropriate to extend the concept to our corporate lives. Could it be that if we were to follow our church's songs to their source, we'd learn a lot about what we value as worshipers and what we hope to become as Christians?

From Old to New

We'll consider a number of song sources, but let's begin with a timeline from old to new. Today's churches have the opportunity to sing songs as old as the Bible itself (e.g., Psalms) or as recent as a song posted to YouTube last night. Unfortunately, most churches focus almost exclusively on one or the other. Those who value a more traditional song repertoire claim to sing songs that have "stood the test of time." This is certainly true. Time has a way of weeding out the chaff of yesteryear, handing down songs with real merit that continue to speak, generation after generation. But those who value contemporary songs argue that worship should speak in a way that is relevant to those currently in our churches and culture. Surely it's true that popular song styles and modern language are the *lingua franca* of our time and represent the easiest way of communicating with those around us.

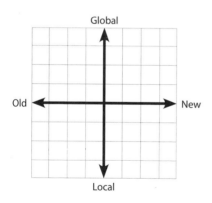

While both sides have valid points, there are problems with focusing on songs only from historic or modern sources. Plenty of old songs continue to be sung out of nostalgia rather than merit, or use words that make little sense to modern worshipers. On the other hand, a steady diet of the latest hits can leave us unmoored from our shared past, pushed along by whatever breeze blows our way.

What if we were to think of our song repertoire a little less in terms of old and new and a little more like "hardcover" and "paperback"? That is, some books are classics—millions of people have read them before us and millions of people will read them after us. The Bible, the works of Shakespeare, *The Art of Worship.* We will read them over and over again, so we'll want these books in a sturdy hardcover or elegant leather binding.[2] On the other hand, the life cycle of the latest detective mystery or tech magazine is much quicker. These paperbacks will be read once and then recycled.

And that's okay.

Both are important because both serve a particular need at a particular time. In the same way that fine china and cloth napkins are inappropriate for a picnic, a dense four-verse hymn in nineteenth-century English may not be the best song for every occasion. Conversely, Styrofoam cups are probably not a good choice for a wedding. "Certainly our God deserves better than *disposable* songs!" you protest. While God is "from everlasting to everlasting," we humans "flourish like a flower of the field; for the wind passes over it, and it is gone" (Ps. 103:15–17). But in God's good grace he chose to send his Son Jesus to our world as a human. Jesus's willingness to become "disposable" for our salvation certainly should help guide our thinking about the forms we use to communicate the gospel. We should strive for a balance of transcendence (otherness; timelessness) and immanence (nearness; immediacy). We seek to communicate the unchanging truth of an eternal God but we use musical materials that are bound by time and human inadequacy, whether three hundred years or three hundred days old.

From Local to Global

We seek to "bring out treasures old and new" (see Matt. 13:52) in our worship, but we also seek to reflect God's transcendence and immanence by the use of both local and global songs.[3] Once again, many churches fall into an either/or approach with their repertoire. Some churches with talented in-house writers rarely sing a song a church member hasn't written. Other churches can't imagine singing anything but what is in their hymnal. The first is missing out on the unity of singing with the broader church, and the second may be closing the door to the near-at-hand works of the Spirit as prophesied in Joel and fulfilled on Pentecost: "your sons and your daughters shall prophesy, and your young men shall see visions, and your old men shall dream dreams" (Acts 2:17; see Joel 2:28).

Why is it important to include songs from both inside and outside our tradition or church? Music powerfully expresses who we are and how we see the world. But it also forms us. Churches who only use music from their own writers or denomination risk getting caught in a feedback loop of self-expression and formation that can lead to an insular, nearsighted faith. We can't imagine that anyone who is not like us could truly love the same God as we do. Indeed, we may not be worshiping the same God but rather a god of our own making that looks just like us and our people.

One antidote to this culturally reinforced idol worship is singing the songs of those outside our community. Adding our voices to Christians outside our "tribe" broadens our perspective. Yes, we all have access to the Bible and the insight of the Holy Spirit, but we don't all have the experience of being persecuted, educated, or hungry. In the same way that a book or movie can let us enter someone else's world, singing with Christians of other times and places lets us enter a deeper understanding of the faith. This may take the form of a hymn from the first centuries of the church, a tender ballad from Latin America, or an exuberant black gospel anthem from the church across the street. Each of these helps us live into our citizenship in the eternal kingdom of Christ rather than our temporary allegiance to our race, class, or local church.

Of course, thinking broadly about our song repertoire shouldn't stop us from writing new songs in our local churches. Indeed, that's where all of these global songs originated. We want to continue to add our voices to the eternal song of God's people.

The Roles of Congregational Song

The perfect balance of repertoire from old, new, local, and global sources doesn't necessarily mean that these songs are the right ones for your particular congregation. The question of music is never only an abstract question. Principles must be applied to actual congregations and songs sung by real people. That's why we also need to consider the role different types of songs play in our congregation's repertoire. Once again, a song is never just a song. Each song helps us *do* something in worship and helps us experience a different aspect of the Christian life. Ron Rienstra jokes that the term "praise team" is too limiting; why not a "lament team" or a "benediction team"?[4] His point is that congregational songs can play all sorts of roles, from confessing sin to proclaiming Scripture. Congregational songs that address a broad spectrum of themes are an important part of forming a congregation in Christlikeness in all areas of faith.

Pastoral   Prophetic

"The role of the church is to comfort the afflicted and to afflict the comfortable." This tongue-in-cheek axiom, attributed to Reinhold Niebuhr, unveils a deep truth about the *pastoral* and *prophetic* roles of worship music. The church and its worship should be pastoral, meeting people where they are and offering them rest in Jesus Christ. "Come to me, all you that are weary and are carrying heavy burdens, and I will give you rest" (Matt. 11:28). But it doesn't stop there. Worship should also be prophetic. When Christ calls us, he calls us *to* something. Consider the examples of the disciples; Christ called them to leave their jobs and follow him, and many of them followed him to their deaths. The peace of Christ is not the same as a comfortable coddling; it is a peace "which surpasses all understanding" (Phil. 4:7).

Unfortunately, many people see worship—and especially the music of worship—as one-dimensional. They assume worship should be relevant, comfortable, and positive—essentially, the Christian version of the music we hear when we're shopping. But this ignores music's role as a way of calling people to deeper, more costly discipleship. As Amos 5:23–24 puts it: "Take away from me the noise of your songs; I will not

William Alexander Percy puts the comfort/affliction dichotomy in stark terms in this hymn of discipleship:

> They cast their nets in Galilee
> just off the hills of brown;
> such happy, simple fisherfolk,
> before the Lord came down.
>
> Contented, peaceful fishermen,
> before they ever knew
> the peace of God that filled their hearts
> brimful, and broke them too.
>
> Young John who trimmed the flapping sail,
> homeless, in Patmos died.
> Peter, who hauled the teeming net,
> head-down was crucified.
>
> The peace of God, it is no peace,
> but strife closed in the sod.
> Yet let us pray for but one thing—
> the marvelous peace of God.[5]

listen to the melody of your harps. But let justice roll down like waters, and righteousness like an ever-flowing stream." Our songs are just noise until they spur us on to lives of justice and righteousness, so let's choose songs that call our congregations to faithful living.

Formation   Expression

In a similar vein, many people define worship as "a time to express ourselves to God." This is certainly true, but do we also give God a platform to express himself to us? This balance between *formation* and *expression* is tricky. Some churches focus entirely on expression—hands are raised, hearts are open, and feelings flow freely. These are all wonderful, biblical expressions of worship, but if worship is only expression, it can become an empty, narcissistic ritual that elevates me and my feelings above all else. To be fair, many of these expression-oriented churches provide ample opportunities for formation; they simply see singing as a time of expression and have healthy expectations for formation during the sermon, personal devotions, and other areas of church life. Different mediums—singing, speaking, praying—are more effective for achieving different goals, but when we use music only for its expressive role we lose a ripe opportunity for music to teach, pray, and proclaim.

Other churches—sometimes in opposition to a recent tide of expressive worship styles—see formation as the primary goal of worship. I recall talking to a woman at a party one time; she railed against what she saw as the vapidity of modern praise music, leaning way too far into my personal space and spitting out, "Doctrine! Doctrine! Where is the doctrine?!" Most people who extol the virtues of formation in worship aren't quite so animated about it but would agree with the basic premise: worship should be part of the discipleship process. Focusing on the formative possibilities of worship music becomes even more highlighted as we recognize that many of those in our congregation won't spend any time outside of church reading the Bible, praying, or fellowshipping with other believers. Though not ideal, one hour of church may be the only chance we get to teach our people the foundations of the faith! Many great pastors throughout history have understood the power of music to teach: John Calvin's *The Genevan*

Psalter, Samuel Stone's collection *Lyra Fidelium* (songs on the Apostle's Creed, including "The Church's One Foundation"), and the many pastor/poets such as Isaac Watts who concluded their sermons with freshly written hymns to cement the teaching in people's hearts.

There are many ways to express this spectrum: doctrine/devotion, revelation/response, information/ecstasy, head/heart. All of these are variations on the same theme—some worship songs express who we currently are, and others help shape us into who God is calling us to become. We should seek a balance between the two.

On a more practical level, worship songs can range from *complex* to *simple*; from a seven-verse creedal hymn with dense poetry and challenging melody to a simple, repeated, "Thank you, Lord." The battle between "highbrow" and "lowbrow" approaches to worship music has gone on for years, with one camp complaining about "mindless ditties" and the other camp suffering through "endless dirges." This brings up an important point: sometimes the argument is less about the music itself and more about people's personalities— whether they're oriented more tov the head  or the heart. *Head* people value ideas, especially complex ideas that need to be teased out with nuanced words. They don't believe the mysteries of God can be accurately portrayed by simple words or music. *Heart* people value feeling, relationship, and immediacy. The many words and sophisticated music of the head people's hymns leave them cold and unmoved.

Neither of these approaches—head or heart—is wrong. And neither is right. God made us all different and then put us into community to complete each other. The problem comes when a community leans heavily in one direction, forcing some people to express themselves in forms that are an ill fit for their disposition. Essentially they spend the worship service "translating" from a foreign mode of communication. Also, the rest of the church loses the benefit of their unique perspective.

Full disclosure: I'm a head person. This became clear to me years ago when I had ongoing tension with two singers on my praise team. We always seemed to be speaking past each other. I would introduce what I considered to be a quality song, and they would never warm up to it. They would describe an amazing worship experience they'd had, and it would just sound tacky or overly emotional to me. At first I thought we were experiencing a traditional-versus-contemporary tension, but I soon realized the tension was more based on personality type. Once I understood our fundamental difference, I made a point of using more heartfelt language that would help me relate to them better. Instead of extolling a new song only for its aesthetic qualities, I'd explain how it moved me on an emotional level. (Even head people have emotions!) This wasn't manipulative; I was simply trying to become more conversant in their language. In the same way, worship directors should identify whether they themselves are head or heart people and which direction their congregation leans, then use language and songs that are inviting to people of all dispositions.

But the complex/simple song spectrum is not only a matter of personality. No matter what your congregation's disposition, it will include members of different ages, education levels, and verbal abilities. If we choose only complex songs, our children may be unable to engage. If our songs require us to read music, it may leave out those with less musical training. If our songs use sophisticated language, members who speak English as a second language may be entirely lost. Is this dumbing down worship? Perhaps. As some have argued, we shouldn't underestimate people's ability to learn complex material nor should we dilute the faith for the sake of simplicity.[6] However, if we're holding on to our complex songs simply because they make us feel more sophisticated than the church down the street, we're losing a rich opportunity to minister to all the people God has given us. We

include both simple and complex music in our services because God calls us to meet people where they are while calling them to deeper and deeper faith.

Some of the issue of complexity is mitigated through familiarity. In her fascinating study of repetition in music, *On Repeat: How Music Plays the Mind*, Elizabeth Hellmuth Margulis shows that repeated hearings allow the mind to comprehend new songs or styles; further, repetition is the primary factor in musical enjoyment. If you are a trained musician, this may be completely foreign to your way of thinking. We musicians are connoisseurs: we can read music (or have better than average ears), have a more diverse repertoire than most people, and are eager to try new music. Our congregations, on the other hand, process music slowly. They like what they already know and are reluctant to try music that veers from the repertoire they had established by the time they were twenty-five.

Is there a hopeless gulf between members and church musicians, between *known* and *new* songs? If Margulis is right, worship directors can use song repetition in our favor. That is, if we use a song frequently enough, its complexity will decrease over time and it will be more likely to become one of the con-

How many songs are too many?

This is the conundrum that Jon Nicol addresses in his practical book, *The SongCycle: How to Simplify Worship Planning and Re-engage Your Church* (FlingWide, 2013). He leads us through the process of introducing, maintaining, and retiring songs in a systematic way. Nicol's math is a sobering antidote to the typical worship director's love of new songs.

gregation's heart songs. Does this mean that your hymn-loving congregation could learn to syncopate, your untrained members could sing in four parts, or your Midwest American congregants could gain an appreciation for global worship songs? Yes—but it will take time, intention, and planning.

While we can assume that every congregation has the capacity to learn and appreciate new songs as they become more familiar over time, no congregation has the capacity to expand their repertoire endlessly. John Witvliet suggests that most congregations really know only two hundred songs or hymns.[7] Let's use this as a starting point. If we take the time to teach our congregation a new song, perhaps in an unfamiliar style, and we repeat it until it becomes a church favorite, we now have 201 songs in our repertoire. However, if we teach ten more songs and repeat them often enough for them to become part of the church's cherished repertoire, it is likely that other songs are now moving out of rotation, soon to be forgotten.

Perhaps we could understand the balance of known songs to new songs as a pyramid. At the bottom of the pyramid are songs that are cherished by the whole congregation—*near and dear*. Sing the first few words of one of these songs and everyone happily joins in by memory. Near and dear songs should form the foundation of a church's singing, freeing them to worship from their hearts without distraction. Hopefully this core of the church's repertoire will not only be well-loved but also versatile enough to be used at funerals, in times of crisis, and in worship services throughout the year.

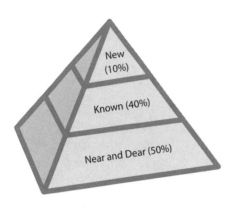

At the next level of the pyramid are songs that are generally recognizable but not lodged quite as deeply into the collective memory as the previous category. These *known* songs might include songs with new words to familiar tunes, recent additions to a church's repertoire, or songs that are still sung but only infrequently. Sing the first few words of one of these songs and people will recognize the song but won't be able to join in without musical leadership and lyrics. These are songs that engage the mind but are not embedded deep in the heart. They are perfect for filling out a worship service with familiar songs that support Scripture and sermon themes. After all, not every song can invoke a warm, fuzzy feeling!

At the top of the pyramid are *new* songs. These songs will challenge the congregation as people attempt to learn a new melody, understand an unfamiliar music style, or grapple with a difficult text. They are more work than play. Why would any congregation want to sing one of these songs? More importantly, why would any worship director plan to sing a song that is not well loved or even familiar—that is, perhaps, downright difficult? Once again, we return to the idea of "comforting the afflicted and afflicting the comfortable." If a congregation sings only songs that are already well loved they become stuck in a nostalgic rut, unable to respond to changes in their community and new movements of the Spirit. On the other hand, if a congregation sings too much new or challenging material they will have no shared song—no foundation from which they can grow.

As a starting place, consider a ratio of 50 percent near and dear songs, 40 percent known songs, and 10 percent new songs. This creates a good deal of stability in each worship service, with half the songs instantly singable, yet also includes a place of challenge in most services—something that explores new territory. An approach like this builds growth and change into the fabric of worship planning while maintaining the trust of the congregation.

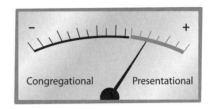

A final spectrum to consider when choosing worship songs is the balance between *congregational* and *presentational* music. Though the Bible instructs us repeatedly, "Sing to the Lord," it's clear that many church members don't interpret this Scripture literally. They stand and watch the band or sit and listen to the choir—seeing themselves as an audience rather than participants.

Some of this is due to a broader shift in modern (Western) culture. Whereas public singing was commonplace years ago, today music making is seen as a specialized practice reserved for those with talent and training. People are used to a clear delineation between performer and audience, and they bring that expectation into church with them.

Unfortunately, many church musicians are all too happy to perpetuate this performance model in worship. Whether they play pipe organ or electric guitar, they see their role as playing *for* the congregation rather than playing *with* the congregation. Church architecture often encourages this, putting musicians on an elevated stage with special lighting and sound reinforcement. With all the visual cues of a classical recital or rock concert, is it any wonder we fall so easily into a performer/audience relationship?

But perhaps the most significant barrier to congregational singing is the choice of songs. People don't sing in church because the songs don't encourage their participation. As Graham Kendrick points out in his excellent video, "Why Aren't We Singing?" many songs are too complex, pitched too high, or too dependent on the band.[8] Furthermore, he suggests there may just be too many songs to learn any songs well enough to sing.

In some ways, we are victims of our own success. The rise of worship music as a genre and radio format has changed the way many Christians define worship. "Worship" is something we do when we are listening to Christian radio in our car, are at a stadium enjoying a concert by our favorite worship artist, or are doing worship aerobics in our living room. While these are all good things for Christians to do, they are better described as *worshipful* rather than worship. The problem comes when we try to re-create these worshipful experiences in our local congregations. A song that sounds great in a huge arena full of teenagers might not work as well in a small, intergenerational church. A song we love to listen to in our car may not be very good for group singing. However, most of us aren't thinking about these distinctions; we just know what we like.

Finally, the growth of seeker-sensitive megachurches has changed our assumptions about what we're actually doing when we gather on a Sunday morning (or Saturday night). Christians used to share a common' under-standing of church: it was a gathering of the faithful to worship God, deepen belief, and be immersed in the symbols and traditions of the faith. But the seeker movement has turned those expectations on their head. Discipleship of believers moved to midweek small groups while the large gathering on Sunday morning was geared toward introducing non-Christians ("seekers") to Christianity in a nonthreatening environment. Symbols of traditional Christianity, from crosses to pipe organs, were removed from the auditorium and replaced by bands that played familiar pop music styles and pastors who spoke without a lot of "Christianese" jargon.

This targeted outreach approach has been very successful in ministries such as Willow Creek Community Church in the suburbs of Chicago. However, the trickle-down effect has been that many churches came to see worship as a show—a concert put on for the entertainment of the people in the auditorium rather than a sacred gathering of the "priesthood of believers." Because of this confusion, many worship directors put the cart before the horse, spending most of their time thinking about lighting, sound systems, and perfecting pop hits but paying very little attention to whether the worshipers were taking part.[9]

Let's be honest: most of us are planning services for believers. Let's cut through the clutter of what worship *could* be and focus on crafting worship services that allow our people to raise their own voices in praise rather than watching someone else do it for them. Think of the congregation's voice as the primary voice of worship: they praise, they lament, they pray. Worship leaders are only there to support and supplement the congregation's voice. This doesn't mean that worship is better the more the people move their mouths; it just means we need to take seriously the congregation's role in the conversation between God and his people. Any time we move away from the congregation's voice we need to consider carefully what is gained by their silence.

Does this mean all choral anthems, vocal solos, and instrumental arrangements should be expunged from worship? No. There are certainly times when the congregation participates through active listening—the sermon, for example—but the bulk of worship's work should be placed squarely on the congregation's shoulders. The further we move from the centrality of the congregation's voice, the stronger justification we need for making that decision.

Song Forms

The above song spectrum may seem like an impossible balancing act. How could one church ever incorporate such a wide variety of approaches to congregational singing? Indeed, no church will ever get the balance just right. But instead of seeing it as an overwhelming task too difficult to attempt, consider it an invitation to explore the great variety of worship expressions God has given us.

Our starting place for this exploration is to reimagine singing itself. In most churches, congregational singing is defined very narrowly. In one church it may mean singing a four-verse hymn with an organ accompaniment. In another church it may mean an upbeat praise song with a verse/chorus/bridge structure supported by a band. Let's question these assumptions. If form really does follow function, we need to explore a broader array of musical forms in order to express ourselves more fully. Different types of musical forms achieve different goals; for example, a multiverse hymn allows for the development of a complicated theological idea but doesn't engage the heart in the same way as a simple, repeated chorus. A variety of musical forms help us engage our whole being—heart, mind, and body—in worship.

Accompanied/A cappella

When was the last time your church sang without the help of any instruments? A cappella singing is one of God's greatest musical gifts.[10] The unadorned beauty of a congregation singing together is surely a taste of heaven on earth. But most of us don't trust our churches to sing by themselves, so we provide the crutch of nonstop accompaniment, be it piano, organ, or praise band. Is it any wonder that the singing in many churches is abysmal? Not so in the Mennonite tradition (and others) where all church members are expected to do their part, adding their voice to the rich harmony.

There is much to commend the tradition of singing exclusively a cappella, but we don't need to ban instruments from our sanctuaries entirely to gain something from it. Periodic a cappella singing breaks the monotony of constant accompaniment, provides moments of congregational intimacy, and builds the congregations' confidence for singing. Try to include at least one moment of a cappella singing in every service. It can be as simple as having the band drop out on the bridge of a praise song or as complicated as teaching four parts of an African chorus by rote. Every congregation is different. We simply need to know our congregation's capacity for singing and provide appropriate challenges for them. Congregational singing is like a muscle—too little exercise and it atrophies, but too much too fast can lead to injury.

Note/Rote

People from Western cultures generally favor word-oriented forms of communication such as books, newspapers, and musical scores. Other cultures favor spoken communication such as face-to-face conversations, storytelling, and memorized or improvised music. Of course, most modern cultures are a blend of these two modes, with an emerging "Twitter culture" rising somewhere in between literacy and orality.

These cultural modes of communication affect the way churches approach worship, with each church favoring certain forms of communicating. One church feels right at home with hymnals and a printed bulletin, while another finds musical notation elitist and prefers words on a screen, and a third worships entirely "off-the-page." None of these approaches is right or wrong. It is simply a matter of being aware that your church has a communication preference and that it can learn from other modes.

When we favor a particular communication style, we inevitably gravitate toward particular song repertoires as well. Churches with a lot of music readers feel comfortable singing from a hymnal. Therefore they will end up singing mostly music that fits neatly on the page: strophic hymns, four-part musical textures, and simple rhythms.[11] Hymns have served the church well for many years, but there are many other modes of singing that will benefit the congregation, such as the meditative prayer made possible by a Taizé song, the immediacy of a call-and-response spiritual, or the hands-free participation of singing from projected lyrics. Of course, the opposite is true as well. Churches that normally sing from memory or projected lyrics would benefit from holding a hymnal in their hands and singing the rich doctrine of hymnody that has sustained the faith of many Christians for centuries.

Leader/People

Congregations would do well to consider the balance between the congregation's voice and the music leaders in their worship. In some churches, the organ or praise band drowns out the voice of the congregation, eventually teaching them their voice is not necessary in worship. Other churches attempt to remove any trace of musical leadership in order to give the congregation full control of the singing. Certainly, the congregation's voice should be primary in worship, as worship is the work of the people.[12] But does that mean that the moment the congregation stops moving their jaws, worship has ceased to be worship?

Perhaps a more helpful way of thinking about the balance between the congregation's and leaders' roles is that God has gifted people in different ways. In the same way that a preacher is gifted to play a specific role in worship, music leaders have been gifted to play a unique role in the music of worship. Too often we understand music leadership as all-or-nothing: the leader sings a solo while the congregation listens or the congregation sings while the leaders play a supporting role. There are many congregational song forms that break this pattern, restoring a more natural volley between leader and people. For example, responsorial psalmody gives the complicated, rehearsed section (verses) to a vocal leader while the congregation responds with a simple refrain. It is common in African and African-American traditions to have a lead singer (what Michael Hawn calls an "enlivener") who feeds the congregation new verses or adds excitement to the singing with improvised vocal lines. Similarly, the repeated refrains of Taizé give the congregation a simple entry point for singing, while more experienced singers can sing in harmony, cantors sing verses over the congregation's refrain, and instrumentalists add descants. Using a variety of musical forms allows us to assign appropriate roles to each group so singing is accessible to the most modest musicians in the church, while those with musical gifts can exercise them fully.

Wordy/Wee

Some people give the impression that hymns with dense texts are intrinsically better, as if congregational songs were weighed by the pound—those with more words are simply a better deal! Certainly some themes are best explored with a multiverse hymn, but there is also plenty of room for simple songs with very little text—what the British would call "wee" songs. These little songs play an important role in worship because they engage our hearts and bodies, allowing us to express a simple emotion clearly and fully.

Does this mean that we need to include Sunday School ditties in worship? Not necessarily. A short song doesn't have to be trite. There are numerous songs that elegantly say one thing simply. Consider the archetypal "wee" songs of the Bible: Isaiah 6:3 ("Holy, holy, holy is the LORD of Hosts; the whole earth is full of his glory"), Psalm 117 (just two verses long, centered on the phrase "Praise the LORD"), and Revelation 4:8 (in which angelic creatures circle the throne day and night singing "Holy, holy, holy, the Lord God the Almighty, who was and is and is to come"). These passages show us there is plenty of room for short, repeated texts. In fact, simple songs can often be disarmingly profound. There's a story that a student once asked famed theologian Karl Barth if he could summarize his theology in one sentence. He replied, "Yes, I can. In the words of a song I learned at my mother's knee: 'Jesus loves me, this I know, for the Bible tells me so.'"[13]

This brings up another important point: worship is not only for smart adults. Our churches are full of worshipers who can't grasp the sophisticated language of many hymns. Children, the mentally disabled, and those new to the language will benefit from simplicity and repetition.[14] Using a wide range of songs, from wordy to wee, enables a wide range of ages and intellects to engage in a variety of modes of worship. Everyone benefits.

Planned/Spontaneous

Some churches plan services weeks in advance, with every minute of worship mapped out and locked down days before the service takes place. Other churches begin worship with little or no idea what songs they'll sing that day, assuming that the Spirit will guide them to sing the right songs at the right moment. There's something to learn from each model. Certainly the Spirit can work both in planning and in the moment. The trouble comes when we become so entrenched in one particular mode that we can't hear the Spirit's voice any other way.

Those who insist on spontaneity often fall into the rut of choosing the same ten songs that always come to mind in the heat of the moment. They would benefit from a more rigorous planning process that allows the input of more people. This expanded planning group would draw on a deeper pool of resources. The added weeks of planning time would allow for extended searches to find just the right song, or may even give adequate time for people to write brand-new songs.

Those who favor long-range planning often fail to improvise in the moment—they have a plan and will stick to it regardless of how the Spirit is moving among the people. One particular Sunday, when I first began in music ministry, I had a light, jazzy choral anthem planned to follow the sermon. The sermon, however, was a gut-wrenching discussion of how we can trust God when so many bad things happen in our lives. This came at a time when a number of people in the congregation were struggling with infertility, disabilities, and broken relationships. I should've acted quickly and announced that we would sing a hymn of consolation instead, but I was new to ministry and was insecure about making the change. As we sang our peppy anthem tears streamed down the cheeks of one of my basses. I had failed to respond to how the Spirit was moving in the moment.

It's best to start with a plan—after all, it's easier to change a plan than make one up on the spot. But remain flexible. You may arrive at the church to the news that a member of the congregation has died. Be ready to choose a different song to respond to this change in atmosphere. You may have rehearsed a song in a particular tempo, but the congregation insists on a different tempo. Don't fight them! Listen and adapt on the spot. Have hand signals ready to guide your musicians in spontaneous repeats or a cappella singing. You can even plan for spontaneity: practice improvising additional verses in the tradition of spirituals or ask the congregation to request a hymn.

Variety

This fluidity between planning and spontaneity accounts for the fact that worship is made up of people—living, breathing people who show up to worship with a variety of joys and concerns. We worship a living God who moves among people in creative and astounding ways. We need to be sensitive to the moment rather than simply executing a plan.

There is such an incredible diversity of song forms available to churches that it would be a shame to limit ourselves to one or two types. Even what we call "hymns" or "praise songs" have a huge range of genres within these categories. The generic term *hymn* can describe Latin hymns from the early church, Lutheran chorales, metrical psalms, the sturdy hymns of Watts and Wesley, early American shape-note tunes, evangelical gospel songs, frontier revival songs, southern and black gospel, and recently written texts exploring modern social issues.[15] Likewise, "praise songs" can include verbatim Scripture songs, upbeat praise choruses, praise-and-worship era pop anthems, and emerging worship repertoire, each with its own unique approach.[16] But this is just the tip of the iceberg. There are many varieties of chant; worship songs from Africa, Asia, and Latin America; Negro spirituals, black gospel, and urban contemporary gospel; liturgical music old and new; and ethnic/folk songs from all over the world.[17] And just when you think you have a good grasp of what's available, along comes something completely different: Taizé chants, Iona choruses, or "harp and bowl" worship from the International House of Prayer.

Each of these songs carries with it the unique perspective of the people from which it comes. It is impossible to sing an off-the-page African chorus without catching something of the communal context that gave it birth. Likewise, singing a majestic cathedral hymn such as "For All the Saints" draws us into the generations of saints who now sing around the heavenly throne. We don't strive for a diverse song repertoire to feel more cultured than the church down the street; we sing a broad range of songs because each of these experiences broadens our perspective of God and the church.

A practical question remains: How can we sing such a wide variety of song styles authentically? In reality, we can't. Even if we dedicated a lifetime to studying only one culture's music, we couldn't hope to fully understand it. However, we can enter the life of these songs enough to be changed by them.

Perhaps we should focus on respect rather than authenticity. While an authentic rendering of a song from another culture may be impossible, we can respect the music enough to learn as much as we can about performance practice in that culture. This will allow us to make good decisions about how we translate the music into our own cultural context.

> ### Song Choice Checklist
>
> **Intrinsic quality:** *Are the words and music well crafted?*
> **Congregational fit:** *What one thing does this song do that none other can?*
> **Appropriate for service:** *Where would we sing this?*
> **Pastoral consideration:** *Does this song meet a particular need?*

One of the ways we do this is to find the right mode of singing for different styles of songs. We may be used to reading hymns from a hymnal, but singing an African chorus from a hymnal pins it to the page like a butterfly in a collection—beautiful, but dead. Even the most note-bound congregation will benefit from learning a song by rote, exercising their ears rather than their eyes and experiencing a little of what the sending culture experiences when they sing. In many modern worship contexts, only song texts are displayed. While some people fear the loss of music reading, some songs are simply easier to sing when worshipers sing the text like they'd speak it rather than dutifully reading syncopations. Of course, hymns have been sung from hymnals for centuries, and that, too, should be respected. The experience of holding a hymnal in your hand, singing parts, and helping a child follow along will continue to bless congregations for years to come.[18]

Choosing Music

There once was a time when many churches sang from a hymnal. One hymnal. A church's pew hymnal offered perhaps five hundred songs from which to choose. Projection and printing technology changed all that. Today the internet, radio, and worship conferences bombard us with songs of every type, from the most remote place and time to the song written yesterday by a teenager in our own congregation. It wouldn't be an exaggeration to say the typical worship planner has access to five hundred *thousand* songs today. How do we whittle this number down to the two hundred or so songs that make for a manageable song repertoire in our church?

Intrinsic Quality

We should sing good music. Most music listeners equate "good" with "I like it," but as shepherds of our church's song, we need to go deeper than that. Each song we sing should have integrity. Like a building, a song needs to be structurally sound—trustworthy—which is a separate consideration from our feelings about the building. How can we evaluate a song's intrinsic quality?

First, the song must be singable by a congregation. A song may have exquisite theological insight and harmonies that draw deep into the well of tears, but it is useless as a congregational song if our congregation can't sing it. A variety of factors affect singability, but generally congregational songs have a limited range, clear rhythmic patterns, and simple forms. So while Bach's "St. Matthew Passion" and John Coltrane's "A Love Supreme" may be intrinsically good music, they are not intrinsically good for group singing. Instead, we look for the simplicity and accessibility that have marked folk songs throughout the ages, from "Frere Jacque" to "We Shall Overcome."

Second, once we have established a song's appropriateness to group singing, we can begin to evaluate the internal musical qualities of the song itself. Does the music have internal coherence or does it sound like two different musical ideas pasted together? Is it satisfying to sing multiple times or does it quickly become tiring? Does the music ennoble our humanity or trivialize it? Are the musical ideas fresh yet timeless? (We are to sing a new song, but novelty quickly wears thin.) All of these questions can be applied to any style of music. There is no "best" style of music, rather better or worse songs within each genre. We evaluate a song's quality within its stylistic context.

Third, the words of a song can come in many different forms, from the simplicity of Scripture songs to the theological nuances of modern hymns. We shouldn't elevate one genre or approach above another but rather evaluate each song within its context. As a baseline, we must insist that each song text is biblical in the sense that it reveals an orthodox Christian faith, free from heresy. However, a single song can only illuminate

For a More Thorough Discussion of Choosing Music

Constance M. Cherry, Mary M. Brown, and Christopher Bounds, *Selecting Worship Songs: A Guide for Leaders* (Marion, IN: Triangle Publishing, 2011).

Charlotte Kroeker, "Choosing Music for Worship," Charlotte Kroeker, ed, *Music in Christian Worship: At the Service of the Liturgy* (Collegeville, MN: Liturgical Press, 2005), 191–205.

Greg Scheer, *The Art of Worship: A Musician's Guide to Leading Modern Worship* (Grand Rapids: Baker Books, 2006), especially chapter 3, "Building Repertoire."

so much truth! It may seem that a song text with a half dozen biblical insights would be better than a song with only one, but often these songs lack focus and end up providing no insight at all. Instead, each song should reveal some aspect of truth. Like a piece in a mosaic, each song fits into our church's whole song repertoire, creating a bigger picture of the God we love. Two extremes should be avoided. On the one hand, we don't want to waste the congregation's time with songs that are the lyrical equivalent of a marshmallow—sugary fluff that doesn't satisfy real hunger. On the other hand, we want to avoid thick, complex theological treatises that are about as inspiring as singing the phone book.

Is it realistic to think a humble, local church musician can evaluate every song that his or her congregation sings? As the gatekeeper for your congregation's songs, it is your duty to sift through songs. But you don't necessarily need to possess advanced skills in theology and aesthetics, or do the job on your own. Sometimes it is best for us to rely on the wisdom of experts. Traditionally, these experts are hymnal editors. They evaluate thousands of songs before the five hundred songs of a hymnal are published. Even if you don't buy a particular hymnal for your whole congregation, there is much wisdom to be gleaned from studying the hymnal's contents.

Collaboration with others in your church is a way to gather group wisdom about song repertoire. In what some would call a post-hymnal age, other experts inform our decisions. Magazine editors, conference worship leaders, bloggers, book authors, and worship forums all have their place in sharpening our decisions about repertoire. Just remember to look for those with objective standards; many song suggestions come from those who wrote the songs or otherwise have a financial interest in your church singing them.

Congregational Fit

Of the five hundred thousand songs available to us, we narrow down the pool to five thousand songs that have good theology and music. (These numbers are only estimates. I don't recommend that you make an actual list!) From this pool of five thousand, we need to choose fewer than five hundred that are appropriate for our particular congregation.[19] What makes for a good fit between a song and a congregation?

We should be striving for a balanced repertoire of songs. Like a good hymnal, our churches should be singing songs that connect with all the major themes of the Christian faith. Can we sing from Genesis to Revelation? Can we sing through the year, from the Annunciation to Ascension? Can we sing of a God who is Father, Son, and Spirit? Can we sing through a Sunday service, from call to worship to communion? Church music leaders should constantly be monitoring their church's song repertoire for gaps that need to be filled and areas in which we have too many songs.

We should also be aware of areas where we need to grow. Perhaps our church's demographics have changed but the songs we sing haven't reflected that change. We can't represent the people in our pews in a song quota system, but certainly each person should feel something of themselves reflected in the song repertoire. The same is true for people of different personality types. An emotional or rational person shouldn't be entirely left out when it comes to singing; feelers and thinkers should each have moments of connection in worship.

That being said, each congregation will have their own personality—their sweet spot. Wise worship planners will find ways of stretching the church appropriately. If your congregation has never ventured beyond the hymnal, don't start with an upbeat rock praise song that requires drums. Instead, begin with a hymn-like praise song such as "In Christ Alone" or "There Is a Redeemer" that has some musical connection with what people already know. If your people have never sung a song from outside their own culture, don't begin with one based on an exotic Javanese scale or sung entirely in a different language. Introduce them to the Kenyan "Kwake Yesu Nasimama (Here on Jesus Christ I Will Stand)" or others with musical traits that will feel familiar.

Appropriate for Service

Once we have established a song repertoire that supports our congregation well, we need to draw from that pool of songs and place them in actual services. This is not easy. There are a thousand things to consider with each song choice. Are there significant events in the life of the church that would affect song decisions? How often has a song been sung recently? What is happening at that moment in the service? What role does the song serve—prayer, reflection, praise? Do you have the right musicians to lead the song?

So many considerations can make the task feel overwhelming. We can't calculate each of these factors like a mathematical equation. Instead, good worship planners gather this information and then imagine themselves in the moment, feeling what their congregation will be feeling, intuitively understanding what song is needed. I often find it helpful to gather three or more songs for every song spot in a worship service. This gives me wiggle room as I finalize songs for each part of the service. A heavy song may be balanced by a lighter one elsewhere. An unfamiliar song may be balanced by a handful of familiar songs.

We should avoid two extremes. On the one hand, some planners pay no heed to any of the theological, emotional, or logistical factors at play in a service. They simply choose their favorite songs. This misses out on the rich way music interacts with the rest of worship and supports our faith. On the other hand, some planners treat a worship service like a grocery list, dutifully finding a song on Nehemiah 8 but overlooking what that moment of worship might need most. Just because a scriptural index of hymns recommends a song doesn't mean it's the right one for your service. The right song in the wrong place is the wrong song. Perhaps instead of a song that simply reiterates the sermon theme, people really need a song that lets them rededicate themselves in this area of their life.

Pastoral Considerations

Finally, we need to take into account our people and their unique needs. We worship leaders can obsess for hours over finding just the right song, but make no connection at all with the people in the pews. There's no sin in letting your people sing songs they like! Don't become so fussy in your worship planning that you leave your people behind. For example, Mary Louise Bringle wrote a beautiful hymn text about the ravages of Alzheimer's, called "When Memory Fades." My own father died from this disease, so I find the way the song speaks of God's unchanging love in the face of dwindling memory to be comforting. I've given this text to people whose spouses are declining from Alzheimer's, but I've never recommended that it be sung at a funeral. Why? Because, pastorally, they don't need to sing about the disease. Instead they need to sing songs they already know well that will tap into a deep well of memories. These hymns are "comfort food" that perhaps have less precision than "When Memory Fades" but nonetheless are just what is needed in a time of grief.

These are a lot of things to keep in mind when planning music for a service! If you are just beginning your journey as a worship planner, don't worry; you'll get better and better at this. Over time you will learn more songs and become more skilled at putting them together. Like an artist learning the mechanics of blending paint, your musical palette will grow into a wonderful burst of color and nuance. Whether you are just starting this journey or have been planning worship for a long time, keep a few general principles in mind.

First, know your congregation. Enter their stream. While we worship planners likely have more experience with the broad scope of worship music than the people in our churches, we shouldn't set ourselves above our people. For one thing, no one likes a know-it-all! More importantly, every congregation possesses collective wisdom. We need to learn what wisdom lies beneath our church's song repertoire before making changes to it. If we know our congregation well, we'll know their "sweet spot"—the songs they sing with all their heart. These heart songs are a source of comfort and identity for the congregation. This should be our starting point as leaders. From there we have a secure center from which we can stretch our congregations a little at a time.

Second, this centering and stretching are the dual roles of the pastoral and prophetic worship leader. Indeed, the congregation should expect to encounter some pastoral, comforting elements and some prophetic, challenging aspects in each service. Of course, there is a thin line between stretching and breaking. We need to be careful we don't cross that line with our congregations. Don't move too fast! Instead, we should stretch our people a little at a time, so they can become comfortable with each new song before moving on to the next. Yes, this may be a painfully slow process for those of us who lead—we are always eager to move on to an exciting new thing—but our people need much more time to become familiar with new material.

Third, because worship leaders focus on the details of worship services, it is easy for us to lose sight of the big picture. We need to periodically step back and assess the overall health of our church's worship, rather than just individual services. This is the difference between the diet and the meal. If a particular service is a complete disaster, it is not the end of the world. If we compromise and sing a song our congregation loves but that we think is mediocre, the church's worship will not unravel. Instead we should take the long view. Five years from now, will our people have a more expansive view of Christ and his kingdom because of the songs we've chosen? Is the congregation's singing getting better or worse over time? What are our people going to sing by heart around a campfire? What songs will they sing at a funeral? These are the questions that should occupy our minds.

The worship leader should aim to be a shepherd of the people's song, a theologian of the heart, an expositor of Scripture in music.

For Discussion

1. Look back at the analysis of your own church's repertoire at the start of the chapter. After reading about the many kinds of music that can be used in worship, do you find particular strengths or weaknesses in your own church's repertoire? What does your church's song repertoire do well? What does it do poorly? What is the one area of improvement you'd like to address first?

2. "A song is never just a song." Reflect on how music functions in the world around you. List all the music you've heard today and describe what the music *did*. (The musical theme before the newscast announced the start of the news and conveyed a sense of authority. The music in the elevator was chosen to soothe your nerves. The songs on *Sesame Street* helped your children remember their letters.) Now apply the same thinking to your worship: choose a half dozen songs from your church's repertoire and describe what they *do* (praise, repent, teach).

3. Flip back to chapter 7, "The Church Year," and chapter 8, "The Fourfold Worship Order." See how many songs support each item discussed (for example, how many Advent songs or benediction songs are in your church's repertoire?).

4. Should church music sound good? Does it sound good in your church? How might "good" differ between the music you hear on the radio and the music you hear in church?

5. John Witvliet suggests churches have about a two-hundred-song repertoire capacity; how many songs does your congregation have their repertoire?

6. If there really are "hardcover" and "paperback" songs, do you have a plan for retiring the "paperback" songs at the end of their short shelf life?

7. I suggest a 50/40/10 percent split for near, known, and new songs. Is this a good balance for your church? Take an honest look at your song choices from the last few services—do they look like a pyramid? An upside-down pyramid? A pear? Draw it.

PART 4

PRACTICE

The Arts in Worship

List any nonmusical arts that were used in your most recent worship service (drama, dance, visual arts, and so forth). How often do you include the arts in your worship throughout the year (such as a Christmas play or art exhibit)? Have any artists been excluded from your church's worship simply because you don't have a category for their art? Are there any areas of worship arts for which you don't have competent artists?

We have focused in great detail on congregational song. Certainly, we spend the bulk of our time in church singing or listening to sermons, but hearing is by no means the only sense we involve in worship. If we are to engage our whole selves—heart, mind, and body—we need to incorporate all of the arts. But we don't incorporate the arts into worship simply to keep all of our senses busy. Instead, we find the art form that best supports what we are trying to accomplish. This is not art for art's sake, but functional art. To adapt the title of Hans Rookmaaker's famous book, we could put it this way: art needs no justification—except in worship.

Unfortunately, functional art goes against the grain of most artists. Actors, dancers, and visual artists spend years honing their skills for the stage or gallery. The idea that they would submit their skills to a larger context betrays everything they've learned about art. Their training has encouraged them to challenge audiences with complex, freestanding works of self-expression. Let's be clear: we should affirm brothers and sisters who are called to create works like this;

Recommended Reading

Frank Burch Brown, *Good Taste, Bad Taste, and Christian Taste: Aesthetics in Religious Life* (Oxford: Oxford University Press, 2000).

Andy Crouch, *Culture Making: Recovering Our Creative Calling* (Downers Grove IL: IVP Books, 2013).

W. David O. Taylor, ed., *For the Beauty of the Church: Casting a Vision for the Arts* (Grand Rapids: Baker, 2010).

Nicholas Wolterstorff, *Art in Action: Toward a Christian Aesthetic* (Grand Rapids: Eerdmans, 1987).

we need more top-notch Christian artists being salt and light in their secular artistic fields, not fewer. But when an artist contributes to worship, it is a very different context—a context in which they play a supporting role. This requires artists to repurpose their training for the task at hand. Just as a concert pianist uses the same keyboard in a very different way when accompanying hymns, a visual artist uses clay or paint in new ways when creating for worship. Some artists will never be able to come to terms with what they see as worship's lowest common denominator art, but others will be surprised to find that the modesty and directness of the worship arts present a lovely challenge.

Certainly the Bible affirms the use of the arts. Genesis makes a point of introducing us to Jubal, "the ancestor of all those who play the lyre and pipe" and "Tubal-cain, who made all kinds of bronze and iron tools" (Gen. 4:21–22). These early craftsmen were followed by Bezalel, an artist who God filled with the Spirit to work on the tabernacle, and the many prophets and poets who acted and rhymed God's message rather than simply saying it:

> Then Moses said to the Israelites: See, the LORD has called by name Bezalel son of Uri son of Hur, of the tribe of Judah; he has filled him with divine spirit, with skill, intelligence, and knowledge in every kind of craft, to devise artistic designs, to work in gold, silver, and bronze, in cutting stones for setting, and in carving wood, in every kind of craft. And he has inspired him to teach, both him and Oholiab son of Ahisamach, of the tribe of Dan. He has filled them with skill to do every kind of work done by an artisan or by a designer or by an embroiderer in blue, purple, and crimson yarns, and in fine linen, or by a weaver—by any sort of artisan or skilled designer. (Exod. 35:30–35)

Andy Crouch makes a convincing argument that in the opening chapters of the Bible God ordained humans to be "culture-makers" who "*make sense of the world by making something of the world.*"[1] Others have proposed the *Imago Dei* (the image of God) in humans is that they mimic their Creator by being "little creators."[2] Indeed, we know God better because of the Ethiopian Orthodox Timkat procession and C. S. Lewis's Narnia. But what does this "culture-making" look like specifically in a worship context?

When using the arts in worship, it is important to understand that a new context calls for a new approach to art making. Whereas a visual artist normally expects to create in seclusion and display the finished artwork in a gallery, the worship context may call for a more collaborative creation process and less highlighted display. For example, ceramic artists may find themselves contributing communion chalices to worship. They use many of the same skills they would use in their fine art context, but in the end their artwork is used as a cup. Does this minimize the art or the artist? No! In fact, this "functional" use of art allows a level of engagement that is impossible in "absolute" (or "high") art. Altarpieces, gospel music, and icons have enriched millions of people and in many places are a community's only contact with art of any kind.

> "So how do we make sense of the world? The two senses turn out to be more intertwined than we might have thought. We make sense of the world by making something of the world. The human quest for meaning is played out in human making: the finger-painting, omelet-stirring, chair-crafting, snow-swishing activities of culture. Meaning and making go together—culture, you could say, is the making of meaning."
>
> —ANDY CROUCH[3]

Does embracing a functional view of the arts in worship mean throwing all aesthetics out the window? Certainly not, but sadly, many churches have taken an entirely utilitarian approach to the use of the arts in worship, with clip art, flannel banners, and slice-of-life sketches filling up mall-shaped churches. We can do better.

Let's commit to three things. First, we need to encourage our church's artists. Whether they create art inside or outside the church, we need to support them. This may be as simple as attending a dance recital or as involved as mentoring them while they explore their calling. Second, we need to find places for artists in the church—not simply to keep them busy but for our mutual edification. Spiritual leaders need to engage artists theologically, and artists need to engage spiritual leaders aesthetically. When deep, respectful relationships are formed, we will see profound works of art sprouting around us, art that pulls us deeper into the mysteries of Christ. Finally, we must encourage worship arts that are fitting. *Fittingness* is a term coined by Nicholas Wolterstorff that means art should support the message and the moment of worship. In the spirit of 1 Corinthians

10:23, projecting a waving American flag behind the lyrics of a hymn may be *permissible*, but it is not *beneficial*.

When great artistic skill and a deep understanding of worship come together, a "disciplined creativity" emerges that is greater than the sum of its parts.[4] Let's examine what that might look like in each area of the worship arts.

For Discussion

1. "Art needs no justification—except in worship." Do you believe this is true? What is the balance between artistic skill on one hand and fittingness to the worship context on the other? Can you give an example of someone who "tamed their muse" for use in worship?

2. In which area does your church need to grow the most?

3. How can you encourage your church's artists in their work inside or outside the church? Can you find new or more effective places for artists to contribute to worship? Are you achieving a "fitting" aesthetic for art in your church's worship?

13

The Gospel Enacted

Drama and Wordsmithing

Before you begin: What is your inventory of words?

Does your church have a drama team or individuals who do dramatic presentations (such as sketches, acted Scriptures, or miming)? What kinds of stories get told in your worship services (biblical stories, life stories, or plots from literature)? How are these stories told (acted, read, or memorized)? How often?

Consider Nathan's prophecy in 2 Samuel 12. He begins by telling David a story. (Who doesn't like to hear a story?) David is quickly caught up in the tale of a pitiful poor man whose only dear lamb—a family pet, really—is slaughtered for a rich man's feast. David is enraged, declaring that the man deserves to die. Nathan's next words are like a sword to David's heart: "You are the man!" The story of the poor man's lamb drew David into Nathan's word from God in a way that a direct "You have sinned, David" would not have done. Jesus, too, harnessed the power of story—the parables. Why would Jesus and Nathan use stories to communicate truth rather than simply being forthright with factual communication?

First, stories engage our emotions and imaginations. David got caught up in Nathan's story and knew without a doubt that the rich man had sinned mercilessly against the poor man. The story lowered his defenses and he saw the truth clearly. If Nathan had skipped the story of the sheep and simply said, "You've abused your power by committing adultery with Bathsheba and murdering Uriah," David would have countered with a thousand excuses, perhaps "She shouldn't have been bathing where I could see her!" or "I didn't *kill* Uriah, I simply put him on the frontline." The impact of Nathan's story cut right through all David's excuses. He knew that *he* was the man.

Second, stories help us see the world from a different perspective. Without Nathan's story, it would have been difficult for David to be sympathetic to the feelings of an average soldier like Uriah. But the story of the poor man's sheep allowed David to step outside of his kingly privilege and see the story (and ultimately his own story) from the perspective of the powerless. We, too, place ourselves in a parable or sermon illustration, experiencing the story from multiple angles, gaining deeper understanding as we try on points of view that we could never have had without the help of the story. In my own congregation, the powerful story of Christ's passion was narrated on Palm Sunday, punctuated only by sung reflections. The congregation played the role of the crowd, shouting "Crucify him!" One parent told me his son was moved nearly to tears, wondering, "How could they do that to Jesus?" That boy understood Christ's sacrifice at a much deeper level because the dramatic presentation of Scripture allowed him to see the passion through different perspectives: Jesus, Peter, and the mob.

Third, stories allow for many layered meanings. They draw us in and let us explore in ways essays or speeches don't. For example, when we hear the parable of the prodigal son, we know that the story is about grace and forgiveness, but that barely scratches the surface of our experience with the parable. We may put ourselves in the shoes of the prodigal son so far from his family. We may identify with the father who longs for his son to come home. We may even sympathize with the older brother who watches as his reckless brother seems to be rewarded for his sins. All of these are valid. The beauty of stories is that they allow all these different meanings to emerge simultaneously.

Fourth, stories compress time. A strange thing happens when we hear the words, "Once upon a time." Instead of hearing those words as an artifact from some distant time and place, we immediately put ourselves inside the story, living it along with its characters. This is certainly how the Israelites experienced the stories they repeated in annual festivals. The exodus from Egypt was not just an ancient tale but a story that became alive again with each retelling. This is more than mere memory; it is what theologians call anamnesis—reliving or "making alive" a memory. As Jeff Barker explains in *The Storytelling Church*, Hebrew grammar makes no distinction between past and present; the stories of God's salvation are not only history but present reality and future hope.[1] We experience the same thing in Christian stories, understanding Christ's work as living and active, as we saw earlier in relation to anamnesis and the Lord's Supper. We remember the story of the Last Supper, we celebrate communion in the present, and we hope for the heavenly banquet to come. In a very real way, stories are timeless.

Types of Worship Drama

Drama and storytelling may be powerful, but how are they used in worship? In recent years, "slice-of-life" dramas have become very popular, in part due to the influence of Willow Creek Church. These dramatic sketches are often used before a sermon to introduce a theme, lower our defenses, or ask a question that the sermon will answer. These are fine as sermon "icebreakers" but rarely move beyond a lighthearted laugh at human nature or a bite-size morality tale.

One of the most compelling ways of using drama in worship is to stage Scripture readings. Old Testament scholar Thomas Boogaart has convincingly argued that what we often consider historical sections of the Old Testament are more properly categorized as plays.[2] They were originally used as scripts to tell stories in worship, and they come alive when acted out. The same principle can be extended to the parables and stories of the New Testament. Dramatic scenes from the Bible are heard with fresh ears when the roles are assigned to actors and staged before our eyes.

Churches without the resources to fully stage Scripture can still honor God's Word with compelling readings. "Choral readings" use multiple readers to bring out the different voices within Scripture readings.[3] Actor Max McLean has presented whole books of the Bible as one man plays and pastor/professor Tim Brown regularly memorizes the Scripture passage from which he'll preach.[4] Such feats of memorization may seem impossible, but at the very least we can honor God's Word by reading it well![5]

Enacted prayer is another way that the dramatic arts can be engaged in worship.[6] In this form of prayer, developed by theater professor Jeff Barker, actors stage a prayer request in the form of a tableau (an acted picture), literally putting flesh on the congregation's prayers. These "picture prayers" allow us to experience prayer in a new way, with eyes open and bodies engaged.

Preaching may not seem like it falls under the category of theater arts in worship, but there are many techniques that preachers can learn from the world of acting. The Word is preached more clearly when *words* are chosen carefully and delivered convincingly. Pastor and theologian Neal Plantinga teaches and writes about the benefits of pastors engaging with good literature.[7] Preachers who engage with good literature are more likely to choose vibrant vocabulary when they speak. Also, preachers would benefit by working with actors on the physical aspects of preaching: Are you using the full range of your voice? Are you comfortable with your body and how you move when speaking? Are you making eye contact with the entire room? Certainly the Word of God has its own power, regardless of a preacher's skill, but an articulate, colorful speaking style will help everyone engage more fully.

There are many other places in worship where the talents of actors, wordsmiths, and poets can be employed, such as testimonies, written prayers, and welcomes. Anywhere there are stories to be told and words to be written, we should aim for good words well delivered. The key is to amplify what worship already does rather than feel obligated to include drama in worship because that's what the big church down the street does.

In fact, there are as many ways for drama to *detract* from worship as there are for drama to enhance it. We've all suffered through poorly conceived skits that leave us feeling uncomfortable for the actors rather than drawn in to the topic. By all means, we should use every talented actor or writer in our congregation, but we also need to have the wisdom to know when dramatic talent is not available. We also need to be careful not to manipulate emotions. Certainly, worship should involve our emotions, but leaders should take care that we're not stirring the emotions for the sake of stirring the emotions. Avoid gratuitous plucking of the heartstrings and instead encourage emotional participation that leads to repentance, commitment, and Christlikeness. Similarly, actors should take care not to overpower the message. If a flowery performance of a Scripture passage leaves the congregation thinking about what great actors we are rather than gaining fresh insight into God's Word, we have failed. Like a frame around a beautiful painting, the artist's work should complement the inherent beauty of worship.

For Discussion

1. If Thomas Boogaart is right and what we often consider historical sections of the Old Testament are more properly categorized as plays, how does that change your understanding of Scripture? How does that change your understanding of storytelling?

2. Look at your initial inventory of your church's use of drama, stories, and words. After reading about a variety of ways acting can be used in worship, are there any areas you would like to explore right away? Any areas you doubt would be effective in your church setting?

3. Improvements in worship are often incremental. Think small for a moment: What is something *you are already doing* in worship that could be improved by applying one of the above ideas?

4. Describe a time when drama or storytelling has detracted from worship in your church or elsewhere. What worries you most about introducing the dramatic arts in your congregation?

14

The Gospel Embodied

Dance and Movement

Before you begin: Take an inventory of movement in your worship.

Is there a tradition of dance and movement at your church? Write a short overview or history. List everything you do with your body in worship (such as stand, sit, raise hands, kneel, process, genuflect, or sway). Feel free to consult a bulletin or video from a recent worship service to jog your memory.

The biblical witness shows a long and sometimes troubled history with dance. After the Israelites crossed the Red Sea and were delivered from the Egyptians, "the prophet Miriam, Aaron's sister, took a tambourine in her hand; and all the women went out after her with tambourines and with dancing" (Exod. 15:20). Throughout Scripture, dance and the joy of the Lord go hand in hand. David followed Miriam's example when he danced "before the Lord with all [his] might" (2 Sam. 6:5). The psalmist praises God for turning his "mourning into dancing" (Ps. 30:11). A celebration with feasting and dancing marked the return of the prodigal son (Luke

15:25). Scripture tells us there is a time to dance (Eccles. 3:4) and we are even commanded to praise God with dance (Ps. 150:4).

Yet a mere seventeen chapters after Miriam's dance of deliverance, we read of dance turned idolatrous. While Moses was in the very presence of the living God receiving the two tablets of the covenant, the Israelites were dancing before a calf made of gold (Exod. 32:19). In the New Testament, Herodias's dance led to the beheading of John the Baptist (Matt. 14:1–12; Mark 6:14–29). Dance can be motivated by joy in the Lord but it can also be misguided by idolatry and indiscretion.

This same tension has dogged dance throughout the history of the Western church. While it's likely that some biblical and Jewish dance tradition carried over into early Christian worship, the early church was also eager to distance itself from the worldly connotations of dance in pagan worship and secular entertainment. There were endorsements and critiques of dance, as well as a move toward spiritualizing dance (dance in your heart but not your body). This dichotomy between spirit and body continued to widen in the Reformation as reasoned faith was elevated over mystery and ritual. However, dance continued in various forms outside worship in mainstream churches. The Shaker communities of eighteenth-century America were known for their spontaneous and choreographed dances in worship, as well as the shaking and twitching that gave them their name. Worship among African-American slaves was marked by ecstatic movement, most notably the "ring shout." This was a precursor to the "praise break" in modern African-American worship and surely influenced Pentecostals who are known for their "dancing in the Spirit."

In the 1960s, as Catholics followed the instructions in *The Constitution on the Sacred Liturgy*[1] toward "full and active participation" in worship, including "actions, gestures, and bodily attitudes," and as some Protestants began to reclaim ritual aspects of the early Church's worship, worship dance began to make a comeback. This resurgence was mostly in the form of "liturgical dance," a form of choreographed dance that supported various actions of worship. Dance has continued to gain acceptance in a variety of forms and in a variety of worship contexts. Today, dance and movement in worship fall into five broad categories.[2]

Five Categories of Worship Dance

Choreographed Dance

Like an anthem sung by a choir, a choreographed dance is performed by a trained group of people for the edification of the rest of the congregation. Often named "liturgical dance," it takes various forms. True liturgical dance is dance that supports and amplifies the liturgy itself. As church historian J. G. Davies points out, "it is not a filler that brings the course of the liturgy to a halt," but "must be integrated with . . . the celebration of the liturgy."[3] Whatever is happening in the worship service—praise, confession, prayer—is embodied by the dancers. This can include processional and recessional dances, seasonal dances, and movements that ritualize common actions such as lifting a cross or kneeling in penance. The simple elegance of dance can help us experience the joy and sorrow of worship in a new way.

Another form of choreographed dance is frequently called liturgical dance but is more accurately named "interpretive" or "expressive" dance. It draws on the traditions of ballet and modern dance, with performances choreographed to music. Unlike true liturgical dance, in which the dance is an integral part of the worship action, interpretive dance pieces tend to be self-contained presentations on a particular theme. These can be powerful dance pieces, but by their very nature they draw attention to themselves and break the flow of worship.

Like the early church, many modern churches see the biblical precedent and hypothetical good of including dance in worship but worry about the danger of introducing the (mostly female) body into the congregation. Could it arouse lustful thoughts and cause some to stumble (see Rom. 14:13–23)? Certainly, dancers should dress modestly and avoid dance moves from our hypersexualized modern pop culture. On the other hand, our bodies are a gift from God. We should embrace the beauty of the body and learn to engage our whole selves in worship.

Unfortunately, this is not as easy as it sounds. For example, I once served in a congregation in which there was a wonderful ballet dancer. She periodically used her gifts in worship, but though she dressed and danced appropriately, some people in the congregation were still uncomfortable with her dancing. Focusing on liturgical dance rather than expressive dance could have mitigated some of this tension; expressive dance stops the flow of worship and forces our attention on the dancer, whereas liturgical dance is part of a song, Scripture reading, or some other worship action. But in the end, even dressing dancers in cardboard boxes wouldn't be modest enough for some people. We need to know our churches—can we effectively introduce dance or would it simply ignite a firestorm of controversy? Thankfully, choreographed dance is only one of many ways to include our bodies in worship.

Spontaneous Dance

Like David's "undignified" dance in 2 Samuel, there is always room in worship for joyous worshipers to break forth into dance. There is a long history of "dancing in the Spirit" in the Pentecostal tradition. It can range from a gentle sway with hands raised to the ecstatic stomping of the "praise break." In some churches, these spontaneous dances have become more formalized; for example, with teams of flag dancers improvising during congregational singing. Another branch of spontaneous dancing in worship is "prophetic dance." As dance instructor Lynn Hayden explains, "Even as someone with the gift of prophecy can hear from God about an individual or situation and deliver it through word or song, so can a dancer with the gift of prophecy hear from God and deliver a message through movement."[4]

Mime

Somewhere between drama and interpretive dance lies mime. While most of us may think of miming and clowning purely as entertainment, the same techniques can be applied to a worship setting. Whereas other dance forms are more abstract in their gestures, mime-dance is more literal. Mime-dancers might act out the words of a song or Scripture, using movement that engages the eyes as well as the ears. Tableaux, such as Tom Long's "Freeze Frame" technique, can create body pictures that literally flesh out what is being said.[5] In my own church, dancers accompany the Apostles' Creed with a mime-dance. It is arresting to say the well-worn creed while seeing it unfold in images before your eyes.

Group Dances

Like many arts, dance in the West has become the domain of professionals. Yet in many cultures dance is a communal activity, with people of all ages and abilities invited to participate. From circle dances to square dances to line dances, group dances are ways of bonding a community together physically as well as emotionally. Israeli folk dances became popular in churches during the 1970s as the Messianic Jewish movement brought Israeli folk songs into churches. Thomas Kane's video series *The Dancing Church* captures a number of group dances from around the world, including a rigorous Easter victory dance from the Ngoma tribe.[6] St. Gregory of Nyssa Episcopal Church in San Francisco has reclaimed dance as a regular part of their worship, inviting the whole church to join a circle dance around the altar during the sharing of peace and communion.[7]

Movement and Posture

Many churches will never adopt a dance ministry, but every church should consider all the ways our bodies can be used in worship. Certainly the Bible shows the regular use of the body in worship, such as raising hands (1 Tim. 2:8), falling prostrate (Rev. 7:11), and kneeling (Ps. 95:6). Like fasting or observing the Sabbath, these physical postures shape our spirits in profound ways. We need to intentionally involve our bodies in worship not only because some people in our congregations are tactile learners but also because ours is an incarnational faith. Jesus's birth as a human being shows us that Christianity is more than a philosophy—it is a faith that takes on flesh.

Perhaps if we replaced the word *dance* with the word *movement* it would free us to think more creatively about this area of worship. Are there places in our worship that would have more impact if our bodies were included? For example, standing when reading Scripture or kneeling during confession are two ways our bodies can move in sync with the spiritual work we are doing in worship. Could moments such as the offering become more active and meaningful if the congregation were asked to come forward with their gifts? Could the movements of the worship leaders be amplified, for example, by holding the Bible overhead and proclaiming, "The

Word of the Lord from the Gospel of John!" or by walking down among the congregation to pray! If you have ever been anointed with oil or had a congregation lay hands on you in prayer, you will understand the power of bodily involvement to focus the heart in worship.

Movement and posture in worship can even serve an evangelistic function. In Robert Webber's video *Ancient-Future Worship*, a man tells the story of his conversion.[8] He and his wife were not Christians but they decided it would be proper to take their young child to church. They sat in the back row. As the procession of cross and Bible entered the sanctuary and passed by their row, they were overcome by the Holy Spirit and fell to their knees in repentance. Though they wouldn't have been able to articulate a theology of the cross, their lives were changed because of its symbolic weight in worship. This man is now an Anglican priest.

The Holy Spirit works through dance and movement, stirring in us sighs too deep for words, truths deep down in our bones, and joy that fills our whole beings. Let us step in time with the work of the Spirit!

For Discussion

1. Heart, mind, body: which is most active in your worship?
2. Does your congregation include dancers, choreographers, or mimes? Are they being utilized in your worship services?
3. Would an attempt to include dance in your church introduce a controversy around modesty?
4. Replace the phrase "dance in worship" with "movement in worship" and then have a discussion about movement and posture in your worship. How could the body be incorporated more fully, and what benefits might that bring?

15

The Gospel Envisioned

The Visual Arts and Architecture

Before you begin: Complete two eyes-closed exercises.

1. When you were small, did you have a picture-book Bible? Can you close your eyes and still see some of the pictures in your mind? Which ones?
2. People often describe a view as "breathtaking." Describe an experience that was visually breathtaking. Have you ever been in a church that was breathtaking, beautiful, or simply gave you a sense of the presence of God? Close your eyes and try to remember the details of that experience before writing it down or sharing it with a group.

The Bible is full of images. From dramatic snapshots like Jesus ascending into heaven (Acts 1:6–11) to symbolic icons like a bronze snake on a pole (Num. 21:4–9), the Bible is an illustrator's dream. Consider the visual feast we find in Exodus. In chapter 24, God calls Moses up to cloud-covered Mount Sinai. The chapters that follow are instructions about God-ordained visual elements: an ark of acacia wood, a lampstand of pure gold, a lamp

Moses Breaks the Tables of the Law

fueled by pure oil of beaten olives, and a bronze basin. If we had any doubt that the Master Architect was concerned with how visual surroundings impact our spiritual lives, chapter 31 ends with God himself creating art: "When God finished speaking with Moses on Mount Sinai, he gave him the two tablets of the covenant, tablets of stone, written with the finger of God" (v. 18). Note that God gave Moses physical tablets rather than a verbal list—God understood that humans need visual aids. Note also that they were *written with the finger of God*—our incarnational God etched the stones himself.

Alas, even while Moses was engulfed in God's glory on the mountain, watching the finger of God carve the words, "You shall not make for yourself an idol. . . . You shall not bow down to them or worship them" (20:4–5), the Israelites were melting their earrings into a golden calf—an idol they could worship while they impatiently waited for God and Moses. Moses came down from his mountaintop experience and was so frustrated with his people's sin that he broke the tablets in a rage. After some serious discipline for the Israelites and intense negotiation with God on their behalf, Moses was invited by God back up the mountain. This time, however, Moses has to bring his own tablets. God instructed him, "Cut two tablets of stone like the former ones . . . which you broke" (34:1).

God's words reflect, perhaps, some annoyance with his chosen servant, Moses—"You broke them, now you've got to bring your own!" More seriously, we see in these passages important principles about art in worship. First, we see that God really does care about art. In these chapters, God is giving direct instructions about worship—one of the few places in the Bible where God hammers out the details of what worship should look like—and they are extremely visual. God dictates the architecture of the tabernacle, provides schematics for the furnishings, and even lists the fabrics and colors to be used. Given this example, how can we settle for unimaginative, colorless sanctuaries?

God's sanctuary fills the eyes (and all the senses) with wonder and awe. God understands that we humans are creatures who rely on our senses, and so ordains art as a window into ethereal truths. They are visions, of a sort, that allow us to experience God in the deepest part of our being. Psalm 27 speaks of this desire to see God's beauty in the sanctuary:

> One thing I asked of the LORD,
>   that will I seek after:
> to live in the house of the LORD
>   all the days of my life,
> to behold the beauty of the LORD,
>   and to inquire in his temple. (Ps. 27:4)

The psalmist also tells us that God's beauty extends beyond the sanctuary: "I believe that I shall *see* the goodness of the LORD in the land of the living" (v. 13, emphasis added). God fills our physical world with visual signs of his goodness not only as signposts for spiritual truths but because they are simply part of God's character.

God's beauty cannot be separated from God's self, just as justice and righteousness are part of God's very being.

Unfortunately, humans are all too ready to pervert God's good gifts. While Moses was receiving instructions in the use of art in worship of the one true God, the Israelites created art that was an idol—a mute, lifeless golden calf. This is, in a sense, art for art's sake; art that ends in itself rather than leading to God.[1] Humans seem to be drawn to gods that are manageable, that work within our time frame and behave as we'd expect. The true God we worship is beyond our ways. As C. S. Lewis puts it when referring to the Christ figure Aslan in *The Lion, the Witch, and the Wardrobe,* "he is not a *tame* lion." Or as Paul states in Romans:

> *"O worship the Lord in the beauty of holiness." (Ps. 96:9 KJV)*

O the depth of the riches and wisdom and knowledge of God! How unsearchable are his judgments and how inscrutable his ways!
> "For who has known the mind of the Lord?
> Or who has been his counselor?"
> "Or who has given a gift to him,
> to receive a gift in return?"
For from him and through him and to him are all things. To him be the glory forever. Amen. (Rom. 11:33–36)

We need to use our artistic skills to help plumb the depths of the riches and wisdom and knowledge of God, rather than to simplify and cheapen the mystery, as if God could be reduced to our level.

One further principle gleaned from these passages is this: art can be used by the Spirit, but art is not the Spirit itself. When God rewrote the tablets of the law, it was on tablets Moses had cut. Moses used his artistic skill to chisel stones into tablets, but they were still—quite literally—blank slates. These tablets were just slabs of stone until the finger of God etched the law onto their stone surface. Even then, the physical stone was only an intermediary step. Ultimately, God's Spirit will do a deeper work: "I will put my law within them, and I will write it on their hearts" (Jer. 31:33; Heb. 8:10). The church's artists should faithfully offer their work for the enrichment of worship, but it is never a substitute for the Spirit's work.

The Visual Arts in Worship throughout History

The tension between art as an aid and art as idolatry ran through both Israelite and early Christian worship. On the one hand, Scripture specifically forbids the making of idols: "You shall not make for yourself an idol, whether in the form of anything that is in heaven above, or that is on the earth beneath, or that is in the water under the earth" (Exod. 20:4). Some Jewish traditions interpreted this to forbid the making of any images at all, while others understood it to simply forbid making images intended for idolatrous worship. Indeed, God himself ordered the making of a bronze serpent on a pole in the desert and golden cherubim to adorn the mercy seat in the tabernacle. Nonetheless, there was reluctance to bring art into worship for fear of falling into the idol worship of Israel's pagan neighbors.

Similarly, the early Christian church was in a pagan culture, surrounded by temples and statues. Idolatry was one of the early believers' primary temptations, as we see from the number of times the New Testament addresses the theme. Many early church leaders discouraged the use of images in worship for the same reason they took great care with food sacrificed to idols: they didn't want to open any doors to idolatry. Instead, they separated themselves from the surrounding culture, creating a distinct lifestyle that supported a unique faith.

As the church grew, the Eastern and Western branches of the Christian church came to view art and architecture differently. The West valued art for its narrative function. Stained glass and other art was considered "the Bible of the poor," a visual exposition of sin and redemption written in paint, glass, and stone. Church art played a crucial teaching role in a largely illiterate context.

In the Eastern church, on the other hand, art played a specific devotional and theological role. Art didn't serve only as a sign of a deeper spiritual truth but, in a sense, was the spiritual truth itself. Eastern art, most famously the icon, served as a portal to a spiritual realm. An icon of Christ or a saint was a proxy for the actual person. A lavishly adorned Orthodox church, its walls lined with icons and its dome depicting Christ as Ruler of the Universe, is a window into heaven itself. In the same way that an embassy is a small piece of a nation's territory on foreign soil, Orthodox worship is a small piece of heavenly ground here on earth.

Throughout the first millennium of the church, the pendulum swung between *iconodules* (those who believe in venerating icons) and *iconoclasts* (literally "image breaker," or those who oppose icons), until the Eastern and Western churches split in the Great Schism of 1054. Icons have been the domain of Eastern Orthodoxy ever since. The Orthodox are careful to distinguish between worshiping an image—which is idolatry—and venerating an icon—which is a form of respect or reverence for the subject of the icon. Still, many Western Christians are uncomfortable seeing people kiss or bow down before an image.

However, art in Western churches was not without its own problems. What began as Bible stories rendered in stained glass became more majestic in the later Middle Ages as Romanesque and Gothic architectural styles soared higher and higher into the sky. Soon, what started as art for the glory of God became intertwined with political opulence. Cathedrals such as Notre Dame and Chartres, for all their beauty, were also totems to the powers they represented: Christendom, the Holy Roman Empire, and European political powers. By the time of the Reformation, even monasteries had become lavish artistic and architectural masterpieces.

These extravagances were among the complaints raised by the Reformers. Calvin felt that if the Roman Catholic Church had been preaching the Word in worship, there would have been no need for religious art—the "Bible of the poor"—to cover the walls of sanctuaries. Luther was more moderate, conceding that images could support the Word. In England, where the Anglican Church swung back and forth between Catholic and Reformed sentiment, Oliver Cromwell's Puritan government took the opportunity to take iconoclasm to extremes, gutting churches and monasteries of their monuments, paintings, and even pipe organs.

The Reformers' iconoclasm mirrored a larger cultural move away from the mysticism—some would say superstition—of the Middle Ages and toward the reasoned humanism of the Renaissance. The Word—and words—was most important to the Reformers. Art, at best, was a distraction from the "real truth" that could be conveyed in speech and print. Though art continued to be created for worship, the church was no longer the leading patron of the arts. Over the next few centuries the art world relocated from the church into the secular domain of galleries and universities. By the twentieth century art had by and large become something like its own religion, with artists as prophets whose goal was self-expression rather than creating art for the glory of God.

Modern evangelicals largely followed in the Protestant Reformers' footsteps when it came to the arts in worship. They weren't as iconoclastic—you can't be an icon breaker when there are no more icons to break—but art and worship had separated so long ago that evangelicals were simply ambivalent about art. What evangelicals valued was the gospel. If they did think about art, it was only about how art could serve the message of salvation. Artist Jack Chick, for example, drew comic book tracts that followed characters to heaven and hell and ended with a plan of salvation that readers could follow. Within worship itself, art was limited to clip art in bulletins and banners of Scripture passages. Art theologian David Taylor described his evangelical upbringing's view of the arts as "ultimately expendable, a luxury far from the center of biblical Christianity."[2] This utilitarian approach was not unusual in evangelicalism. Evangelicals took the same approach

> **For Further Study**
>
> Christians in the Visual Arts, http://civa.org/.
>
> *Faith & Form Journal*, http://faithandform.com/.
>
> Hans R. Rookmaaker, *Art Needs No Justification* (London: InterVarsity, 1978).
>
> Francis A. Schaeffer, *Art and the Bible* (Downers Grove, IL: InterVarsity, 1973).
>
> W. David O. Taylor, *For the Beauty of the Church: Casting a Vision for the Arts* (Grand Rapids: Baker, 2010).

with music, for example, which was seen as bait for a salvation message or a warm-up for the sermon. In the areas of visual art and architecture it meant evangelicals were comfortable with warehouse-style churches and aluminum siding as long as the Word was preached. This is a long way from the Sistine Chapel! Later evangelical iterations like Willow Creek even stripped their meeting halls of crosses for fear it would turn off the unchurched they were trying to attract for the gospel.

In recent years, some churches have attempted to incorporate the visual arts more fully into their worship, understanding that what we see and what we believe often work hand in hand. They have been more intentional with the symbols in their sanctuaries and the way their worship spaces speak of God's glory and gospel truth. There has also been a movement to bring artists back into the church, with shepherds such as Francis Schaeffer, Hans Rookmaaker, and David Taylor providing a theological framework and hospitable call to Christian artists who are trying to figure out how their art and faith connect.

Given the variety of ways art and architecture have been used throughout the history of the church, how should modern churches approach the visual aspects of worship?

Architecture

Any discussion of the visual side of worship must begin with building design. A church's architecture is—quite literally—set in stone. Once those stones are set, it becomes infinitely more difficult to make fundamental changes to the worship area. For example, if the floor is sloped like a movie theater it will create good sight lines but won't allow for future changes in the seating arrangement. If the building incorporates a lot of natural light into its design, projection will be more difficult.

Further Reading on Architecture

Environment and Art in Catholic Worship by National Conference of Catholic Bishops (Chicago: Liturgy Training Publications, 1993).

Richard Giles, *Re-Pitching the Tent: Reordering the Church Building for Worship and Mission* (Norwich, UK: Canterbury Press, 1996).

Richard Kieckhefer, *Theology in Stone: Church Architecture from Byzantium to Berkeley* (New York: Oxford University Press, 2004).

Chris Stoffel Overvoorde, "Does It Fit? Guidelines for Critiquing Worship Space," *Reformed Worship*, September 1994, http://www.reformedworship.org/article/september-1994/does-it-fit-guidelines-critiquing-worship-space.

Mark A. Torgerson, *An Architecture of Immanence: Architecture for Worship and Ministry Today* (Grand Rapids: Eerdmans, 2007).

James F. White and Susan J. White, *Church Architecture: Building and Renovating for Christian Worship* (Nashville: Abingdon, 1988).

Perhaps because church buildings are such permanent structures and no building committee wants to leave an unusable worship space for future generations, there has been a move toward "multipurpose rooms." This "all things to all people" approach seems like a wise one on the surface: isn't it good stewardship to create a sanctuary that can also serve as a fellowship hall and community theater? Yes—and no. While some flexibility is wonderful, too often the competing uses of a multipurpose space keep it from doing any one thing well. Church historians James and Susan White are adamant about the focus of church architecture: "The worship offered by a Christian community is the sole reason for a church building to exist."[3] This is not to say that a church building *can't* serve other roles such as Sunday school, food pantry, or community meeting hall, but those secondary roles must not trump the primary role of the church building: worship.

More difficult to discern is how a church may be used in the future. How many sanctuaries have been built around a choir loft only to find their choir program dwindling a few decades later? Perhaps the same thing will be said of today's worship spaces, with their massive projection screens, in the future when worship is followed on smartphones! Predicting the future of worship may seem the job of a prophet rather than a building committee, but it is safe to assume that congregations will continue to do the same things they've always done: hear the Word, take communion, perform baptisms, and sing together. Any building that focuses on these timeless actions will be well prepared to serve its congregation in the future.

Though all church structures enable speaking, singing, and other actions of worship, there are as many ways of achieving this as there are buildings. In his book *Theology in Stone*, Richard Kieckhefer discerns three basic patterns of church design: Classic Sacramental (long buildings with the altar as the focus), Classic evangelical (auditorium-style space with the pulpit as the focus), and Modern Communal (multiple areas and focuses that accommodate the movement of people). James and Susan White suggest three functions of worship that architecture can support: hospitality (How does a space invite people in?), participation (How does a space allow people to take part?), and intimacy (How does a space make people feel close/distant from God and others?). James VanderMolen and

Ron Rienstra see many worship architecture issues boiling down to the interplay between the horizontal and vertical — the horizontal axis makes us aware of other worshipers and the vertical axis makes us aware of God.[4] Added to this are the many practical issues that affect a worship space such as light (How much natural light does the building let in? Where does the light draw the eye? What does it illuminate?), acoustics (How much reverb/ echo does the sanctuary have? Does it have any "hot spots" of sound concentrated by domes or parallel walls?), and transitional space (Is the entry area welcoming? How does the building move people from gathering area to worship space?).

All of these details are concrete (or wood or glass) answers to fundamental questions:

What does your worship space say about God and God's people?

What does your worship space encourage?

What does your worship space discourage?

The first question concerns what Ron Rienstra calls "theophanic expectation."

I find helpful the concept of "theophanic expectation." (The roots are Greek: *theos* = God; *phainein* = to show.) How does the particular configuration of architectural space and the elements placed within it shape a congregation's expectations about how and when and where God "shows up"? When you step into the room, what is the first thing your eyes are drawn to? Where do your eyes move? What does the room put at the "center" of the assembly of the people? If the horizontal axis of the building says something about how we relate to one another, and the vertical axis represents the in-breaking of the Divine, how do those two axes align? Are their foci clear and strong?

In some buildings, you'll see a huge pulpit in front of rows of pews. These say "God is going to come to us when a book is read and preached by a single individual." In other churches, the seating is in the round, which suggests, theologically, that we find God in our interaction with one another. In other sanctuaries, the dominant feature of the worship space is a large and immovable table (or altar) that says "*Here* is where God shows up." Still other congregations put amps and instruments and assorted gear (and the people using them) front-and-center.[5]

The next two questions—what does a worship space encourage or discourage—are perhaps more down to earth but no less important. No worship space can do everything equally well. Instead, each space will emphasize one aspect of worship and minimize others. For example, a sanctuary with a sumptuously long reverb will make any choir or pipe organ sound beautiful but will be a nightmare for preaching intelligibility.

Environment

All of this architectural advice is well and good, but most of us don't have the luxury of building a new church from the ground up. We need to do the best we can with the buildings we have. Even though there may be significant deficiencies in our church structures, we can still make substantial improvements to our sanctuaries by renovating or restructuring our worship environment. To do this we ask the same questions as an architect would: What does our worship space say? What does it encourage or discourage?

A particularly successful renovation provides a good example. The Mulder Chapel at Western Theological Seminary in Holland, Michigan, was

Mulder Chapel, 1954

built in 1954 with rows of pews focused on a raised pulpit, reflecting the Reformed emphasis on preaching. An organ loft at the back of the long sanctuary reflected the hymn-singing legacy of the chapel. But as time went on and the leaders of the seminary asked the questions—What does our worship space say? What does it encourage or discourage?—they found the space focused so exclusively on enabling preaching that other acts of worship such as communion or liturgical dance were nearly impossible. The rigid rows of pews barely allowed worshipers to interact or move; that is, they encouraged preaching but discouraged community. The pipe organ had a substantial footprint, but the sanctuary didn't accommodate the music of a community that had grown to include piano, guitars, and percussion.

Mulder Chapel, 2015

This led to a comprehensive renovation. The pews were removed, a fa-çade gave the sanctuary walls a curve that focused the room's orientation to the center of the space, and an oculus (circular skylight) further focused the attention on the center of the room, where a communion table, cross, Bible, and baptismal font now resided.

Western Seminary's approach produced a beautiful, functional worship space, but there are as many ways to approach renovating as there are worshiping communities. Your community may answer the question of what (who) your worship space encourages (includes) or discourages (excludes) by renovating for wheelchair access. Another community might address acoustic problems to encourage congregational singing or tear down a wall to open up space for a growing congregation.

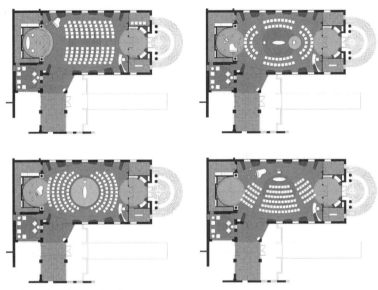

Mulder Chapel, Four Seating Arrangements

Complete renovations are not the only way to address problems in a church building. Sometimes a simple restructuring is all that's needed. Once again turning to Western's Mulder Chapel, we see that changing the orientation of the seating provides flexibility for worship in the round, intimate gatherings, and lecture/recital hall–style seating. Churches with pews bolted to the floor won't have this flexibility, but what the sanctuary communicates can still be substantially changed by altering the lighting design, rearranging the furnishings (especially up front), or even simply using a different color of paint.

Symbols

Once the structure and environment of the sanctuary are arranged in a way that supports the congregation's worship, we can turn our attention to the symbols of worship. Worship symbols are items like the cross, an open Bible, and a baptismal font that serve as a visual theology—a visual index of what the congregation believes to be important about the Christian faith. This may seem so easy that it's not even worth discussing—just put a communion table up front with a number of Christian symbols and you're done. Unfortunately, it's not quite that simple.

The first question is what symbols we should use. This depends in part on the church's denomination and tradition. Most Christian congregations display a cross prominently in their sanctuary. Many congregations indicate their reliance on Scripture with the symbol of the pulpit or a display Bible. Catholic congregations often have large baptismal pools near the entrance of the sanctuary to symbolize that we pass through the waters of baptism to come into God's presence. A church that believes in adult baptism is more likely to have their baptism pool visible only in services in which baptisms are performed. The same is true of churches that place a lot of importance on communion and celebrate it frequently; they will prioritize the communion table and elements visually in their sanctuaries. Word, table, cross, and baptismal font are the most frequently displayed worship symbols. Others include candles (light of Christ), dove (Holy Spirit), *ixoye* (fish symbol of early Christianity), and three-sectioned Celtic knots (representing the Trinity).

Almost as important as *what* symbols a church displays is *how* those symbols are displayed. Which symbol dominates? In some churches the pulpit is a massive structure that requires a staircase to ascend. No matter how much the church values communion, the visual symbols tell a different story: the preaching of the Word dwarfs all other worship elements. Sometimes practicalities lead us to obscure the importance of symbols. For example, many churches, in their rush to retrofit their sanctuaries with projection screens, covered over the symbol of the cross. What does it say about our worship when a screen scrolls down over the cross during the singing? I served in a church that had a high view of baptism yet kept the baptismal font in a back hallway except on baptism Sundays. Even worse, when the pastor would officiate a baptism, he'd pull the liner bowl out of the wooden font and walk down to meet the baby. The bowl looked suspiciously like a metal dog dish! A church that values baptism should be more careful with how it uses baptismal symbols. Other churches dilute the symbolic power of their worship by having multiple versions of the same symbol; for example, having a cross *and* a Christian flag. The cross is already the symbol of the Christian faith; there is no need for a flag with a cross on it. Simplify and centralize.

Finally, we need to be sure we don't inadvertently promote some visual elements to the status of religious symbol. The most frequent offender in US congregations is the American flag. A flag is a political symbol. The sanctuary should be reserved for symbols of the faith.[6] There are numerous other visual elements that vie for prominence in our sanctuaries. Projection screens and other technology can so overwhelm the visual field in some sanctuaries that symbols such as the cross or Bible are rendered visually powerless. We've all seen churches that make room for a praise band by pushing the communion table off to the side. The "theophanic expectation" that is communicated visually is that we are more likely to meet God in the music than in the Lord's Supper.

Visual Art

Structural forms of visual art such as architecture and worship symbols are parts of the sanctuary that will generally remain constant from week to week. But this certainly doesn't exhaust the possibilities for including visual art in worship. We now turn our attention to forms of art that are newly made for worship services.

Like all of the arts in worship, we don't simply use the visual arts to keep our churches' artists busy, but because the visual arts allow us to preach the gospel in unique and powerful ways. For example, an art exhibit called *The Father & His Two Sons: The Art of Forgiveness* featured dozens of art

Return of the Prodigal Son by Christian Rohlfs

works all based on Jesus's parable in Luke 15:11–32.[7] Each one focused on a different aspect of the parable, helping viewers explore the parable from different angles and in greater depth. Similarly, Henri Nouwen wrote an entire book meditating on Rembrandt's painting *The Return of the Prodigal Son*.

Why are these visual depictions of the parable so powerful? Can't the Word of God stand on its own without the help of a painting? Yes, certainly. But in the same way preacher after preacher has plumbed the depths of this parable and returned with some new insight for their congregations, works of art can give us unforgettable ways of connecting with Scripture.

The visual arts can be used for many parts of worship, including prayer, testimony, and confession. We already considered icons, which in the Orthodox Church constitute an important form of prayer. Author Sybil MacBeth suggests that drawing our prayers can be a powerful way of communicating with God.[8] MacBeth focuses on private prayers, but there is no reason the same principle shouldn't be applied to the corporate setting. A recent trend has seen artists painting during the preaching, creating a work that visually reflects the themes of the sermon. Depending on how well-implemented this is, it could provide an excellent way of letting the eyes hear the sermon. Another trend has been "cardboard testimonies," in which church members write a problem they had on one side of a sheet of cardboard and then turn the sheet over to reveal how God intervened in their life. Seeing these compact testimonies one after another gives powerful witness to God's work in those around us. Though not art in a strict sense, it shows how creative effort can turn something common—a testimony—into something we experience with new eyes.

> "In worship, our emotions, bodies, and imaginations have a vital role, and the arts serve to bring them into an intentional and intensive participation."
>
> —David Taylor[9]

Most often the visual arts in worship take the form of an installation. In my own church each new season of the year is accompanied by an art installation that reflects the themes and colors of the season. At Pentecost, long stretches of fabric painted with fire flow along the ceiling from the center of the sanctuary to the exits. At Christmas, stars undulate slowly overhead, reflecting light and shadow on the walls. Communion chalices and banners pick up these same visual themes.

Would worship still be pleasing to God without communion chalices to match the season? Certainly. However, beautifying the worship space deepens our experience of worship, allowing our whole beings to come before God.

Graphic Design

Graphic design is a form of visual art that focuses on the combination of visuals and text. Unlike "high art" meant to be savored in a gallery, graphic design is meant to communicate to viewers instantly and is found everywhere, from magazine layouts to billboard advertisements. Graphic design is used throughout worship, from the sign pointing the way to the bathrooms to the typeface used in the hymnal. The question is not whether you should use graphic design in worship but whether you're going to use it well.

In a sense, a church's use of graphic design begins well beyond the walls of the sanctuary. Most churches have a website. A church website is often a church's first form of hospitality. Does the website winsomely communicate the mission and values of the church? Does it inform visitors how to prepare for worship? (What do people wear? Is childcare provided? Are they welcome to participate in communion?) Does it give directions to the church? Is there an email address or phone number for those with questions? Are service times and other information kept up-to-date? Don't underestimate the power of a website to communicate to visitors if they are welcome at a church.

Courtesy of Ben Coleman and City Church. ©BRDDG, LLC; www.brddg.co

Once a worshiper arrives at a church, the form of graphic design they need most is "wayfinding," or the signage that helps them navigate a church building. This may seem like a trivial concern to long-term church members, but for a visitor who needs to get one child to the bathroom and another to Sunday school before finding a seat in the sanctuary, it is a vital form of hospitality.

After worshipers are settled into their seats and the service starts, a feast of graphic design commences. Most churches use some form of worship material in printed or projected form that allows worshipers to follow along with the service. It might be as simple as a piece of paper that gives the outline of the service or as complex as a projection screen that accompanies every moment of the service. At a basic level, these are practical tools that give worshipers the forms, words, and music they need to get through the service. Yet at another level the graphic design of worship materials says a lot about what we believe and how we believe it. Whereas art beautifies the message, graphic design is the tone and inflection of worship's visual surroundings. Would worship still be pleasing to God despite mismatched typefaces and tacky clip art? Yes. Is God still glorified when the choir sings out of tune and the preacher delivers a sermon in monotone? Yes. But in all these cases, worship won't be as effective or communicate as fully as it could.

To give an idea of how something even as simple as typography communicates beyond the words themselves, take a look at four renderings of the phrase, "I love you" below. With a simple change of typeface and punctuation, they communicate very different things. Which one would you use for your spouse? Your dad? Nuance is important. Worship should be so much more than simply conveying facts about God!

I. LOVE. YOU.

I love you.

I love you . . .

I love YOU.

Graphic design doesn't only enhance the aesthetics of our worship environment; it also serves an educational function. In the same way signage helps us navigate a building, graphic design guides us through the service. The way words are laid out on a page gives us instructional cues (read this; the leader will read that) and establishes hierarchy (headings tell us where we are in a service; footers give us extra information).

In my own congregation, worshipers follow the service using a printed order of worship. Because there are many words in our services and we include music for all the songs, this worship booklet can be overwhelming. We decided to redesign it to make it more user-friendly. First, we created a series of headings and subheadings that not only clarified where we were in the service but also educated the congregation about what elements were used each week in our services. Next, we made better use of white space and dividing lines to break up the text and make it easier for the eye to scan. Even though this is less efficient than large blocks of text, it makes the service feel lighter and less wordy. Finally, we established consistent ways of using typefaces, from indicating when the congregation should read to listing copyright information. This kind of detail may seem a long way off from the vision of ecstatic, effortless worship portrayed in Revelation, but the reality is that, this side of heaven, attention to the details can lead to more engaged, heartfelt worship.

Psalm 132

¹ O Lord, remember in David's favor
all the hardships he endured;

² how he swore to the Lord and vowed to the Mighty One of Jacob,	¹¹ The Lord swore to David a sure oath from which he will not turn back:
³ "I will not enter my house or get into my bed; ⁴ I will not give sleep to my eyes or slumber to my eyelids, ⁵ until I find a place for the Lord, a dwelling place for the Mighty One of Jacob."	"One of the sons of your body I will set on your throne. ¹² If your sons keep my covenant and my decrees that I shall teach them, their sons also, forevermore, shall sit on your throne."
⁶ We heard of it in Ephrathah; we found it in the fields of Jaar.	¹³ For the Lord has chosen Zion; he has desired it for his habitation:
⁷ "Let us go to his dwelling place; let us worship at his footstool."	
⁸ Rise up, O Lord, and go to your resting place, you and the ark of your might.	¹⁴ "This is my resting place forever; here I will reside, for I have desired it.
	¹⁵ I will abundantly bless its provisions; I will satisfy its poor with bread.
⁹ Let your priests be clothed with righteousness, and let your faithful shout for joy.	¹⁶ Its priests I will clothe with salvation, and its faithful will shout for joy.
¹⁰ For your servant David's sake do not turn away the face of your anointed one.	¹⁷ There I will cause a horn to sprout up for David; I have prepared a lamp for my anointed one.

¹⁸ His enemies I will clothe with disgrace,
but on him, his crown will gleam."

Graphic design can even bring clarity to a sermon text. When a friend preached on Psalm 132, he requested that the psalm be printed in columns.

Once I heard the sermon, I understood. Verses 2–10 and 11–17 are mirrors of each other. He could have spent ten minutes explaining how the psalm mirrored itself in its second half; instead the congregation was able to see the mirror clearly and refer to it throughout the sermon. And this all because of simple graphic design!

Few worship directors and church leaders have skills in graphic design. We can't be experts in everything. If you don't have the expertise to address these issues, find a graphic designer who can help you. A designer can identify the most distracting aspects of your church's visual materials and set up templates that will keep you on track. This doesn't necessarily need to cost a lot of money. You may very well find someone in your congregation who would be happy to help. Even if you have to hire someone, it's a wise investment. It doesn't make sense for a church to pay thousands of dollars for computers, printers, and projectors but not pay a few hundred dollars to make the things they produce look good!

Art in worship is a functional art. All of the visual arts, from architecture to graphic design, must serve worship. Art should complement rather than compete with the environment and message of worship. For example, I often hear musicians pray for humility before leading worship, "Dear God, don't let people see us, but let them see only you." Then they walk out into the middle of an elevated stage, the house lights dim, and their image is projected larger than life on a screen as they begin to sing. No matter how humble and transparent the musicians try to be, the architecture and lighting are screaming, "Look at me!"

Sometimes the art is simply distracting. Many of us have been in worship services in which the song lyrics are projected over video footage of the Grand Canyon. Beyond the fact that the church should provide motion sickness bags at each seat, such a busy background distracts us from the worship act at hand: singing. The visual artists of the church should apply Paul's admonition that "All things are lawful, but not all things are beneficial" (1 Cor. 10:23). Just because we *can* use a moving background behind lyrics doesn't mean we *should*.

You will notice that the above examples of unfitting and distracting visual art involve technology. This is not to say that only modern multimedia arts can overshadow the worship context, but it is certainly a lot easier to do when technology is involved. Technology allows anyone to create materials for worship—whether skilled or not—and project them to a size that dwarfs all else. Proceed carefully! Having said that, modern technology also enables churches to engage the arts more easily and cheaply than ever before. Take advantage of the opportunity to be creative, experimenting with visual arts that fit your church context.

For Discussion

1. Draw a Bible story (alternative: diagram a theological concept).

2. On a span from iconodules (those who believe in venerating icons) to iconoclasts (those who oppose icons), where are you? What do you think is an appropriate use of art? What goes too far?

3. Close your eyes. Imagine your own church's worship space. Name everything you see, whether it's art, architecture, or simply part of the room. What spiritual significance do these objects have?

4. Find two or more pictures of different types of sanctuaries/worship spaces. Discuss what each one might say about God or our "theophanic expectations." Where would your attention be drawn? What might you feel in each of these spaces?

5. What does your worship space say about God and God's people? What does your worship space encourage or discourage?

6. If you could go back in time and talk to the committees and architects who designed your church's sanctuary, what would you ask them to change?

7. Look at the printed and projected materials in your own church. Do they communicate clearly? Do they enhance the text they support, whether it's a sign for the nursery or a Scripture passage? Do you use typefaces consistently between printed and projected materials? Does the color palette of your projection match the color palette of your church or the church season?

8. After reading the variety of ways the visual arts have been used in the church, what is one thing you'd like to try in your church?

16

The Gospel Intensified

Technology in Worship

Before you begin: Consider worship unplugged.

You may know the show *MTV Unplugged*, on which popular bands perform their songs acoustically. Let's do a thought experiment on worship unplugged. Unlike the MTV show, let's imagine a church service with no electricity at all. How would that change things? Obviously, worship without electricity would have no sound system. What would the music sound like? Ensembles would have to balance their volume acoustically like a bluegrass band or string quartet. Musical forms would favor group singing like hymns or call and response forms like work songs. Preachers could no longer whisper into a microphone but would have to project their voices. Congregations, by necessity, would have to be small—maybe two hundred people maximum. Church buildings would be lit by natural light or candlelight. In the absence of projection screens, worshipers would sing from hymnals or memory.

Continue along this line of thinking, considering all the ramifications of worship that is entirely unplugged from electricity.

The walls of Jericho fall.

When we think of technology, we may think of stage lighting, digital keyboards, and smartphones, but this is only the most recent wave of technology to be used in worship. Indeed, technology encompasses any tool that enables, supports, or amplifies worship, from the pipe organ to the printing press. Like today's innovations, many previous technologies were demonized, overused, and eventually integrated into worship. Defining worship technology expansively allows us to learn from history and gain wisdom for our own churches' use of modern technology.

Audio

Technology is usually broken into two categories: audio and visual (or A/V). Obviously, audio—sound—has been around as long as ears, but the means of projecting sound have changed throughout history. One of the most striking examples of sound amplification in the Bible is Joshua 6, in which the walls of Jericho crumbled to the ground when Israel shouted. That must have been some shout! In that same story we see the use of the shofar, a ram's horn that called Israel to worship and war. Joshua 6 gives us a sampling of the two types of audio technologies available the first millennia of civilization. First was technology built into the human body: the voice, the ears, hands for clapping, and feet for stomping. Added to that were musical instruments: horns, flutes, stringed instruments, and tambourines. It is important to note that these all require significant human effort. When the Bible says to praise with loud songs (Ps. 47:1) it assumes that the worshiper will be investing a lot of energy into creating the loud praise. The shout of Jericho is a far cry from turning up the modern praise singer's microphone!

Music technologies accompanied—or perhaps initiated—many of the musical advances of the Renaissance and following historical periods. New tuning systems paved the way for tonal and chromatic harmonies. Pipe organs put orchestral colors within the reach of churches. Trumpet valves and other innovations made it possible for instruments to play music too difficult for previous generations.

The real watershed came in the twentieth century as mass media made its way into the church. Early adopters like Aimee Semple McPherson (pastor of Angelus Temple in Hollywood) leveraged the technology of Broadway and Hollywood, paving the way for televised worship such as Robert Schuller's *Hour of Power* and slickly produced megachurches such as Willow Creek. Mass media values soon found their way into local congregations, and low-cost digital technology meant every church could afford a sound system and electronic instruments.

If it is true that "we shape our environments, then our environments shape us,"[1] these changes in modern worship environments have shaped our worship in ways we, perhaps, didn't anticipate. Live broadcasting of worship made churches very time conscious, as they had exactly sixty minutes for each service. Even those that weren't broadcasting cast aside historical worship service paradigms and took their cues from late-night talk shows and rock concerts. Multimedia worship artist Stephen Proctor says it well: "modern worship has borrowed the liturgy of the rock concert, which forms worshipers into fans and critics."[2] Beyond the philosophical question of how all this technology shapes us spiritually, on a practical level many churches today can't even imagine having worship without a digital sound system, cue sheets, or in-ear monitors.

Audio technology allows churches to do many good things in worship, but we should challenge the assumption that applying technology will always make things better. Technology allows us to amplify our worship to larger-than-life proportions, so we can hear a whispered melody across a ten-thousand-seat auditorium, but perhaps what we really need is worship that is human-sized. Have our sound systems dulled our ability to "be still, and know that I am God" (Ps. 46:10), taken away the intimacy of blending our voices with that of our neighbor, and made us forget the unabashed joy of singing a cappella so loudly that the room reverberates with praise? And as a practical matter, are the thousands of dollars we invest in sound equipment going to yield benefits if volunteers aren't trained to run it?

Sound level	Examples	NIOSH daily permissible noise level exposure *(hours per day)*
0 dB	Threshold of hearing	
60 dB	Normal conversation	
70 dB	Loud singing from three feet away	
85 dB	String instrument/city traffic from inside car	8
88 dB	Woodwind instrument/subway train	4
90 dB	Brass instrument/train whistle (500 feet)	2
94 dB	Loud classical music/average headphone level	1
97 dB	Piccolo/lawnmower	.5
100 dB	Motorcycle/timpani or bass drum	.25 or less
112 dB	Discotheque/rock concert/symphonic music peak	0
120 dB	Threshold of pain/rock concert peak	0
194 dB	Loudest possible sound	0

Examples are approximate levels; much depends on distance from sound and peak versus average sound level
3dB increase will generally be heard as a change in volume
10dB increase is perceived as twice as loud

One area where the question of audio technology becomes most pressing today is the volume of worship. Sound systems, amplifiers, and pipe organs have given us the ability to reproduce the volume of Jericho's "great shout" week after week, with no more than the turn of a knob. Some churches pride themselves in sound levels averaging above 90 decibels (dB) and peaking over 100 dB, because it gives them a modern, "immersive" worship sound. The United States' Occupational Safety & Health Administration (OSHA) has set 90 dB as the limit for eight hours of work. This is the *legal* limit rather than a *healthy* limit. The National Institute for Occupational Safety and Health (NIOSH) sets safe sound levels much lower. Given that churches include babies and elderly people who may be more susceptible to hearing damage, wouldn't it be wise to err on the lower side of these standards?[3] As shepherds of our congregations, we need to seek the well-being of our people. This may be one area in which we decide to follow the law of love rather than the law of the land.

Visual

In the earliest days of faith, truth was communicated orally. Psalm 78 gives a good sense of how God's commands were passed down from generation to generation:

> Give ear, O my people, to my teaching;
>   incline your ears to the words of my mouth.
> I will open my mouth in a parable;
>   I will utter dark sayings from of old,
> things that we have heard and known,
>   that our ancestors have told us.
> We will not hide them from their children;
>   we will tell to the coming generation
> the glorious deeds of the LORD, and his might,
>   and the wonders that he has done.
> He established a decree in Jacob,
>   and appointed a law in Israel,
> which he commanded our ancestors
>   to teach to their children;
> that the next generation might know them,
>   the children yet unborn,
> and rise up and tell them to their children,
>   so that they should set their hope in God,
> and not forget the works of God,
>   but keep his commandments. (Ps. 78:1–7)

It wasn't until the invention of the printing press and Gutenberg's Bible that average Christians could be expected to read Scripture for themselves.

Today we take it for granted. But it wasn't only Scripture that was affected by mass printing. Hymnals and prayer books became standard equipment in churches. These tools allowed for more participation of lay people and the dissemination of new hymns that would have been impossible previously. However, some things were lost too. I can just imagine the older folks shaking their heads and saying, "When we were kids, we memorized the Bible on our parents' knees; kids today just read it in these newfangled books!" Perhaps it didn't happen quite like that, but the point remains: each new communication technology encourages some things and discourages others.

After Gutenberg's printing press, the technologies that had the greatest impact on worship were the mimeograph, photocopier, and overhead projector. Each advance allowed churches' worship materials to become more localized and immediate. Gone were the days of waiting for a denomination to come out with a new hymnal. Churches could add new songs and worship materials every week. As James White pointed out regarding A. B. Dick's invention of the mimeograph in 1884: "Gutenberg made it possible to put prayer books in the hands of the people; Dick made prayer books obsolete."[4] By the time digital projection, the internet, and smartphones came along, churches had the power of thousands of printing presses at their disposal.

Churches also gained access to a whole world (literally) of songs and resources. Tapping into the wealth of worship from around the world was certainly a blessing, but it created some difficulties as well. How were local worship directors supposed to sort through the millions of options available to them? Previously, this was the work of denominational publishing houses. Now the task fell to the local church. Some churches tapped into mass media: songs from the radio and sermon illustrations from popular preachers. Others aligned themselves with a particular style or "brand" of worship such as Willow Creek, the retuned hymn movement, or Hillsong.

Today visual technology doesn't only affect worship behind the scenes. It also has a huge impact on the visual environment of worship itself. In many churches, the projection screen is the focal point of the worship space. Whereas screens were previously used simply to project lyrics and other text, they are now part of a multimedia experience. Preachers illustrate sermon points with a scene from a movie. Song lyrics may have moving backgrounds. Even church announcements can take the form of a projected video montage. Recently, there has been a movement toward "environmental projection," a form of projection that is used more for atmosphere than verbal/written communication. Images are projected that synchronize with stage lighting or coordinate with the colors and themes of the auditorium's overall visual design.

This opens up amazing opportunities for artists and technicians to use their skill for the Lord. Technology allows a sanctuary to have an entirely different visual design every week, with teams of designers working together virtually and bringing all elements together on Sunday morning. This is a long way from the four years Michelangelo needed to complete painting the Sistine Chapel ceiling!

However, this same technology can create a burden for churches. In a consumer-driven culture churches feel the pressure to "keep up with the Joneses." If the church down the street is projecting images on its side walls, the other churches in town don't want to be left behind. To keep up, many churches hire massive tech teams to run lights, sound system, and projection, and to produce multimedia content. This can have the effect of letting the technology run the show. A live production with so much to coordinate requires a stage manager calling cues over headsets. The cue sheets from which the tech team works are scripted down to the second, and worship leaders tell stories of being in the middle of a prayer and hearing a voice over their in-ear monitor, "Thirteen seconds over time. Wrap it up." We soon lose sight of what is important in worship, and we wonder why.

How Can We Use Technology Wisely?

In an increasingly "always on" world, it is easy to let our technology rule us. We interrupt face-to-face conversations to check text messages, we stare over each other's shoulders to see the TV at restaurants, and we are distracted by a barrage of beeps and blinks. Inevitably, this unsettled part of our culture seeps into our worship. It becomes a frantic parade of images, sounds, and movements that holds our attention but never reaches our souls. Psalm 62 paints a very different picture of communicating with God:

> For God alone my soul waits in silence;
>> from him comes my salvation.
> He alone is my rock and my salvation,
>> my fortress; I shall never be shaken. (Ps 62:1–2)

We need to challenge the assumption that A/V technology is good or even necessary in worship. Just because technology permeates every aspect of our culture doesn't mean it should permeate our churches. On the other hand, Pandora's box is already open. We can't act as if all this technology doesn't exist. Instead, we need to treat each new technology for what it is: a tool to be used—or not—to achieve a particular goal. We've all seen a child pick up a hammer; she is just as likely to put a hole in a wall as she is to build a deck. The same is true of technology in worship. If a technology simply enables us to make superficial kitsch faster and bigger, it is not the right tool. We must control our technology rather than allow our technology to control us.

To discern wisely what technologies to use in worship and when, we should ask ourselves the same questions we do of art:

What does our technology say about God and God's people?

What does our technology encourage?

What does our technology discourage?

Technology is never neutral. In the same way that architecture and art encourage or enable some aspects of worship while discouraging others, different technologies are appropriately applied to different aspects of worship. For example, leveraging social media and scheduling software to bring a church's musicians together makes sense. Who would want to go back to those pre-email afternoons making twenty phone calls trying to change a rehearsal time? In this case, the technology enables us to efficiently achieve the spiritual goal of including people in ministry. But the same technological efficiency when applied to the worship order may not be as helpful. Does a sixty-minute service scripted down to the second allow worshipers to quietly linger as the Spirit moves during singing? Does the tyranny of the clock dictate that the community can't stop and pray for a family who has experienced a tragedy?

We also need to look at the unintended consequences of our decisions. It is no secret that people are not singing in worship as much as they used to, and the problem seems to follow the same trajectory as the rise of praise bands, sound systems, and concert-style lighting.[5] Though there are exceptions to this rule and no scientific studies to prove the correlation, it seems pretty clear that as churches have used technology to create excitement on the stage and have dimmed the lights in the auditorium, people have responded by playing the role given them: passive audience. Graham Kendrick says it well:

> Much of the church has embraced a performance style. I think, to a great extent, we have copied the "concert" model, so that what's coming from the platform is almost complete in itself. We're surrounded by screens and all sorts of personal devices that deliver entertainment to us, that deliver performances to us, and we've come to expect that what happens on that screen is going to do something to us. It's going to entertain us or it's going to inspire us, it's going to make us laugh or cry and it's very easy to find ourselves in a church context and what's happening at the front is just another screen, and we are looking to that screen to do something for us.[6]

These are practical examples, but there are deeper ways in which technology shapes our faith. When we pattern our worship in the image of the culture around us—rock concert, talk show, or lecture—we are reducing worship to just another entertainment option. More wholesome, to be sure, but not of a different category. Has the church ceased to be a refuge from the busyness that surrounds us? Has it lost its ability to be "in the world, but not of it" (see John 17)?

Perhaps we could learn something here from Amish culture. The Amish are a strain of Anabaptists who settled in Pennsylvania in the eighteenth century and adopted a simple lifestyle. They are known for shunning the trappings of modern life and can still be encountered riding their horse-drawn buggies near their communities. But the Amish are not technological Luddites, never-adopters who reject all modern devices. Instead, they selectively discern which technologies will bring their community together and which will weaken it. In an excellent article about the Amish relationship to the cell phone, journalist Howard Rheingold found that the Amish weigh each modern device for its potential dangers. There is no question, for example, that the automobile is faster than a horse-drawn carriage. But the Amish decided that cars would make it too easy for people to take a day trip to the city or beach on a Sunday rather than visiting shut-ins and enjoying communal dinners. The Amish banned landline phones because they feared they would disrupt face-to-face conversation in the home; however, they have adopted cellphones for business and travel. One of the Amish men interviewed stated,

> We don't want to be the kind of people who will interrupt a conversation at home to answer a telephone. It's not just how you use the technology that concerns us. We're also concerned about what kind of person you become when you use it.[7]

What if churches took a similar discerning stance about their use of technology? What if we asked ourselves honest questions? *If this microphone enables me to speak or sing louder, whose voice is quieter because of it?* Sometimes we simply need to ask *Why?* I remember being at a conference where I kept running into the same three people having long, earnest conversations about environmental projection. What was the best projector? How could they sync their screens? Could they put together a system on their budget? I wanted to walk over and say, "Do you realize that the church of Jesus Christ has survived for two thousand years without environmental projection, and your church will likely be just fine without it too?" We need to ask whether we need a given technology at all, have the fortitude to act on the answer, and commit to continued discernment.

What Is So Good about Technology?

All this may sound overly critical of technology in worship. Churches need to hear this message, because many have uncritically adopted technologies that have drawn them very far from the heart of worship. Others have resisted any innovations at all, as if their worship would be pure if they reject any technology later than the book. Let's consider some positive things that technology allows us to do.

First, multimedia technology allows churches to engage people with a wider variety of learning styles. Especially in the area of preaching, churches have worked for years with the assumption that everyone can understand and retain a sermon simply by hearing it. But educators know that different people learn in different ways. Whether you subscribe to VARK learning styles (visual, aural, read/write, kinesthetic) or Howard Gardner's multiple intelligences, the idea is the same: sometimes a picture (or a video or an action) really is worth a thousand words. This doesn't diminish the role of preaching in worship but rather supports it. The same is true for other parts of worship. A well-placed visual image accompanying the lyrics of a song can draw in a person who is not as naturally engaged by singing.

Second, technology can introduce a sense of awe into our worship. This may seem counterintuitive after our discussion of all the ways technology can distract us and keep us from being still before God. However, most of our church sanctuaries are missing the grandeur of the cathedrals of old, which had awe built into their very structures. Instead, we have very ordinary rooms that convey nothing of God's otherness. Projection screens can give us a canvas big enough to paint a picture of the glory of the Lord. Sound design, lighting, and images can all contribute to bringing a little taste of heaven into our everyday lives.

Third, technology can help foster connections between people, and between their lives and worship. Gone are the days of church as the center of a community's life. Many families commute to worship from out of town and everyone is trying to squeeze in church between eighty-hour work weeks, night classes, and soccer practice; a tightknit church family is a rarity. Social media can be a way to keep church members connected during the week. Blogs and emails can keep church leaders connected to worshipers. Think how much more fully people would engage in the sermon if they received an email with next week's Scripture passage and could tweet their questions or email articles to the pastor throughout the week. Yes, anything like this takes time, but if it results in deeper community and richer engagement with the Word, it is worth it.

Fourth, the true power of multimedia is in the "multi." It is the combination of sensory approaches that allows multimedia technology to become more than a sum of its parts. For example, I once attended a worship service that ended by asking us to quietly visit baptismal bowls that were stationed

Further Reading on Technology in Worship

Eileen D. Crowley, *Liturgical Art for a Media Culture* (Collegeville, MN: Liturgical Press, 2007).

Elizabeth Steele Halstead, "Visual Arts: Images and the Screen Showcase" *Calvin Institute of Christian Worship*, April 13, 2012, http://worship.calvin.edu/resources/resource-library/showcase-visual-arts-images-and-the-screen/.

Brad Herring, *Sound, Lighting and Video: A Resource for Worship* (Burlington, MA: Focal Press, 2009).

Stephen Proctor, "The (Newly Enhanced) Guidebook for Visual Worship," September 3, 2013, http://illuminate.us/the-newly-enhanced-guidebook-for-visual-worship/.

Quentin J. Schultze, *High-Tech Worship? Using Presentational Technologies Wisely* (Grand Rapids: Baker Books, 2004).

James F. White, *New Forms of Worship* (Nashville: Abingdon Press, 1971).

Susan J. White, *Christian Worship and Technological Change* (Nashville: Abingdon Press, 1994).

around the room. As Gavin Bryars's spacious and repetitive "Jesus's Blood Never Failed Me Yet" played, we each walked up to the bowls, perhaps to pray, perhaps to dip our fingers in the water. As I hovered over the water, I could see a message undulating through the water and glass: "You are forgiven." In an instant, my auditory, visual, and tactile senses were infused with a new understanding of forgiveness: *I have been washed clean, once and for all, through Jesus's sacrifice.*

Finally, technology is very well-fitted to amplifying what is already there. This could be as simple as bringing an acoustic guitar's volume up enough

Image courtesy of Stephen Proctor, http://illuminate.us. Used by permission.

Multimedia communion table.

to play with a piano. A purist might complain that musicians should be able to blend their volume without technology. That is perhaps true, but few of us have musicians or acoustic spaces that allow for unlimited musical possibilities unaided by a sound system. In this case, the technology enables the musicians we have to play in the sanctuary we're in. Stephen Proctor tells his church's arts team, "Creativity must be the subtle amplification of our worship. Subtlety is key. Immersive environments should slow you down and stir your imagination, not create more noise."[8] We can see Proctor's philosophy at work in the above picture of the communion table with the sketch of Christ projected behind it. The communion table is already ripe with meaning; when combined with the image of Christ stretching wide his arms (In crucifixion? In welcome?) the image and the idea are sealed in our hearts.

If technology amplifies what is already there, it is also true that technology can't bring sense to a poorly constructed sermon, give a church a vision for worship, or bring creativity where there is none. Churches will find that technology serves worship best when it functions as a frame, a complement to an imaginative and well-constructed service.

For Discussion

1. What advantages or disadvantages did you find in unplugged worship? Were there any points that could be applied to your church's worship?

2. Tell about a meaningful moment that was made possible by technology. Recall a time when technology ruined the moment in worship. Are there any lessons to be learned from these two occasions?

3. List every item of technology your church uses in worship. What specific gift does each item enable? What potential danger does it introduce?

4. What is one technology you wish your church had? What would that piece of technology allow you to do that you can't do now?

5. What is one technology you wish you could eliminate from your church? Why?

17

The Gospel in Time

Worship Pacing and Other Intangibles

Before you begin: What just happened?

Fishermen and country singers often tell tales of "the one that got away." Worship directors often have similar stories—worship services that turned out very differently than planned. Tell a story about one of those times. Maybe you had an energetic service plan and it ended up being very reflective in the end—or flat as a pancake. Or you expected an ordinary Sunday but for some inexplicable reason the congregation sang like never before and participated wholeheartedly throughout the entire service. Positive or negative, it left you scratching your head and wondering, *What just happened?* As you recall this story, see if you can pinpoint anything that may have accounted for this unexpected outcome of the service.

When worship directors plan services, we may think of ourselves like engineers: we put together the right elements and everything will run smoothly. But we all know this is not the whole story. Some services run exactly as expected but others go in directions we never could have anticipated, for good or ill. Worship services are more than a sum of their parts. There is often a mysterious X factor for which we simply can't plan. Certainly some of this X factor is the work of the Spirit. "The wind [of the Spirit] blows where it chooses, and you hear the sound of it, but you do not know where it comes from or where it goes" (John 3:8). All we can do is be attentive and responsive to it.

Sometimes, though, that X factor is an aspect of worship that happens "off the page." It is not part of our worship plan but is nonetheless important. These factors include the pacing of the service, the mood of the day, and the interaction between leaders and people. It is not the songs but what happens between the songs. It is not the words that are used but how they're said. We'll look at some of the areas that can quietly make or break a service.

Time

Worship takes place in time; it has a beginning, an end, and a tempo that leads us along between those two points. Too often we approach worship planning like a butcher, weighing our worship by the pound, but we would benefit from thinking more like an architect who has to look beyond the schematic design and imagine how a room would *feel* with an extra window or raised ceiling.

Whereas an architect works with the beyond-the-page element of space, worship directors work with the element of time—the pacing with which the elements unfold. Too often we give a great deal of attention to the worship elements themselves but leave the pacing of those elements to chance. For example, the opening of worship will retain its energy if the pacing remains brisk and each element segues quickly into the next. But many services have the wind sucked out of them when an upbeat opening song ends and the congregation waits for a leader to walk slowly up to the podium, check to see if the microphone is on, then start speaking. At times like these, thirty seconds can seem like an eternity (and not in a good way). Or an otherwise terrific praise set never really ignites because every song ends with an awkward pause as the musicians shuffle their pages to prepare for the next song. These are moments that would benefit from rehearsing the transitions. Who will start the next song? Will they begin without a break? What is the tempo? If someone is coming to the platform to speak, do they (and the sound operator) know their cue so they can be in place with the microphone on?

The same is true on the other end of the spectrum. When we want to lead the congregation into quiet reflection, we need to slow down the tempo before we get there. The music relaxes, the spaces between elements get longer, and the leader's voice becomes more subdued. Churches need to learn how to embrace silence. But deep silences don't just happen—they are prepared. It is important to note silence is very different from "dead air." Dead air, a term borrowed from radio, is the awkward, unplanned silence that happens when someone misses their cue. Rich, reflective silence takes place when the people have been prepared and sit in stillness before the Lord.

Worship Lessons from Mr. Rogers

If you have never seen the video of Fred Rogers accepting the Lifetime Achievement Award at the 1997 Emmy awards, do yourself a favor and watch it.[1] This humble Presbyterian pastor and children's TV host begins by saying, "So many people have helped me to come here to this night. Some of you are here, some are far away and some are even in heaven. All of us have special ones who loved us into being." Then he does something unforgettable.

He asks the crowd, "Would you just take, along with me, ten seconds to think of the people who have helped you become who you are, those who cared about you and wanted what was best for you in life? Ten seconds; I'll watch the time." Suddenly the glamorous audience of famous actors is transformed. For ten seconds they are thoughtful, appreciative, and even reverent.

What can a worship leader learn from Mr. Rogers? First, he transitions well, easing the audience from applause to silence with his own heartfelt thanks for those who had shaped him. Next, he doesn't demand—he invites. An invitation to join someone is much more winsome than an instruction. Finally, he assures people that he'll monitor the time. Silence can be very uncomfortable for some people; knowing that it is a short time and that someone will watch the clock allows the audience to clear their minds of everything but the silence.

Be like Mr. Rogers: lead with sensitivity and quiet confidence; you will gain the trust of your people. Is this emotional manipulation? No, it is simply good leadership. We want to prepare people for what comes next in a service, so we give care to worship's pacing in our planning and rehearsing.

The Church Calendar

Pacing within a worship service is important, but we should pay attention to the pacing of a church's calendar too. We worship directors too often fall into the temptation of trying to plan big, complicated services week after week. This only leads to exhaustion. We need to distinguish between *ordinary* weekly worship and *festival* services—Easter, Christmas, and other special events.[2]

Our ordinary services are the mainstay of our worship diet. Like breakfast last Tuesday, individual services may not be particularly memorable; however, they give us the ongoing nourishment we need. The congregation learns to arrive at church ready to be fed rather than overwhelmed by spectacle. The musicians and artists of the church can settle into a steady pattern of serving the church. Even though these services are fairly humble affairs, it is good to build in one special moment in each service. Perhaps something as simple as a creative way of praying, a song sung in a different language, or a guided reflection in response to the sermon—not a big production, but something that reminds us, even in our ordinary weekly services, that we are engaged and ready to hear what the Spirit is saying.

Festival services, on the other hand, are the "all hands on deck" and "pull out all the stops" services. These services take a lot of planning and use more of our worship volunteers. Special services such as Christmas Eve or Easter morning are highlights of a church's year, in part because they occur infrequently. Even in these relatively extravagant services, we need to remain focused on glorifying God rather than our musicians or ourselves. It is very easy to cross the line from inspiring to spectacle.

One church guards itself from becoming too reliant on its art by "cleansing its palate" every few months. They strip the sanctuary of all decorations and hold a sparse service in order to wean themselves from a constant visual and musical feast. These cycles of feasting and fasting are a healthy part of a Christian's life and can become part of a church's discipline as well.

Mood

Some church leaders are uncomfortable considering the mood of a service—seeing it as emotional manipulation—whereas other leaders focus entirely on mood. We need balance. It is healthy to remain focused on the content of worship, but people are more receptive when the content is delivered well. We should consider ways the worship's message and mood can work together.

Do you remember going to church on the Sunday after the Twin Towers fell on 9/11? The air was thick with the tragedy, and people arrived at worship full of disbelief and sorrow. Some worship directors forged ahead with their service plans as if nothing had happened, even bragging that upbeat praise would remind worshipers that God reigns regardless of our feelings. Other churches were more sensitive to the mood of the nation and quickly adapted their services to include lament, prayer, and somber reflection.

Most Sundays will not present worship directors with such pressing choices, but the principle remains: people have emotions and they shouldn't be required to leave them at the doors of the church. Instead, we dignify the humanity God gave us by including it in our worship. We respond sensitively when national or personal tragedies hang over our congregations and we "rejoice with those who rejoice [and] weep with those who weep" (Rom. 12:15).

We support the scriptural message of a given service with an appropriate ambience; the character of a service focusing on repentance should feel different than one on rejoicing in the Lord. This can be achieved in a number of ways. Most importantly, leaders need to be sensitive to their people. We all know people who are socially tone deaf—they tell jokes at inappropriate moments or deliver heartfelt words in a flat, lifeless tone. Church leaders need to be more emotionally engaged than that. We need to read the room quickly and adapt our demeanor accordingly. This can be as simple as using the tone of our voices to transition from a quiet moment to a joyous one.

Our physical surroundings have an impact on our emotions too. Lighting, for example, changes how we experience things. A candlelit dinner feels romantic while the fluorescent lights of a government office feel impersonal. In worship, we can light our sanctuary in a way that supports a mood of joy or of reflection. Posture also plays an important role in how we experience worship. Yes, we can praise or repent in our thoughts, but when we stand with arms stretched to heaven or fall to our knees with our heads bowed low, we understand these actions more fully. Even the temperature of a room can make a difference in how we engage in worship. Some church sanctuaries are kept at temperatures so uncomfortably cool that they also feel emotionally cold. I hope we don't cause our people to identify with the child in "The Little Vagabond" by William Blake: "Dear Mother, dear Mother, the Church is cold / But the Ale-house is healthy & pleasant & warm."[3]

Scripted versus Spontaneous

Some churches rehearse their services thoroughly, with every word read or memorized. They see anything less as haphazard. Other churches' worship is completely improvised. They avoid preplanned worship because it doesn't feel authentic and heartfelt. There are advantages and disadvantages to both scripted and spontaneous worship.

Scripted worship—services that are planned and rehearsed ahead of time—give leaders time to make thoughtful decisions. Words can be carefully considered. Artists can be enlisted in creating work for the service. Transitions can be rehearsed. This leads to a service that runs smoothly and lets worshipers participate without distraction. However, it can also lead to a service that feels lifeless and impersonal. A worship service, after all, is not a theatrical production; it is living people coming before a living God.

Spontaneous worship—services that are mostly improvised in the moment—provide the life and immediacy that scripted services often lack. They allow leaders to follow the Spirit, read the congregation from moment to moment, and allow each person present to contribute in some way. When leaders are sensitive and the congregation is engaged, spontaneous worship can be truly exciting. However, it can also devolve into randomness and cliché.

Both approaches can learn from the other. Churches most comfortable with a scripted mode of worship don't need to become entirely spontaneous but could find places to improvise within their existing structure. Prayer requests could be taken from the congregation and prayed for on the spot. Sections of the service could be introduced extemporaneously to create a more personable atmosphere. The service plan itself could be changed at the Spirit's nudging. For their part, spontaneous churches could identify sections of the service that would benefit from carefully crafted words. They could also experience the blessings of planning services in advance—discovering that the Spirit works both in the moment and in the planning.

Jazz offers a good paradigm for integrating both preparation and spontaneity. Many people are amazed that jazz musicians can just "make up" music on the spot. But it doesn't work quite like that. Jazz musicians first have to learn to play their instruments. Then they learn their chords and scales. Then they commit hundreds of tunes to memory. Only then are they ready to "make up" music. The reality is that good improvisation is created in the moment but is based on hundreds of hours of diligent work. To hear what this might sound like in worship, listen to Dr. S. M. Lockridge's sermon, "That's My King."[4] It is a masterful improvisation that is clearly based on years of experience and ample rehearsal.

The Role of the Congregation

Worship directors give a great deal of thought to what we will say or do when standing in front of the church on a Sunday morning, but do we give as much thought to the role the congregation will play? If worship really is the "work of the people," we need to pay more attention to how the people take part. Yes, it is easier to assess how well you played a difficult piano accompaniment or how eloquently the sermon was delivered than it is to assess how well the congregation sang or how much they understood, but it is vital nonetheless.

We need to take stock of who in the congregation is invited to take part in leading worship. Can lay church members read Scripture or lead prayer? Are amateur musicians involved in the music? Are there places for young people to lead? Do you reinforce social norms by only having the majority ethnic group in front of the church, or do you send the message "all are welcome and all are important" by including a wide variety of ethnicities in worship leadership? In my own church, the majority of the congregation is white and highly educated. One Sunday, one of our less-polished members read Scripture. A friend told me later that the man sitting next to her—a man who had recently returned from prison—leaned over to her and asked, "Does this mean *anyone* can read Scripture?" He hadn't seen anyone like himself up front, so he assumed that Scripture reading was only for other people. Our services are always sending subtle messages about who is welcome. As you can imagine, those who feel relegated to the fringes have a very different experience in worship than the "insiders." This has a huge impact on the spirit of our services.

Another important question is how we invite people to respond. When worship is compelling, people will react to what they've experienced. This may be as general as a hearty "Amen" or as specific as a prophetic word from the Lord. In between these is a whole range of responses: testimonies, altar calls, silence, or asking questions. Even though these spontaneous responses can be unpolished, worship directors would do well to plan for or even encourage them. There is nothing more powerful than hearing the testimony of someone who has been given new life in Jesus Christ. There is nothing more beautiful than the deep silence that settles on a congregation caught up in prayer. Of course, we can't (or shouldn't) manufacture these moments, but we should be open to them and leave space for them to happen.

Finally, we need to consider the mysteries of the faith—those spiritual factors that infuse our worship with eternal meaning. In my church, for example, I regularly see people coming forward for communion with tears in their eyes. I wonder what the Spirit might be doing in their hearts that is moving them to tears. This is nothing I can manufacture. The same is true of prayer, preaching, and so many other elements of worship. We can prepare the words of a prayer or sermon, but the actual work is that of the Spirit. The words we speak are only the tip of the iceberg. Likewise, we can prepare the bread and cup of communion, but without the work of the Spirit these are just common food items. This should keep us humble! Yes, we are called to important work in worship, but ultimately the work is not our own. "Neither the one who plants nor the one who waters is anything, but only God who gives the growth" (1 Cor. 3:7).

We cannot quantify these intangible, off-the-page aspects of worship, and we certainly can't micromanage them. All we can do is be sensitive to the Spirit and our people, knowing that our plans are only the starting point for what happens in worship.

From dance to architecture to the intangibles of worship, the point is clear: the way we shape worship will ultimately shape our congregation's affections. Just like children, our congregations come to love things that are familiar. Worship directors have the great responsibility and opportunity to help our congregations learn to love good things—things that will sustain their faith over a lifetime.

For Discussion

1. If festival and ordinary services could be plotted on a graph, with Easter being at 100 and the simplest service at 0, map out the last few months of services to see the pacing of your services. Do you see an ebb and flow? Are you trying to do big productions too often or are your services overly ordinary? (Take into account the resources your church has, realizing that your "festival" may be another church's "ordinary.")

2. Are there people in your congregation who bring expectations of festival worship into ordinary weekly worship services?

3. Are there moments in your worship services that consistently have dead air (awkward gaps due to poor planning or leading)? How can you address this?

4. Does your church ever include intentional silence?

5. Think about a recent national or congregational tragedy. How did it affect worship that Sunday?

6. Is your church more scripted or spontaneous? Name three places in your church service that would benefit from the other mode.

7. List all the people who have been up front in recent worship services. Do you notice any trends (age, race, gender, social or marital status)? What message might this be sending?

PART 5

PEOPLE

Ministry would be great if it weren't for people. These words have been uttered by anyone who has ever worked in a church. All the principles (biblical theology of worship), past (history of worship), and practice (the arts in worship) we've studied become exceedingly more complicated when applied to the real world, especially a real world that is populated with people very different from us.

On the other hand, the messy world of people is exactly where ministry happens.

My story of ministry is a good example of this. My background is in music; to this day, music is where I am most comfortable. Music is reliable and logical. Notes have never let me down. People, on the other hand, are frustratingly undependable. They make decisions based on emotions, they change their minds, and they often clash with one another. (Unresolved dissonance, in musical terms.)

When I began in music ministry, I loved the music part of my work but found the ministry side of things draining. Over the years, however, God

---

"The day we find the perfect church, it becomes imperfect the moment we join it."
—CHARLES H. SPURGEON

"Those who love their dream of a Christian community more than the Christian community itself become destroyers of that Christian community even though their personal intentions may be ever so honest, earnest, and sacrificial."
DIETRICH BONHOEFFER

"I don't want to belong to any club that would have me as a member."
—GROUCHO MARX

"God is great, beer is good, and people are crazy."
—BILLY CURRINGTON

has done a work in my heart. I have come to see the people side of music ministry as an opportunity rather than a burden. Perhaps it is because I realize that I, too, am a fickle, argumentative human being. God has had mercy on me, so I have more empathy for those around me. Also, I have come to see the depth of need in those around me: dig beneath the chipper exterior and you'll find a lifetime of pain, fear, and doubt. God wants to heal these wounds, and worship is one of the ways God uses.

Of course, these realizations don't always make day-to-day ministry any easier; there's still that guitarist who can be so irritating, the influential congregation member who complains to anyone who will listen, and the fellow minister who has never been a team player.

What follows is an overview of the people of ministry. We'll begin with a wide-angle view of our worship in the context of the world and culture. Then we'll narrow our focus down to the congregational level: those in the pews, fellow worship leaders, and partners in ministry. We'll conclude with how worship directors can care for our own souls and how we can mentor future generations for ministry.

18

The World

Before you begin: What is your church's cultural profile?

Every church has a culture, but it takes time and honesty to discern. Start by taking an inventory of your church demographics. Are the people generally rich or poor, educated or blue collar? Does your region support a dominant profession such as technology, education, or military? What is the age distribution of your members? Now dig a little deeper. Does your congregation lean liberal or conservative? Is there a dominant ethnic group? Is there a significant segment of the congregation that is related by blood or marriage? Is there a "vibe" or personality to the congregation? How would you describe it? How would a visitor or someone who used to attend your church describe it? Given your church's cultural profile, can you identify any unwritten rules of your community? Are there any unspoken assumptions that might not be immediately apparent to a newcomer?

As much as stained glass may dim it, there is a whole world outside the walls of our churches. Christians often use the phrase, "in the world, but not of it" to describe our hope of living on this earth while being detached from its temptations. While it is healthy to separate ourselves from the sinful aspects of our world, there is no way we can untangle our "Christian" lives from our "regular" lives. Nor should we. God made us both creatures and new creations.

Worship and Culture

In the same way that our faith and humanity are fused together in one body, each congregational body is intertwined with its culture. Our culture, language, and place in history all impact how we worship. It is important to understand this, because many of our worship conflicts are actually caused by cultural assumptions so deeply ingrained in us that we hardly know they're there.

A particularly useful tool for allowing us to examine the way culture and worship interact is the *Nairobi Statement on Worship and Culture*.[1] This document was born of conversations within the global Lutheran church, which was trying to discern the good and bad of culture in an increasingly diverse international coalition of churches. According to the Nairobi Statement, there are four ways worship and culture interact: transculturally, contextually, counterculturally, and crossculturally.

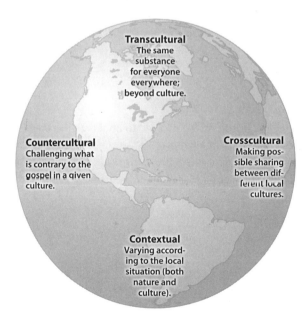

Transcultural
The same substance for everyone everywhere; beyond culture.

Countercultural
Challenging what is contrary to the gospel in a given culture.

Crosscultural
Making possible sharing between different local cultures.

Contextual
Varying according to the local situation (both nature and culture).

Transcultural worship elements transcend their cultural context. Christians in every time and place hold things in common such as the Word of God, communion, and prayer. We could express this using language from Ephesians 4:5, "One Lord, one faith, one baptism." Transcultural worship elements are the unchanging worship practices to which we all hold fast.

Though every Christian church shares some universal components, local churches will practice these worship elements differently according to their cultural context. The Nairobi Statement labels this interaction between worship and culture *contextual* and defends the contextualization of worship based on the person of Jesus Christ. That is, the transcendent Son of God became human and lived in a particular cultural context—born Jewish and working class, living under Roman rule. If God became imbedded in a local context, it gives us permission—even an obligation—to adapt to our own cultural context in worship.

If God is both transcendent and immanent, how might we reflect that with worship that is both transcultural and contextual? A simple example would be reading the Bible (a transcultural worship element that all Christians share) in a local language (a contextual adaptation). That is, perhaps, obvious. Things get more difficult when we come to a transcultural worship element like communion. Does Jesus's example in the upper room obligate every church to use bread and wine, or can we adapt these food items to local custom? For example, is grape juice an acceptable substitute for wine? What about cultures in which rice is a food staple rather than wheat—is Jesus, the Bread of Life, adequately represented in a rice cake? In each of these cases we have to discern what the transcultural requirements are and what contextual adaptations can or should be made.

One of the difficulties of this discernment process is that every cultural context—just like every person—has both blessed and sinful traits. Worship is *countercultural* in that it resists those things in a culture that go against the grain of the gospel. For example, American culture is blessed with an understanding of individual rights and freedoms but is plagued by individualism and consumerism. How might these cultural norms seep into worship? Perhaps the cultural emphasis on the individual might lead to a healthy understanding that each person must take responsibility for their faith but weaken our ability to worship in unity as the body of Christ. In

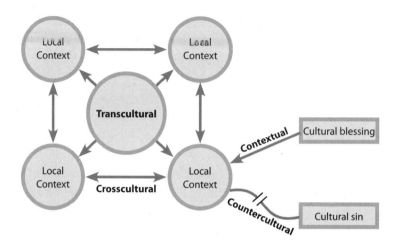

contrast, more hierarchal/respect-driven cultures may more easily align with the command to "Honor your father and your mother [and by extension, elders]" (Exod. 20:12) but have difficulty following Jesus's example to "let the little children come" (Matt. 19:14). Worship is the place where we identify our culture's besetting sins and practice replacing them with gospel habits.

Finally, our worship should be *crosscultural*. As local churches develop worship practices that resonate with the gospel, we share them with churches from other cultures and receive others' local practices into our church. This creates a network that displays the diversity of God's people and the unity of the body of Christ (1 Cor. 12:12–26). Our own cultural lens will always be somewhat out of focus, so we rely on Christians of other cultures to help us see a more complete picture of God. Some may be suspicious this is a "politically correct" multicultural agenda. No, it is simply a way of living out our prayers that God's kingdom come on earth as it is in heaven (Matt. 6:9–13), knowing that worship in heaven will include a great multitude "from every nation, from all tribes and peoples and languages" (Rev. 7:9).

The Local Church and the World

It is often said that theologian Karl Barth encouraged preachers to "Take your Bible in one hand and the newspaper in the other." This is a good principle for churches as well. Too many churches shut their eyes to the world around them, focusing solely on the words of Scripture. While this may seem like a spiritual approach to life, in essence it connotes that Christ can only be Lord of individual hearts, not Lord of heaven and earth.

How can worship "take the newspaper in one hand"? We can begin by praying for the needs of the world (1 Tim. 2:1–3). As I write this, refugees are pouring out of Syria and flooding across Europe, North Korea is ramping up its nuclear weapon capabilities, and Chile is recovering from a tsunami. Creation is groaning for redemption (Rom. 8:22) and we should intercede for it.

We need to be aware of the world around us, because it impacts the life of the church. The world is changing rapidly. We are moving into a post-Christian era that will be fundamentally different than the centuries preceding it. The Western church will soon face situations familiar to much of the church elsewhere in the world, in which God and country do not smoothly align. With this shift in culture comes a shift in the demographics of the church. The relationship between sending and receiving churches is changing, and the West is already moving from the mother/daughter relationship it has had with the global church toward a model of partnership.

People in the Pews Are People of the World

When I first began working at my current church, I was advised to be careful about who I talked about, and with whom. In our Dutch-American community, almost everyone is related in some way.[2] Indeed, I could have gotten myself into a lot of trouble: A is the sister of B, and B's father-in-law is C, who chairs the committee with his childhood friend, D.

The same principle applies to a church's relationship to the world. We can no longer assume that those inside the church are "us" (racially, culturally, and/or politically similar) and those outside are "them" (everyone else). Even the smallest towns have significant migrant populations. Children marry outside their family culture. Parents adopt children from other countries or races. Everyone in the pews has a story that extends beyond the church; we can't assume that it is the same story as ours. Their story might include a spouse who is in prison, a child who is gay, or a friend who is an undocumented immigrant. This doesn't mean we can't have convictions about these issues, but we need to realize that each of these issues touches real people in our pews.

Similarly, churches send a strong message about who is welcome at a church by the people they include in worship leadership. When people visit a church and don't see anyone like themselves up front, they'll likely think this church is for others but not for them. This is tricky terrain for churches to navigate. On the one hand, we want to make sure everyone feels welcome. On the other hand, we don't want to dutifully fulfill ethnic or socioeconomic quotas. We need to find a balance that acknowledges the church's majority group while also making room for outsiders to feel welcomed. To achieve this it is often necessary to tip the balance in favor of the outsider. That is, insiders already feel welcome by nature of being insiders; outsiders, on the other hand, need a lot more attention to feel truly welcomed. It is important to remember that outsiders are not only ethnic minorities; outsiders could also be young people, the tattooed and pierced, or political conservatives.

We can no longer assume the people coming through the doors of our church have a shared racial, cultural, or life story. All of the hospitality we can muster is fueled by the belief that we are called to be one in Christ. Our shared story is the gospel.

For Discussion

1. Name the biggest people problem you're dealing with in your church right now. It could be a personality clash, a group conflict, or an unresolved tension. Write it down and keep it in mind as you read the following pages; perhaps you will gain insight into the root of the problem.

2. Play the Bread of Life game. Using the Nairobi Statement as your guide, evaluate the appropriateness of using the following communion elements: bread and wine, crackers and grape juice, sake and rice cakes, pizza and cola, coconut meat and milk, and nachos and diet soda. (All of these are reported to have been used in worship services, some in a youth setting and others in specific cultural contexts.)

3. Does your church refer to at least one international current event in worship each week, whether in prayer or elsewhere? If not, how do you think doing so would be received? If so, does it feel authentic or obligatory? Can you think of ways to make prayer for the world more connected to the life of your congregation?

4. Before you began this chapter, you were asked to create a cultural profile of your congregation. Now identify the outsiders to that profile. It may be the rebellious daughter who went to college and came back punk, a person or group of a different race, or a demographic in the neighborhood that is not represented within the church. How could you welcome them more fully?

19

The Congregation

Before you begin: What is your relationship with your congregation?

How would you describe your relationship with your congregation? Affirming? Cautious? Adversarial? What has contributed most significantly to the state of the relationship?

Worship directors put much of our energy into upfront worship leading. Most of our work during the week ramps up toward that hour on Sunday. This is the time when we are most visible to the church, and it is likely the most intense, stressful part of any worship director's week. The worship service is the most public part of our job, but is it the most important?

In *The Training of the Twelve*, Scottish minister A. B. Bruce makes the point that, though Jesus interacted extensively with the crowd, the bulk of his investment went into preparing the disciples. Jesus knew that crowds were difficult to win over and could turn into a mob in a moment. Consider the sequence of events in John 6. Jesus feeds the five thousand. (Who doesn't like a good meal?) But when he talks about himself being the Bread of Life, many disciples turned back, leaving only the twelve. By the end of the gospel story, the crowd he had fed on the mountain joined the chant of "Crucify him!"

Our church is our "crowd." While we have a less dramatic relationship with our crowd than Jesus did with his, the principles are the same. We can only have so much impact on a large group of people. The relationship is mostly public and impersonal—we can't sit down and chat with each person unless we are in a very small congregation. People will project their hopes and fears onto us without knowing who we really are. As is the case with politicians, actors, and pastors, people will know our *persona* rather than our person. We shouldn't take any of this to heart. Instead we should focus on the things we can do to have the best relationship possible with our congregation. Let's look at some effective ways of navigating congregational waters.

The First Season

There are two broad seasons in a worship director's ministry with a church: the first few years, while the church and worship director get to know each other, and the sustained season of ministry once the relationship has settled. Because this first season lays much of the foundation for the future, it's important to get it right.

The first thing for a new worship director to remember is to try to be a boat rather than a dam. Churches are like wide, slow rivers. They may look placid, but underneath the surface are powerful forces already moving unquestionably in a particular direction. The worship minister who arrives intending to block or redirect that river is unlikely to prevail against the current. This may be hard to accept. Shouldn't our training and experience make a congregation want to follow us, their new leader? Yes, perhaps—in time—but first we will have to gain the church's trust.

Instead of trying to dam up what is already happening in the church, put your boat in their water and flow with their current. Learn the church's history. Listen to people of the church to find out what they value about their worship. Find out who the stakeholders and powerbrokers are. Discern what undercurrents are at play in the church's worship life. Churches don't always align with our own worship philosophy, but there is usually an underlying wisdom that has grown with time in their unique context. Become familiar with it. The best way to enter a church's current is what I call the Zaki Rule, named for Anne Zaki, who passed on the advice to me when I began ministry at my current church. It is a simple, two-point plan:

1. Don't make any major changes for a year.
2. Write down everything you'd like to change.

The first part of the rule puts you in a listening posture that will allow you to learn your new church's worship context. It also helps build trust among the congregation. A new worship director is enough of a change already; there's no need to shake things up further with clever initiatives and new directions. The second part of the Zaki Rule allows you to compile a list of problem areas that will eventually need to be addressed. At the end of the year, patterns will have emerged that will present priority areas for future work.

The Sustained Season

Once the worship director is settled into the church for the long term, there are a number of things that help maintain a healthy relationship. The most important is the worship director's character. Too often, those in the worship arts appeal to the "artistic personality" as an excuse for a lack of sanctification. Let's be clear: being an artist doesn't excuse being short-tempered, self-centered, or sullen. There is not one set of standards for Christians and another for Christian artists, with the latter getting a free pass on a wide range of sins and character flaws. Let's drop the diva mentality and dig into the difficult, rewarding work of serving our congregations!

Communication and education are other keys to a thriving relationship between worship director and congregation. Most people in your congregation simply don't think much about worship; they just know what they like. And what they like has been shaped primarily by the culture (pop radio, prominent churches, and so forth) or by what they've done for years in their own congregation. Most people won't change their values unless presented with a compelling reason to do so.

The worship director needs to communicate with the congregation, helping them arrive at a deeper understanding of worship. All the obvious channels of communication should be used to their full potential: church newsletter, announcements, printed worship materials, and Facebook posts. Don't overlook face-to-face communication. Share your vision at elders' meetings, Sunday school classes, and choir rehearsals. Remember that each person in these groups has a spouse or friends; these conversations will soon ripple through the whole church. What is the main message? Worship is not primarily about preference, entertainment, or being "right"; it is a life-giving opportunity for the congregation to come together to "Taste and see that the LORD is good" (Ps. 34:8).

Yet no matter how winsomely a worship director communicates, it is still hard to take away a congregation's fear of the unknown. One way to reduce anxiety is to make use of the trial period. For example, if church leaders simply announce that the decision has been made to hold weekly communion, the church will fear the many unknowns. What if it doesn't go well? Is the church heading in a strange new direction? Who made the decision, and why wasn't the church included in it? On the other hand, if the church leaders announce that weekly communion will be held during the season of Lent, this gives a clear ending point that eases the anxiety of those who are wary of the decision. The trial period lets everyone experience the new thing together. One of the most compelling ways to change someone's values is for them to experience something that transcends their previous paradigm. Once they have a chance to experience this formerly frightening thing, they may even exclaim, like the Dr. Seuss character, "Say! I like green eggs and ham!"

Still none of this hard work guarantees a congregation will buy in to the worship director's vision. In fact, it would be folly to expect 100 percent buy in from any congregation. Generally speaking, 5 to 10 percent of a congregation will love everything the worship director does and 5 to 10 percent will vehemently resist it. Both of these minorities will be vocal in their support or resistance. The remaining 80 to 90 percent will be happy to follow any leader they trust. Once a worship director begins to lose that middle 80 percent, it becomes harder and harder to lead effectively at the church. This can be due to a variety of reasons. It may simply be a poor fit between worship director and congregation—a clash of values that will never be resolved. It may be that the church is fundamentally unhealthy—is it a surprise that one hour of worship each week won't heal decades of infighting? All we can do is be as "wise as serpents and innocent as doves" (Matt. 10:16) in the congregation in which God has placed us.

For Discussion

1. How much time do you spend on various aspects of your ministry? Is most of your time spent leading worship or preparing for worship? What part of your time goes into conversations/ministry, administration, Scripture study, practicing your art, and prayer?

2. "Be a boat rather than a dam." Discuss the tension between going with the congregation's flow and leading them in a particular direction. Your church hired you for your expertise, so shouldn't you use that expertise?

3. What do you think a poll of the congregation would reveal—what percentage strongly supports you, what percentage strongly resists your leadership, and what percentage is the happy medium? Do any of these numbers worry you?

4. Are you the type of person who likes to be popular? Does it bother you when you hear through the grapevine that someone has criticized your work? If you are sensitive to critique, what can you do to protect your heart?

20

Worship Leaders

Before you begin: How would you handle Julie's solo?

Julie, the pastor's daughter, has asked to sing a solo. Julie is known for her devotion to Christ and her passionate singing. She is also known for being painfully out of tune. What do you do?

Worship directors enjoy personal, regular interaction with their church's fellow worship leaders. This team of musicians, artists, coplanners, and tech volunteers are a worship director's "twelve," in the terminology of A. B. Bruce. These people are the heart of the worship ministry and a worship director's confidants, colaborers, and emotional support. We need a plan for fostering these relationships, growing a strong community of leaders in our church.

Who Should Lead Worship?

Many appeal to Luther's principle of the "priesthood of all believers" to say that anyone who wants to take part in leading worship should be allowed to do so. This egalitarian approach may appear kind, but it doesn't hold up under scrutiny. When Peter calls us "to be a holy priesthood" (1 Pet. 2:5), he does not indicate that we will all have the same roles in that priesthood. In fact, if you look at the Levitical order to which Peter refers (1 Chron. 23–26), we see the priesthood divided into a variety of roles: temple priests, singers, instrumentalists, gatekeepers, and treasurers. The same principle is at work in the New Testament church, where we are called to be "one body" with "gifts that differ according to the grace given to us" (Rom. 12:5–6). We must discern the unique gifts each member brings to that body (see 1 Cor. 12).

However, when it comes to worship, many members feel called to be the mouth. That is, more members feel called to sing a solo than lead junior high Sunday school. This is due to a number of factors. People love music; it gives them great joy to sing and they want everyone to share in that joy. Music is more subjective than many other areas of service; we expect a certain level of skill from the person overseeing the church's finances, but we're not as sure how to evaluate musical skills. We also may believe that if God looks on the heart, we too should overlook musical deficiencies. (Do we take the same heart-oriented approach with those who drive the church bus? . . .) Finally, it must be said that leading music is more glamorous than serving in the nursery; it is inevitable that pride enters the equation.

In the end, we worship directors need to discern who is right for the worship ministry. (Just as the church's leadership discerned that we were right to lead it.) Every church will have a different pool of people to draw from, but generally we should look for volunteers with an active faith, strong musical talent, a desire to grow, and an ability to work on a team. People with an active faith will be able to throw themselves wholeheartedly into the spiritual side of worship leadership rather than just filling a musical role. But that music role is important too. Worship leaders should have talent, and should also have honed their musical skills enough that they can lead the congregation confidently and without distraction. In both faith and music, they should display a desire to grow. This humble curiosity is essential, as they will be asked to stretch to new levels of playing and leading. Finally, they need to be team players. Divas and rock stars make for good reality television, but churches need musicians who want to serve.

All of these traits apply to nonmusicians as well. Music teams are the most regular, public teams of a worship ministry, but we want all of our worship volunteers, from those who run the sound board to those who lead prayer, to be faithful, skilled, growing team players.

Who Shouldn't Lead Worship?

The question of who should be excluded from leadership roles is much more sensitive than setting guidelines for who should be included. No one likes to tell people no, but the reality is that choosing some people to take part in a worship ministry necessitates rejecting others. There are a hundred factors that go into these decisions. Each worship director must discern what is best for their church community, but there are three specific types of people who are unlikely to contribute to the worship leadership.

First, there will always be a number of people in a church who have more desire than skill. They have good hearts, strong faith, and teachable spirits, but they simply don't have the artistic skills needed to lead. It may sound ruthless to exclude them from leading worship, and it will feel even worse to tell them this in person. The only consolation a worship director has is that making a hard decision about a person's role in worship frees that person to pursue other areas of ministry that will be more beneficial for the church body, and ultimately the individual as well. Of course, a church is not a cutthroat studio gig, with the best player always getting the job. Sometimes a person's spiritual contribution is strong enough that it outweighs their musical deficiencies. But don't rob the church of an elder or teacher simply because turning someone away from worship leadership makes you feel bad.

Second, the prima donna is a personality type that rarely contributes positively to worship leadership. The Italian term, meaning "first lady," was originally used to refer to the lead role of an opera but has now come to describe a person who thinks of themselves as better than those around them. Paul cautions "not to think of yourself more highly than you ought to think, but to think with sober judgment, each according to the measure of faith that God has assigned" (Rom. 12:3). He was writing about how our individual gifts fit together to build up the body of Christ, but he may

as well have been talking about church musicians! There is a certain type
of person who is more than happy to sing a solo but is not interested in
coming to weekly rehearsals. They become disgruntled if anyone else gets
an opportunity that they don't—*After all*, they think, *I am the better musician.* The best way to deal with this personality is offer them the same opportunities and responsibilities as everyone else—regular rehearsals, group
singing, and supportive roles. If they prove they have a servant spirit in the
small things, it shows they may be ready for higher-profile contributions.

Third is the thorn. There is much debate about the "thorn in the flesh"
that Paul mentions in 2 Corinthians 12:7. Was it a chronic illness? Sexual
temptation? Failing eyesight? We don't know. What we do know is that
every worship director seems to have one in the form of a person who just
can't accept anyone else's leadership. This person questions the worship
director's every decision, spreads ill will in conversations at coffee hour, and
resists the leader's every move, whether openly or with passive-aggressive
comments. Who knows what motivates these thorns? It is likely that the
worship director represents a loss of power for this person. Perhaps the
thorn was previously the unofficial leader; the installation of a paid or
official worship director makes them feel demoted. Perhaps they don't
think much of the worship director's qualifications. Perhaps they are just
argumentative jerks who refuse to submit to authority!

Unfortunately, there is not much we can do to change another person's behavior. We can, however, manage our own behavior. We shouldn't
stoop to the level of the person who is causing problems. If we have been
given authority to lead, we need to exercise that authority confidently and
lovingly. We shouldn't brood about the person later or gossip with others about their behavior, but instead go directly to the person to resolve
the conflict (Matt. 18:15–17). Often, when a person wants to undermine
another person's leadership it is not in the form of a direct attack but in
passive-aggressive barbs and sarcastic side comments. If this becomes a
trend, deal with it forthrightly: "John, your comments seem to indicate
that you're unhappy about the way I'm leading rehearsal. Is there a problem you'd like to discuss with me later?" Sometimes addressing an issue
directly is enough to make a person realize they are creating tension within
the larger team.

No matter how the person responds, we need to remain patient and loving. Like Paul dealing with his thorn in the flesh, we should turn to prayer.

> Three times I appealed to the Lord about this, that it would leave me, but he said to me, "My grace is sufficient for you, for power is made perfect in weakness." So, I will boast all the more gladly of my weaknesses, so that the power of Christ may dwell in me. Therefore I am content with weaknesses, insults, hardships, persecutions, and calamities for the sake of Christ; for whenever I am weak, then I am strong. (2 Cor. 12:8–10)

In all of these cases, the goal is not to exclude people from ministry but to help discern the best place for them. We want our worship ministry to be a place where people can serve and grow, free from the distractions of ego and dissension.

Fostering Growth

Once we have assembled a good group of people skilled in various areas of worship, how do we foster an environment in which the ministry and its people can grow? First, we must cherish them. They are the heart of the worship ministry. We should foster them like we would our own children, identifying their gifts and encouraging them to use them to their fullest. Many people just need a little support and direction to bring their talents to a higher level. We should challenge our musicians and artists to work hard, but not set the bar so high that they become frustrated (Eph. 6:4).

One of the ways we encourage our church's worship leaders to use their gifts more is by highlighting our own gifts less. Yes, many of us have more training and experience than our volunteers and could probably get better, quicker results in many areas of leadership. However, a ministry should focus more on the process of growing people's gifts than on manufacturing an efficient product. Worship directors need to move from a leader-centered, "celebrity" approach to a more distributed leadership approach in which everyone uses their gifts. We've all seen churches in which one person plays the piano, sings all the solos, plays the transitions between songs, and even reads Scripture and prays. Why not share the wealth? Vocal solos could be assigned to each person on the music team. Different sets of instrumentalists could be responsible for different introductions and transitions. Scripture readers could be enlisted from outside the music team. This distributed approach takes the spotlight off the worship director and allows each volunteer to make a substantial contribution to the service. Of course, in the real world of ministry, efficiency is sometimes necessary. Five minutes before the service starts, with two more songs still to rehearse, it is entirely reasonable for the worship director to play the transition between the songs.

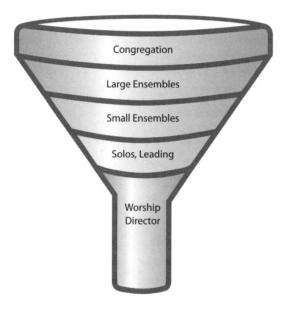

A good way of identifying and honing gifts throughout the whole congregation is to create ongoing opportunities for all levels of musicians. (Musicians are the regular focus of initiatives like this, but the principle applies to all the worship arts.) Like the opening of a funnel, the congregation as a whole is invited to take part in large, unauditioned ensembles. In my own church, this includes the adult choir (open to teens and older), the Joyful Noise Orchestra (band and orchestra instruments of all abilities), and the "Guitarchestra" (guitars, mandolins, and accordions). These large ensembles are an entry point for the music ministry and open to all. They also serve the function of letting the worship director identify those who have more advanced skills.

Moving down the funnel we have smaller ensembles with more focused, skilled leadership: praise bands, chamber choirs, string quartets, and so forth. These small ensembles are often populated with people from the large ensembles; "graduating" musicians to the next level may be less stressful than holding auditions. The next level of the funnel is those who are ready to serve in highly focused areas of worship: singing solos, leading rehearsals, and planning services. This is an opportunity for the worship director to work individually with the most promising worship volunteers.

In any growing, thriving ministry that is consistently encouraging church members to use their gifts at higher levels, there are bound to be some who become worship directors in their own right. This is wonderful news for God's kingdom! We shouldn't feel threatened by these growing leaders but foster their continued growth. Worship directors should make it our goal to work ourselves out of a job. At the very least we should aim to work ourselves into an occasional vacation!

The above assumes a fairly large congregation with a paid staff and a large volunteer pool. Many of us minister in much humbler circumstances. The same principles apply but are practiced in a more intimate setting. Be faithful and creative wherever God has placed you.

Remember that the community a worship director tends to is not a *program* but a *ministry*. The arts are not separate from ministry, and they are not a means by which we do ministry—they are ministry. Don't underestimate the power of the arts to reach people's souls. In the same way that a preacher's words are a ministry to the people of the church, those of us in the worship arts sing, dance, and paint God's love into people's hearts.

One of the most poignant examples of this I've ever experienced was when one of our church members was dying of cancer. Margaret was a saint of a woman who had been a part of the church's worship for years, though not recently. As we prayed for her one night in choir rehearsal, someone mentioned how blessed Margaret had been by recordings of the church services. Even in her weakened state, each Sunday morning she would sit in her recliner with a CD of the previous week's service and a bulletin in her hand, following along. We decided that we would visit her.

One Sunday afternoon we squeezed into her living room and sang songs from that morning's service as well as any hymns she requested. The only one in the room who wasn't crying was Margaret herself! That rewarding visit was ministry to Margaret, to her family, and to the choir itself. Our singing drew us closer together and closer to God.

For Discussion

1. Some might read these guidelines for including or excluding candidates from worship ministry as too strict. Others might never even consider anyone at a less than professional level. Where do you draw the line? Are you more likely to exclude someone for poor skills or for lackluster faith?

2. Describe a time when you had to address a thorny issue about team membership: someone who caused dissension on the team, someone to whom you had to say no, or a team member who was caught in a moral failure.

3. Does your church have a policy about non-Christians being involved in the worship arts? What is it? If you don't have a set policy, write one now. This will come up sooner or later.

4. What ensembles do you have in your church? What opportunities for other worship artists? Who might be falling through the cracks?

21

Pastors

Before you begin: Consider two sides.

Worship directors: the pastor keeps cutting the final song in worship because the services are running long. How should you address this? Make sure you're able to articulate why this matters to you.

Pastors: you feel like the worship director is not being a team player. Any suggestion you make is taken as a criticism. How should you address this? Consider things you may be doing that contribute to the worship director's feelings of being criticized.

Working with volunteers is one type of relationship—the worship director is a "boss" who leads with love. The relationship between church staff—especially the pastor and worship director—is something else entirely. Both the pastor and worship director contribute to worship planning and leading, but they come from very different backgrounds. The pastor is usually trained at seminary with a strong focus on the Word and reasoned faith, whereas the worship director usually comes from an arts background with a stronger focus on emotions and intuition. Too often this leads pastor and worship director to be suspicious of one another, and think, *All the*

worship director cares about is music, or *The pastor doesn't care about
what I do as long as people don't complain*

How can we grow healthy relationships among the church staff? Pastors
and worship directors need to realize they are on the same team. Perhaps
Paul, with his one body/many members illustration, would have called the
preacher the mouth and the worship director the ears and eyes. In any case,
both are using different means to work toward the same goal. Pastors need
to trust the worship director is doing more than warming the people up for
the sermon. Worship leaders need to trust that pastors know the people in
the pews and can provide wisdom about what they need.

The best way to build trust between the pastor and worship director is
to spend time on the relationship—not just working on services together
but sharing life together. Deeper bonds will grow when time is set aside
for reading Scripture, sharing meals, and praying together. Prayer is especially important; it establishes that spiritual work must be done in the
Spirit; further, it is extremely hard to hold a grudge against someone you
pray with regularly.

One of the keys to the pastor/worship director relationship is recogniz-
ing the power difference between the two. A senior pastor generally has
more power within the church structure than the worship director. The
worship director is often a lightning rod for conflict within the church.
Pastors, use your seniority to protect your worship director and foster his
or her growth. Too often churches see their worship directors as playing a
purely functional role. They fulfill tasks—similar to the janitor or recep-
tionist—and are not part of the "real" ministry of the church. If pastors
want their worship leaders to be more than musicians, mentor them in
ministry! Include them in study of Scripture for future services, in visiting
the sick, or any other important aspect of ministry.

Both the pastor and worship director need to defend one another's honor.
Never let a congregation member speak ill of the other. Like parents in
front of children, present a united front and work out any disagreements
later, in private.

Naturally, much of the pastor's and worship director's time will be spent
working on worship services. Like it or not, there is a weekly "gig" that
requires a lot of attention. Most people don't understand just how much

energy and time Sunday morning requires—a poll of the congregation would probably uncover that the congregation sees the pastor and worship director as working one hour per week! Perhaps the comparison to a wedding would help people understand: "If your wedding were Sunday, would you be busy today?" Indeed there are a myriad of details to attend to when planning a service. Try to make the planning process as smooth and sustainable as possible.

The preaching pastor is generally the person to establish service Scriptures and themes for coming months. Pastors have little to lose and much to gain by plotting out service themes well in advance. The sooner a pastor reveals preaching plans, the sooner the church's worship artists can begin to brainstorm about materials that will complement those themes. There is always the possibility that a sermon will change direction as it gets closer to the date, but it is easier to change a plan than not have a plan at all. Pastors who don't unveil their sermon themes until mere days before the service are virtually guaranteeing that their sermons will always be accompanied by a generic worship service. This is truly a missed opportunity.

A wise pastor will insist on weekly meetings with those who plan worship. Too many worship-planning teams schedule meetings only when something goes wrong. Be proactive. Schedule regular meetings to pray, evaluate past services, do long-range planning, and work out details for impending services.

Worship directors will often say there are two extremes of pastors: those who micromanage ("Here are the three songs I want on Sunday") and those who are hands off until there's a problem ("I'm hearing that people want more upbeat songs"). More helpful is a pastor who gives parameters within which the worship director can work ("I'll be ending on a quiet, reflective note. Can you leave fifteen seconds of silence and then begin a reflective song about confession?"). This displays trust in the worship director's abilities, giving ample creative freedom while also providing a context within which they can make informed decisions.

Likewise, worship directors are known to hold their ideas too dearly. When anyone questions the wisdom of a song they've chosen, they act as if pulling out this thread would make worship unravel. One way to mitigate some of this all-or-nothing atmosphere is to establish a 3-to-1 protocol. That is, for every song or other worship element needed, the worship director brings three possibilities to the planning meeting. The first option might be an adventurous long shot—something to stretch the congregation. The second option would be something creative but not too far out of the sweet spot. The third option would be more run-of-the-mill—something that gets the job done but may not be the worship director's first choice. Having multiple options keeps the planning team from yes or no decisions—and keeps worship directors from facing rejection for suggestions they hold dear.

We can hope for rich, deep relationships between pastors and worship directors, but that may not always be the case. Human beings are complex. At the very least we should expect a cordial and productive work atmosphere. At best we can hope for something more spiritually enriching, but it would be unwise for a worship director to expect a pastor to play the role of both coworker and spiritual director. We need to take responsibility for the state of our own souls, as we'll discuss in the next section.

For Discussion

1. Worship directors, do you feel like your pastor understands the arts? Pastors, do you feel like your worship director understands theology?

2. How much time do the pastor and worship director spend together in your church?

3. What is your planning schedule in your church? (How long before a service does the preacher give Scriptures and themes to the worship director? When is the first draft of the service complete? At what point are changes no longer made?) Is this a good schedule for everyone involved? How could it be improved?

22

You

Before you begin: Who are you?

What kind of a person are you? Are you extroverted or introverted? At heart a musician, pastor, counselor, teacher, or coach? More interested—to borrow words from the ACT Inventory—in data, ideas, people, or things? There are no right or wrong answers. If you have the opportunity to take a Myers-Briggs evaluation or an Enneagram test, it can be very helpful. At the very least discuss your self-evaluation with a trusted friend to get their feedback.

Of all the worship director's relationships, the most important is our relationship with God. Worship is, after all, spiritual work. We who plan and lead worship need to attend to the health of our own souls so we can lead from a place of wholeness. No, this doesn't mean that worship directors must be sinless! But we do need to have integrity. Our lives need to display the redemption and sanctification we profess to our congregations.

Spiritual

Too often, church leaders feel pressure to be perfect. We know our lives are on display; any whiff of sin would bring dishonor to the gospel or at the very least be fodder for our detractors. In public we maintain the façade of the perfect Christian, but in private we feel ashamed of our shortcomings. Some of this is inevitable—indeed, we shouldn't confess the details of our sins to the whole church—but left unattended these small, secret sins can create a fissure that will only grow wider with time. We have all seen the effects of this: the "perfect" pastor or worship director is suddenly caught in a scandal that would make even a nonbeliever blush. Truly, we need to live with Jesus's words in mind:

> Nothing is covered up that will not be uncovered, and nothing secret that will not become known. Therefore whatever you have said in the dark will be heard in the light, and what you have whispered behind closed doors will be proclaimed from the housetops. (Luke 12:2–3)

Another spiritual liability of being in ministry is that we pass along the things of God to our people but don't let God's truths plant themselves deep into the soil of our own lives. We begin to view Scripture as a tool to be wielded with the expert precision we've developed over the years rather than life-giving words for our own hearts. We become comfortable with worship and start to approach it like a technician rather than a worshiper. We know that the right set of songs and musical arrangements can produce a convincing atmosphere and we soon forget what it's like to simply bask in God's presence. God can still use us—after all, God was able to prophesy through Balaam and his donkey (Numbers 22–24)—but we should desire the same transformation for ourselves that we proclaim to our congregations.

How can we attend the needs of our own souls amid the hectic pace of ministry? First, we can apply our work to our own heart before passing it on to our congregations. I often tell people that God placed me in ministry not because I'm such a good Christian but because God knew I needed to be in church all week long! Worship directors need to take advantage of the rich blessings our work affords. We get to study

---

Some Books That Get to the *Heart* of the Matter

Rory Noland, *The Heart of the Artist: A Character-Building Guide for You and Your Ministry Team* (Grand Rapids: Zondervan, 1999).

Richard J. Foster, *Celebration of Discipline: The Path to Spiritual Growth* (New York: HarperCollins, 1978).

Dallas Willard, *The Divine Conspiracy: Rediscovering Our Hidden Life In God* (New York: Harper Collins, 1998).

Scripture, pray, and discuss the faith as part of our daily work. With a little extra effort we can fully reap the benefits of this immersion in the things of God by applying Scripture study to our own hearts and praying through the worship services we plan before asking our congregations to do so. Let us not become immune to the Spirit through familiarity.

Second, we need to develop spiritual practices that will sustain us in ministry. The spiritual disciplines are to the faith what physical exercise is to the body: they make us stronger and healthier.[1] Especially important for those in ministry is the discipline of Sabbath. Walter Brueggemann calls Sabbath an "act of resistance."[2] Indeed, when even the church holds up the "Protestant work ethic" as a virtue of faithful Christians, it is easy for ministers to feel pressured to work all the time. This only leads to burnout. The reason God gave the Sabbath is to remind us that we plant and water, but it is "only God who gives the growth" (1 Cor. 3:7). We should work hard, but in the end we have to trust the Spirit is working in ways we don't understand and can't manufacture. Other spiritual practices especially helpful for worship directors are praying Scripture (traditionally called *lectio divina*), singing the psalms, and finding a place to worship without having to lead.[3]

Third, everyone in ministry should meet regularly with an accountability group or spiritual mentor. This is our inner circle, with whom we trust the most intimate parts of our lives. These spiritual confidants are there for us through thick and thin, supporting and praying for us in areas of our lives we don't share with anyone else. Because they know us so well, they can provide a reality check for us, encouraging us when we are discouraged, giving advice when we're having a conflict with a church member, or rebuking us when we're headed down the wrong path. This is also the group to whom we can confess sins and temptations. How many church leaders would still be in ministry today if they'd had an accountability group to help them root out their secret sins before they grew in their hearts and blossomed into public disgrace?

Personal

For our spiritual lives to flourish, our personal lives need to be healthy too. A surprising number of church leaders seem to have distorted pictures of who they are as human beings. They act as if they can do everything equally well, when it's clear to everyone around them that this isn't the case. We are all some combination of amazing gifts and glaring weaknesses. The sooner we understand and accept our unique temperament, the better we'll be able to lead.

Some people find it helpful to take a personality assessment such as Myers-Briggs, Enneagram, or DiSC. All of these tools lead to similar places: uncovering who we are at our core and how we relate to other people. For example, introverts need time away from people—counterintuitive, perhaps, for someone who is in ministry. Most of these assessment tools will also give insight to the types of conflicts we might have with those of other personality types. It can be a major revelation to discover a colleague is not wrong but simply sees the world a different way than we do.

> "Know thyself."
> —SOCRATES
>
> "To thine own self be true."
> —SHAKESPEARE
>
> "You betta check yo self before you wreck yo self."
> —ICE CUBE

We need to understand our "besetting sins"—those personal dispositions that dog us our whole lives. Which sins do we fall into most readily? Power? Sex? Bitterness? Each of us is tempted differently and needs to put up different barriers to accommodate our unique set of weaknesses. If we are driven workaholics, we need to establish a schedule that includes Sabbath and time for family. If we are prone to anger, we may need to have a friend who's periodically willing to read an email before we send it out.

Similarly, we need to know our personal weaknesses. Are we disorganized? Inarticulate? Have no stage presence? Poor with people? None of these eliminates the possibility of a long and fruitful life of ministry. However, we need to be discerning and honest about our weaknesses. We need to work as hard as we can to improve those areas. We need to set up structures and support to accommodate our weaknesses so they don't become liabilities. For example, a person with poor organizational skills might rely heavily on software calendars and to-do lists, or even hire an assistant. A person who has poor stage presence but is great with people behind the scenes can identify volunteers to effectively play that up-front role. Every Moses needs an Aaron (Exod. 4:10–17).

Professional

Worship directing is a strange profession in that most people enter it through another area of training. Historically most come from the field of music, but in recent years this has broadened to include backgrounds in theater, writing, dance, visual arts, and technology. In almost every case, the worship director will have a "hands-on" skill—a performance area with which they serve the church. For musicians, the performance area is usually piano, organ, guitar, or conducting.

Each worship director enters ministry with training in a particular field, but each of us also has a particular disposition as a person. This is similar to pastors—some approach the pastorate like CEOs, others like professors. Worship directors typically fall into five categories. The *performer* is a person who lives for the stage. They shine when they're in front of people, in the moment, and often have a larger-than-life persona that projects well from the stage. The *creator* is most excited by composing, writing, and brainstorming. The *therapist* is a people person who loves spending time on relationships and building community. The *teacher* excels at research, teaching, and mentoring. The *director* is organized and detail-oriented, able to strategize and mobilize teams to implement a plan. Of course, none of these dispositions are exclusive.

Understanding our disposition is the key to who we are and how effective we are in ministry. Each disposition has strengths and liabilities. For example, the therapist is likely to value consensus, building a ministry with strong buy in from all involved, but this focus may come at the expense of rigorous rehearsal or thoughtful planning. A director may have a ministry that runs like clockwork but lacks creative spark. Of course, we all have to be capable in each area to some degree. By understanding our strengths, we will be able to more adequately address our areas of weakness.

Knowing our fundamental disposition is also the key to knowing what gives us joy. We feel most fulfilled when we work within our disposition.

For example, I am a creator by disposition but a director by necessity. I find the most joy when I am composing music or planning a service, but much of my day is spent organizing volunteers or attending to the thousands of details that go into a worship service. When most of my time is spent where I find the least joy, ministry quickly becomes a chore. Is it selfish to orient our work toward what makes us happiest? No. Obviously, every job includes tasks we find less fulfilling than others, but we simply won't last long in a job that is all outside our area of fulfillment.

Performance Areas	Personal Dispositions
Piano	Performer
Organ	Creator
Guitar	Therapist
Conductor	Teacher
Nonmusical Worship Arts: theology, theater, writing, dance, visual arts, tech	Director

Our specific combination of training and disposition defines our ministry. Each of us has a unique way of relating to the world and approaching ministry because of who we are and what we've studied. For example, I am a combination of creator by nature and a composer by training. Because I lack a true performance area, I've had to compensate by writing music for the musicians I have, improving my secondary performance areas (conducting and guitar), and fostering teams of musicians, especially keyboardists. Each of us has our own story. A director with a theater background will be strong in stage management and service flow but will need to trust the musicians of the church to lead congregational singing. A performer/pianist will be able to lead worship with finesse but will need to learn how to incorporate other musicians and teach the congregation.

Pay

Worship directing may be a full-time paid position or part-time volunteer work. Whatever our context, we want to have long, fruitful ministries where God has placed us. Sadly, this is rare. The infrequency of "long and fruitful" worship ministry became clear to me recently when a friend called to ask my advice on proposing a sabbatical to his church. He told me he was calling me because I was one of two people he knew who had been at the same church for more than seven years! Why do worship directors often have such short tenures at churches?

For one thing, worship is often a source of tension at churches, with people taking sides and the worship director getting caught in the middle. It is easy for worship directors to become casualties of these worship wars, no matter how good they are. More consistently, though, money is the factor that prohibits worship directors from staying in ministry longer. Many people assume that worship ministry should be an avocation—that we should all be "tentmakers" like Paul (Acts 18:1–4). Indeed, in many contexts this will be necessary. Unfortunately, many churches with healthy finances still leave worship directors out of their budgets. Jesus said, "Where your treasure is, there your heart will be also" (Matt. 6:21). What does it say about a church's values when the worship budget is so low in its financial priorities?

Low pay for worship directing is not only a problem of "muzzling the ox" (see 1 Tim. 5:18) at a local level. It ripples throughout the church. It forces talented leaders to leave for full-time pay elsewhere, whether in another church or a different profession. (People do need to make ends meet, after all.) It gives worship directing the reputation of being an avocation—a hobby—which discourages talented people from entering the field. We can't simultaneously expect mature leadership from our worship directors while paying them the wages of a junior barista at Starbucks!

Once again, this depends on context. In churches with volunteer pastors it is reasonable for the worship director to volunteer as well. In larger churches a good rule of thumb is that ministry staff such as worship directors are paid 60 to 80 percent of what the senior pastor earns. Neither worship director nor pastor should be given an unreasonably large job description compared to their salary. This is a matter of justice. Regardless of context, churches and their leaders need to cherish those who devote their time to worship. Thank them often. Take them out for a meal. Keep their pianos tuned.

My prayer is that as an awareness of the importance of worship continues to grow, a new generation of talented worship directors will sprout up, finding churches that support them with stable incomes that allow them to concentrate on ministry.

For Discussion

1. Do you find it hard to be a public worship figure but also foster your private spiritual life? What areas of your faith and vocation remain separated? How can you change that?

2. Do you practice the spiritual disciplines, especially the Sabbath? Do you have an accountability group or spiritual director?

3. Assess your professional weaknesses. Be honest. What structures or people could you put in place to help you in these areas?

4. What is your performance area? What is your disposition? How do these combine in your ministry? What are your strengths and liabilities?

5. Few people like to talk about money, especially in ministry, but our churches will benefit from honest discussion. How long has your worship director been at your church? Compare your worship director's salary to the average income of the congregation, a comparable professional (a schoolteacher, for example) in your community, and the pastor's salary. Is it a reasonable wage for your context?

23

Mentoring

Before you begin: Spend another moment with Mr. Rogers.

Mr. Rogers asked the crowd at the 1997 Emmy awards to take "ten seconds to think of the people who have helped you become who you are, those who cared about you and wanted what was best for you in life," and now it's our turn. We don't have the time restrictions Mr. Rogers had in his acceptance speech, so take as long as you need to write down the names of people who have had an impact on you as a worship director. Share at least one name with others, describing how that person changed your life. Finish with prayers of thanksgiving for these people.

In the previous sections we focused on the relationships of worship, slowly narrowing our focus to the individual worship director. But we all know our ministries are the result of the many people who have encouraged us, disciplined us, and modeled faith and ministry for us. We can't pay these people back for their gifts to us, but we can share their gifts with others. As Jesus said when he sent out the disciples: "Freely you have received; freely give" (Matt. 10:8 NIV). May our ministries be marked by giving.

What Is Mentoring?

In *The Training of the Twelve*, A. B. Bruce points out that Jesus's ministry had three spheres: the crowd, the twelve, and the three. The crowd was Jesus's public life: preaching on the mount, feeding the five thousand, teaching in the temple. The twelve, of course, were his disciples with whom he shared his daily life. The three were his inner circle: Peter, James, and John, in whom he invested intentionally.

Jesus	Worship Directors
Crowd	Church
Twelve	Worship Leaders
Three	Mentees

We can draw important lessons from Jesus's approach to ministry. Jesus was clearly an inspired teacher, but he didn't assume his public teaching would fully form his followers. Instead Jesus placed great weight on modeling the faith for his disciples. Anyone who has been parented knows how potent this form of teaching and learning can be. Experiencing someone's belief system in the context of real life is as powerful and authentic as learning gets. Jesus's method of handing down the faith was focused and intentional. He didn't call two hundred disciples and hope that some of them would work out. Instead, he narrowed his focus to the twelve and three; manageable sizes for intimate teaching opportunities. Jesus didn't start a movement or write a book, he planted seeds. Jesus entrusted the entire future of the Christian church to the small band of disciples with whom he ministered. This is a bold move.

What are the parallels for worship directors? We could see the crowd as our church, the twelve as our fellow worship leaders, and the three as a few people whom we mentor. Like Jesus, we interact with our crowd but we live with our twelve and we invest in our three. In the end we, like Jesus, give away our ministry, trusting the Spirit to enable those who come after us to carry it on.

What Jesus called *discipling*, we typically call *mentoring*. What does an intentional mentoring relationship look like? There are no rules, but a few principles will guide us. At its most fundamental level, mentoring is simply opening our lives to another person. Like Jesus explaining parables to the disciples once the crowd had dispersed, the mentor grants his or her mentee a "backstage pass" that allows for questions and a personal glimpse into the mentor's life. In a context such as worship directing, there may be some apprentice aspects to mentoring; the mentor and mentee may come together around a task like planning services or learning gospel piano. The mentor may play the role of spiritual director, helping the mentee sort through faith questions and discern a path for the future. It will certainly include the mentor identifying and naming gifts in the mentee, encouraging the mentee's innate talents to blossom into skills and providing the mentee a model of the faithful Christian life.

Likewise, there are no rules stating whom a worship director should mentor. The mentor should be older or more experienced than the mentee, as life experience is exactly what is imparted in the relationship. The mentee is generally drawn from the mentor's ministry circle, giving them opportunity to interact. It is important that the mentor and mentee like each other. Mentoring shouldn't be a chore, after all. We identify potential mentees simply by keeping our eyes open to see people the way Jesus does: everyone has huge potential to contribute to God's kingdom; they just need love, skills, discernment, and someone who believes in them.

Too often church leaders see the gifted people around us as threats. We fear that any accolades a young leader receives will somehow detract from our own stature. This is rat race thinking rather than kingdom logic. Our goal should be to give away as much of our ministry as possible. We may be training our own successor or we may be growing a future worship director for another church, but we are making disciples just as Jesus commanded (Matt. 28:19).

Take, as an example, the relationship between Paul and Timothy. Paul is a seasoned minister who is pouring himself into young Timothy, his "true son in the faith" (1 Tim. 1:2 NIV). We hear in 1 and 2 Timothy an echo of their relationship. Paul knows Timothy's background, including the faith of his grandmother Lois and mother Eunice, and is eager to place Timothy's future on sure footing as well. His letters to Timothy are full of advice on leading a church, keeping the faith, and even endearing personal details about their relationship: "Do your best to come to me soon. . . . When you come, bring the cloak that I left with Carpus" (2 Tim. 4:9, 13). We hear in these words the way the mentoring relationship has changed: Paul the mentor is now Paul the friend, hoping Timothy will encourage him with a visit. That has been the goal all along: to foster Timothy to the point where he can carry on Paul's ministry himself. Paul follows the template that Jesus established with the disciples, multiplying the kingdom through intentional, focused relationships. He exhorts Timothy to do the same:

> You then, my child, be strong in the grace that is in Christ Jesus; and what you have heard from me through many witnesses entrust to faithful people who will be able to teach others as well. (2 Tim. 2:1–2)

What might this look like in the worship director's context? A show-and-tell approach is good. Mentors needn't prepare a lecture but rather simply explain the behind-the-scene process. Why would anyone care to know how we approach service planning or preparing a rehearsal? Because they will have no paradigm for those tasks otherwise. We are not responsible for showing them the definitive way to oversee a worship ministry, or the best way, just our way. Mentees will mimic, adapt, or even reject our approach when they begin their own ministries, but it's better to have an approach to reject than to have no approach at all.

Real-Life Examples

Let me flesh this out with examples from my own life. I have mentored a number of people over the years, meeting for coffee, Bible study, mini-lectures, and spiritual discernment. For the last ten years I've regularly taken on student interns, and have developed a protocol for these relationships. The mentoring begins with a gift assessment. (In a typical situation the worship director would observe gifts in week-to-week worship at the church, but these students are mostly new to me.) Here I get a sense of the mentee's innate talents, what skills they've developed, the areas in which they can serve the church, and the areas in which they need to grow.

I make it clear they have complete access to me. They can ask any question they want, and I encourage them to do so. I require them to join every ensemble or committee for which they're qualified. I want them to see me run rehearsals, chair meetings, and lead worship—their involvement will allow them to absorb my leadership style. My leadership may not be exemplary, but when they prepare for their first worship committee meeting they'll be thankful to have someplace to start. I often unpack rehearsals and services with them later, soliciting their feedback, inviting questions, and discussing why I made particular choices. Like Jesus explaining a parable to the disciples later, I want them to observe what I do and hear why I did it. This is a powerful form of learning.

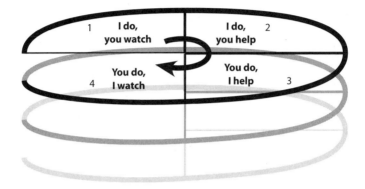

After that we settle into a rhythm of doing and discussing. I begin to assign tasks using an apprenticeship model that slowly hands off responsibility to the mentee. The first step in this learning model is "I do, you watch." They look over my shoulder and ask questions while I do my work. The next step is "I do, you help." I give small tasks to the mentees to get them started. For example, I give them the broad overview of a service I'm planning and ask them to find five songs that might work as a hymn of reflection. The following week we discuss their choices and choose the most appropriate of the five for the service. This helps me, gives them a taste of the work, and allows them to take part in my decision-making process.

Soon they will be ready to take on tasks themselves. "You do, I help" is the next step. They lead part of a rehearsal or plan a service, always with me there to assist and encourage. Throughout this process they are learning by enculturation—learning without even knowing they're learning. The mentoring process imprints subtle lessons such as rehearsal pacing, planning schedules, and dealing with conflict. Finally they're ready for "You do, I watch," at which point I watch as the bird leaves the nest and flies off to build its own nest and begin the process again.

Indeed, the joy of mentoring is watching our young charges grow into mature worship directors in their own churches, adapting what they've learned to their new context and adding unique twists based on their own set of skills. We also experience the fruit of mentoring closer to home. Teaching our philosophy and practice of ministry to someone else clarifies our own thinking. Too often in ministry we react rather than reflect; mentoring provides an opportunity for self-reflection that allows us to mature too. Mentoring keeps us fresh. As we age it is too easy to become set in our ways. Time spent with a younger mentee gives us a personal glimpse into new music styles, worship trends, and cultural shifts. It can even open our eyes to new ways of thinking and fresh solutions to intractable problems.

Because mentoring happens across generations, a healthy bridge is built that creates understanding between young and old, rather than suspicion. If every church member were a mentor or mentee, we would have no more generational worship wars! Finally, mentoring brings the satisfaction that we have helped build God's kingdom in some small way. May we all have people in our lives, both mentors and mentees, about whom we can give thanks like Paul:

> I thank my God every time I remember you, constantly praying with joy in every one of my prayers for all of you, because of your sharing in the gospel from the first day until now. I am confident of this, that the one who began a good work among you will bring it to completion by the day of Jesus Christ. . . . And this is my prayer, that your love may overflow more and more with knowledge and full insight to help you to determine what is best, so that in the day of Christ you may be pure and blameless, having produced the harvest of righteousness that comes through Jesus Christ for the glory and praise of God. (Phil. 1:3–6; 9–11)

For Discussion

1. Do you think the parallel between Jesus's spheres of ministry and our own is helpful? Do you spend more of your time with the larger church or investing in the lives of your worship leaders and mentees?

2. List the mentors and mentees currently in your life. List a few people who you would like to mentor or by whom you would like to be mentored.

POSTLUDE

Ending with a Funeral

Yesterday was Benjamin Nsengiyumva's funeral.

Benjamin was born in 1943 in Rwanda, the son of farmers. He led a humble life that included marrying Felicite, raising twelve children, and working for the government. But when the Rwandan civil war broke out in 1990, all that changed. When violence sweeps through a country like it did in Rwanda, innocent families gather their children and any belongings they can carry, and then they run for their lives.[1]

Benjamin and his family became separated in the chaos, and no one heard from him again. They had to assume that he was one of the eight hundred thousand people who died in the Rwandan genocide.

Benjamin Nsengiyumva

After some time living in refugee camps, Felicite immigrated to Grand Rapids, Michigan, with her children and grandchildren. I got to know Felicite because we lived in the same apartment complex. Her grandchildren and my boys were the same age and would play together while she and I sat on a park bench watching. She spoke very little English, but we communicated with gestures and single-word sentences. Sometimes we'd sing hymns together.

In 2014, the family got a call. Benjamin was alive! After nearly two decades, Benjamin and Felicite were reunited in America, and Benjamin got to see many of his grandchildren and great-grandchildren for the first time. He settled into his new life in Grand Rapids, but it wasn't very long before Benjamin discovered he had cancer. It spread quickly, and he was soon in the hospital with no more options for treatment.

Benjamin died as he lived—a man of deep faith, ready to rest safely in the arms of his Savior. Though the family was heartbroken, they accepted the year they had with him as a gift.

This book began with a funeral, and it ends with one too. Benjamin's funeral was remarkable in many ways. It was a powerful testament to the faith of Benjamin and his family. A few days before the funeral I asked Felicite how she was doing. "Sad," she answered, looking down and shaking her head slowly. "So sad." Yet there she was in the funeral procession, singing with her family. It was truly a moving sight to see a long line of relatives marching slowly behind the casket, singing the hymns that had sustained them through childhood, genocide, and now the death of the family patriarch. My pastor, Jack Roeda, articulated it well in the sermon: "To sing on your deathbed is a remarkable thing. To sing looking death in the face is a testimony to the faith that he who is on our side, Jesus, is stronger than the one on the other side." This is a faith that can simultaneously grieve and hope.

> But we do not want you to be uninformed, brothers and sisters, about those who have died, so that you may not grieve as others do who have no hope. For since we believe that Jesus died and rose again, even so, through Jesus, God will bring with him those who have died. (1 Thess. 4:13–14)

The group that assembled for the funeral provided a glimpse of things to come. Naturally, the Rwandan community came out in full force. But Benjamin's non-Rwandan church friends came out too. Black, white, young, old, resident, refugee, all united in one Lord. It looked suspiciously like a scene prophesied centuries ago:

> And there was a great multitude that no one could count, from every nation, from all tribes and peoples and languages, standing before the throne

and before the Lamb, robed in white, with palm branches in their hands. They cried out in a loud voice, saying, "Salvation belongs to our God who is seated on the throne, and to the Lamb!" (Rev. 7:9–10)

In that funeral, we experienced a taste of that prophesied future worship, even while Benjamin was experiencing it in its fullness. This is the hope of the Christian life. This is the work of worship. This is the rehearsal for heaven.

> Heaven opened to Isaiah, showing him God's glorious throne.
> Lord of might, high and exalted; temple flowing with his robe.
> Seraphim flew all around him, humbled at the holy sight.
> As they circled they were singing, calling out with all their might.
>
> > "Holy, Holy, you are holy,"
> > every angel voice proclaims.
> > "All the earth reflects your glory,
> > every tongue sings out your praise!"
>
> Seraphim continue singing, cherubim still lift their praise.
> Earth and all its creatures worship, moon and stars are still amazed.
> Now above creation's chorus comes another fervent cry:
> all of earth's redeemed are singing, "Glory to the Lord on high!"
>
> > "Holy, Holy, you are holy,"
> > every angel voice proclaims.
> > "All the earth reflects your glory,
> > every tongue sings out your praise!"
>
> One day heaven will be opened and before the Savior's throne,
> saints from every time and nation will begin their endless song:
> "To our God of all salvation, to the high and holy Lamb,
> to the blessed Holy Spirit be forever praise. Amen!"
>
> > "Holy, Holy, you are holy,"
> > every angel voice proclaims.
> > "All the earth reflects your glory,
> > every tongue sings out your praise!"[2]

Notes

About Me (Or, Confessions of a Failed Pentecostal)

1. "There is not a square inch in the whole domain of our human existence over which Christ, who is Sovereign over all, does not cry, Mine!" (Abraham Kuyper, 1880 Inaugural Lecture, Free University of Amsterdam).

Chapter 1 What Is Worship?

1. William Temple, *Readings in St. John's Gospel* (1939; repr., Wilton, CT: Morehouse Barlow, 1985), 67.

2. Bob Kauflin, *Worship Matters: Leading Others to Encounter the Greatness of God* (Wheaton, IL: Crossway, 2008), 59.

3. Ibid.

4. John Witvliet, "On Three Meanings of the Term Worship," *Reformed Worship* 56 (June 2000), 46–47, http://www.reformedworship.org/article/june-2000/three-meaning-term-worship.

5. Bruce T. Ballinger, "We Have Come into His House," © 1976 MCA Music Publishers, ADO Universal Studio, Sound III Inc. (admin. by Universal Music Corp.).

6. Pope Paul VI and the Second Vatican Council, "*Sacrosanctum Concilium* (Constitution on the Sacred Liturgy)," December 4, 1963, http://www.vatican.va/archive/hist_councils/ii_vatican_council/documents/vat-ii_const_19631204_sacrosanctum-concilium_en.html.

7. Frederick William Faber, "There's a Wideness in God's Mercy," 1854.

8. Nicholas Wolterstorff, "An Interview with Nicholas Wolterstorff," *Hearing the Call: Liturgy, Justice, Church, and World* (Grand Rapids: Eerdmans, 2011), 417. Wolterstorff expands on this image of the heartbeat of worship: "The best image I have for expressing the connection is the image of a heartbeat: systolic and diastolic. The church assembles and it disperses. In both its assembling and its dispersing it is living before the face of God, but in two different ways. . . . For me, the two belong together. Worship in assemblies is of deep importance, and doing justice and struggling for shalom when dispersed is of equal importance. . . . You can't have a heartbeat without having both the systolic and the diastolic phases."

Chapter 2 What Is Biblical Worship?

1 Anglicans have their own three-legged stool: Scripture, reason, and tradition. John Wesley, an Anglican before founding the Methodist movement, added *experience* to these three, forming what came to be called the *Methodist Quadrilateral*.

2. Ron Rienstra, *Disciples: Worship* (Grand Rapids: Faith Alive Christian Resources, 2008), 14.

3. Eric Werner, *The Sacred Bridge: Liturgical Parallels in Synagogue and Early Church* (New York: Schocken Books, 1970), http://archive.org/stream/sacredbride007175mbp/sacredbride007175mbp_djvu.txt.

4. N. T. Wright, "How Can the Bible Be Authoritative?" accessed March 3, 2016, http://ntwrightpage.com/Wright_Bible_Authoritative.htm.

5. Ed Setzer, "Dumb and Dumber: How Biblical Illiteracy Is Killing Our Nation," *Charisma Magazine*, October 9, 2014, http://www.charismamag.com/life/culture/21076-dumb-and-dumber-how-biblical-illiteracy-is-killing-our-nation.

Chapter 3 Who Is the Audience of Worship?

1. This exercise comes from *The Worship Sourcebook*, second ed. (Grand Rapids: Faith Alive Christian Resources, 2013), 25.

2. Matt Redman, "The Heart of Worship," © 1999 ThankYou Music (admin. by Capitol CMG Publishing).

3. Søren Kierkegaard, *Purity of Heart Is to Will One Thing*, trans. Douglas Steere (New York: Harper and Brothers, 1948), 180–81.

4. And if we are truly performing for an "Audience of One," why are the worship leaders elevated on a stage facing the people? Or, as Glenn Packiam puts it, "When the worship leader and the Object of our worship occupy the same visual space, the worshipper is easily confused—consciously or subconsciously—about Who the Center truly is." (Glenn Packiam, "What Does the Visual Layout of Our Worship Service Say?" *Glenn Packiam's Blog*, February 11, 2012, http://glennpackiam.typepad.com/my_weblog/2012/02/what-does-our-worship-service-visually-communicate.html).

5. Ben Pasley and Robin Pasley, "I Will Not Forget You," © 1999 Universal Music, Brentwood-Benson Tunes (admin. by Brentwood-Benson Music Publishing, Inc.).

6. James B. Torrance, *Worship, Community and the Triune God of Grace* (Downers Grove, IL: InterVarsity, 1996).

7. Historically named *perichoresis*, or "circle dance."

8. Richard Leach, "Come, Join the Dance of Trinity," © 2001 Selah Publishing Co., Inc. www.selahpub.com. Reprinted by permission.

9. Lester Ruth, as quoted in "Worship As Dancing on Jesus's Feet," *Zac Hicks's Blog*, May 27, 2014, http://www.zachicks.com/blog/2014/5/27/worship-as-dancing-on-jesus-feet.html. Reprinted by permission.

10. Lester Ruth, "*Lex Amandi, Lex Orandi*: The Trinity in the Most Used Contemporary Christian Worship Songs," *The Place of Christ in Liturgical Prayer: Trinity, Christology, and Liturgical Theology*, ed. Bryan D. Spinks (Collegeville, MN: Pueblo Book/Liturgical Press, 2008), 354.

Chapter 4 What Does Worship Do?

1. James K. A. Smith, "Redeeming Ritual," *The Banner*, February 2012, http://www.thebanner.org/issue/2012-02-01.

2. Jason Fitzgerald, "What's the Ideal Runner's Diet Plan? Matt Fitzgerald Says . . . " *Strength Running*, June 2014, http://strengthrunning.com/2014/06/runners-diet-plan-matt-fitzgerald -interview/.

Chapter 5 Learning from the Past

1. Solomon also said, "Of the writing of books there is no end. This too is vanity." But that didn't stop me from writing this book . . .

2. Bernhard W. Anderson, *Out of the Depths: The Psalms Speak for Us Today*, third ed. (Louisville: Westminster John Knox, 2000), 31.

3. Werner, *Sacred Bridge*.

4. Elmer L. Towns and Vernon M. Whaley, *Worship Through the Ages: How the Great Awakenings Shape Evangelical Worship* (Nashville: B&H Publishing, 2012).

5. *Evangelical* comes from the Greek word meaning "the good news." Evangelicals as a movement are known for four core beliefs: personal conversion, high regard for Scripture, centrality of Christ, and evangelism. See Larry Eskridge, "Defining the Term in Contemporary Times," *Wheaton College: Institute for the Study of American Evangelicals*, accessed March 3, 2016, http ://www.wheaton.edu/ISAE/Defining-Evangelicalism/Defining-the-Term.

6. Quentin J. Schultze, "Orality and Power in Latin American Pentecostalism," *Coming of Age: Protestantism in Contemporary Latin America* (Lanham, MD: University Press of America, 1994), 65–88.

7. "Who We Are," *St. Stephen Antiochian Orthodox Church*, accessed March 3, 2016, http ://www.protomartyr.org/who.html.

Chapter 6 Liturgy

1. The name *mass* is derived from the final words of the Latin worship service, *Ite, missa est* ("Go, it is the sending").

2. In Matthew 6:7–8, the King James Version uses the term "vain repetitions." The NRSV calls them "empty phrases." "When you are praying, do not heap up empty phrases as the Gentiles do; for they think that they will be heard because of their many words. Do not be like them, for your Father knows what you need before you ask him." It is interesting to note that these instructions precede the Lord's Prayer, one of the few things that Protestants do recite repeatedly.

3. Pentecost may have looked very different if the apostles had spent the day at the mall!

4. George Santayana, *The Life of Reason: Or the Phases of Human Progress* (New York: Charles Scribner's Sons, 1905), 284.

5. Albert A. Goodson, "We've Come This Far by Faith," ©1963 Manna Music, Inc. (admin. by ClearBox Rights, LLC).

Chapter 7 The Church Year

1. There are also daily and even hourly cycles inherited from monastic life called daily prayer, the divine office, praying the hours, or common prayer. For the sake of simplicity we won't address those here.

2. There are many places to find lectionary readings. An excellent online source for the Revised Common Lectionary is http://lectionary.library.vanderbilt.edu/.

3. *Call to Worship: Liturgy, Music, Preaching, and the Arts*, accessed March 4, 2016, http ://www.presbyterianmission.org/ministries/calltoworship/.

4. *The Text This Week*, accessed March 4, 2016, http://www.textweek.com/.

5. "This Week's Sermon Starters," *Center for Excellence in Preaching*, accessed March 4, 2016, http://cep.calvinseminary.edu/current-sermon-starters/.

6. See "Reverse Lectionary," *The Lectionary Page*, accessed March 4, 2016, http://www.lectionarypage.net/ReverseLectionary.html, or "Scripture Index," *The Text This Week*, accessed March 4, 2016, http://www.textweek.com/Scripture.htm.

Chapter 8 The Fourfold Worship Order

1. See "The Mystery Worshipper," *Ship of Fools*, accessed March 10, 2016, http://shipoffools.com/mystery/index.html.

2. Like all generalizations, this quick overview of communion practices is helpful in painting a broad picture but poor at describing the uniqueness of each denomination and congregation. For example, this doesn't accommodate churches of the Restoration (Stone-Campbell) Movement that celebrate communion weekly but understand it as an ordinance. It is also unable to indicate the many evangelical churches that are beginning to adopt sacramental/Eucharistic practices.

3. Catholics recognize seven sacraments: baptism, confirmation, Eucharist, penance, anointing of the sick, matrimony, and holy orders. Protestants recognize just two, communion and baptism, but some denominations see these as ordinances rather than sacraments. Though all sacraments are important, this book focuses only on communion because of its great impact on worship.

4. A variation on "those tiny, square, oyster-cracker things." Elesha Coffman, "Divided by Communion," *Christianity Today*, August 8, 2008, http://www.christianitytoday.com/history/2008/august/divided-by-communion.html.

5. A. H. Ackley, "I Serve a Risen Savior," © Copyright 1933. Renewed 1961 Word Music, LLC.

6. Read more at "An Early Christian Eucharist," *Christianity Today*, August 8, 2008, http://www.christianitytoday.com/history/2008/august/early-christian-eucharist.html.

Chapter 9 The Psalms in Worship

1. Thomas Day, *Why Catholics Can't Sing* (New York: Crossroads, 1992), 118–19.

2. Guy Deutscher, "Does Your Language Shape How You Think?" *New York Times* (August 29, 2010), MM42, http://www.nytimes.com/2010/08/29/magazine/29language-t.html.

3. Walter Brueggeman, *The Psalms and the Life of Faith* (Minneapolis: Augsburg Fortress, 1995).

4. While we don't fully know the original context of the psalms, there are a number of studies that give us some good ideas. Suzanne Haïk-Ventoura, *Music of the Bible Revealed* (North Richland Hills, TX: BIBAL, 1991) and Sigmund Mowinckel, *The Psalms in Israel's Worship* (Grand Rapids: Eerdmans, 2004) are a good starting point.

5. Joseph Gelineau, "Music and Singing in the Liturgy," *The Study of Liturgy*, rev. ed., Cheslyn Jones, Geoffrey Wainwright, Edward Yarnold, Paul Bradshaw, eds. (New York: Oxford University Press), 493–507.

6. Slightly modified from Gelineau, "Music and Singing in the Liturgy," 504.

7. This approach is reminiscent of Curt Sachs's classification of "logogenic" (word-born) versus "pathogenic" (emotion-born) melodies in primitive cultures, as described in *The Rise of Music in the Ancient World: East and West* (Mineola, NY: Dover, 2008).

8. Werner, *Sacred Bridge*.

9. You can hear this approach on Alex Mejias and Rashad "Shad-E" Lowary's "Whom Shall I Fear? (Psalm 27)," on *Arrabon 2: Songs of Joy & Lament*, http://arrabon.bandcamp.com/track/whom-shall-i-fear-ps-27-feat-alex-mejias-shad-e.

10. This approach can be seen in *Psalms for All Seasons* (Grand Rapids: Faith Alive Christian Resources, 2012) and *Sing! A New Creation* (Grand Rapids: Faith Alive Christian Resources, 2001).

11. See, for example, David Diephouse's rendering of Psalm 106, "Thanks Be to God, Our Savior."

12. Eelco Vos and the Psalm Project have made it their mission to modernize the music of *The Genevan Psalter*, which was once so prominent in their homeland of Holland. See http://www .thepsalmproject.com/.

13. For "retuned" settings of metrical psalms, see *Indelible Grace Hymn Book*, http://hymnbook .igracemusic.com/hymns/search?utf8=%E2%9C%93&tag=Psalm&meter=&commit=Filter +Hymns, and the Cardiphonia psalm compilations, *Songs of the Psalter*, http://cardiphonia .org/.

14. Roman Catholics are required to sing a responsorial setting of a specific Psalm each week. These paraphrases would be sung as "hymns" elsewhere in the service.

15. A similar debate has gone on in Bible translation circles for years. Some favor "formal equivalence"—a literal translation that follows the form and syntax of the original language, also known as word-for-word translation; others favor "dynamic equivalence"—which translates the meaning of the original text in forms that are indigenous to the new language (sense-for-sense translation). If you have ever used Google translate, you will understand that a literal translation is not always the best!

16. It should be noted that the words *responsorial* and *metrical* are widely used terms. I coined application of the terms *paraphrase* and *extract* for the purposes of this chapter.

Chapter 10 The Senses, the Arts, and Worship

1. The *Shema* derives its name from the first word of Deuteronomy 6:4–5, *hear*.

2. St. Augustine, *Confessions*, R. S. Pine, trans. (New York: Penguin, 1961), 238–39.

3. For more on this shift, see Lester Ruth, *"Lex Amandi, Lex Orandi*: The Trinity in the Most Used Contemporary Christian Worship Songs," 354. Ruth states it this way: "This emphasis on the use of musical sets to facilitate an experience of God erodes a classic understanding of Jesus Christ as the mediator between humans and God the Father. Typical use of CWM [contemporary worship music] places expectations on music to mediate worshipers' approach to God. Perhaps displacing Christ as mediator with the Father goes hand in hand with the central focus on an exalted, divine Christ in CWM. If worship's primary end is communion or intimacy with the Son, not with God the Father, need for Christ as mediator is itself lessened. Mediation is shifted to the music. Thus prayer in CWM is not to the Father through the Son but to the Son through the music."

4. James L. Mays, *Psalms: Interpretation, A Bible Commentary for Teaching and Preaching* (Louisville: John Knox Press, 1994), 116.

5. Harold M. Best, *Music Through the Eyes of Faith* (New York: HarperCollins, 1993), 42.

6. Pierce Pettis, "Nothing but the Truth," © 2001 Universal-Polygram International Publishing, Inc. / Piercepettisongs (ASCAP). Used by permission.

7. Sylvia Dunstan, "All Who Hunger," © GIA Publications, Inc., 1991.

8. Pettis, "Nothing but the Truth."

9. Gilbert K. Chesterton, *Orthodoxy* (New York: John Lane Company, 1908), 85.

10. Banning Eyre, "Album Review: 'Beware the Fetish'" *NPR*, August 11, 2014, http://www .npr.org/2014/08/11/339611060/album-review-beware-the-fetish.

11. Jaroslav Pelikan, *The Vindication of Tradition: The 1983 Jefferson Lecture in the Humanities* (New Haven, CT: Yale University Press, 1984), 65.

12. James K. Smith, *Imagining the Kingdom: How Worship Works* (Grand Rapids: Baker Academic, 2013).

13. "Ten Core Convictions," *Calvin Institute of Christian Worship*, March 5, 2012, http ://worship.calvin.edu/resources/resource-library/ten-core-convictions/.

Chapter 11 The Gospel Intoned

1. Anne Porter, "Music," *Living Things: Collected Poems* (Hanover, NH: Steerforth Press, 2006). Reprinted by permission.

2. Graham Kendrick, "Why Aren't We Singing?" *Graham Kendrick's Blog*, accessed March 4, 2016, http://www.grahamkendrick.co.uk/news-blogs/item/587-why-aren-t-we-singing.

3. Lest you consider me a curmudgeonly killjoy, let me make it clear that I see no need for restraint outside of worship; play or listen to anything you want! In fact, I wish more Christian musicians would pursue a calling to be a jazz pianist, metal guitarist, or pipe organ virtuoso in the broader musical market rather than trying to fulfill those dreams in a worship setting.

4. As quoted in Andy Parks, *To Know You More* (Downers Grove, IL: InterVarsity, 2004), 222.

5. Recently there has been a slew of writings on the benefits of group singing, including Anna Haensch, "When Choirs Sing, Many Hearts Beat As One," *NPR Health Shots*, July 10, 2013, http://www.npr.org/sections/health-shots/2013/07/09/200390454/when-choirs-sing-many-hearts-beat-as-one; Karen Loew, "How Communal Singing Disappeared from American Life: And Why We Should Bring It Back," *The Atlantic*, March 28, 2012, http://www.theatlantic.com/entertainment/archive/2012/03/how-communal-singing-disappeared-from-american-life/255094/; Stacy Horn and Ari Shapiro, "'Imperfect Harmony': How Singing With Others Changes Your Life," *NPR*, June 3, 2013, http://www.npr.org/2013/06/03/188355968/imperfect-harmony-how-chorale-singing-changes-lives, an interview with Stacy Horn, author of *Imperfect Harmony: Finding Happiness Singing with Others* (Chapel Hill, NC: Algonquin Press, 2013); and Daniel Levitin, *This Is Your Brain on Music: The Science of a Human Obsession* (New York: Plume/Penguin, 2006).

6. If you want to experience how uninspiring a movie can be without its soundtrack, look online for the final scene of *Star Wars Episode IV: A New Hope* stripped of its music, such as "Star Wars Minus Williams—Throne Room," YouTube video, 2:14, uploaded by Auralnauts on September 10, 2014, https://www.youtube.com/watch?v=Tj-GZJhfBmI.

Chapter 12 A Balanced Congregational Song Repertoire

1. Robert Bayley, "Made in God's Image: Two New Hymns on Healing Sexual Identity," *Reformed Worship*, March 2009, http://www.reformedworship.org/article/march-2009/made-gods-image.

2. I'm kidding. *The Art of Worship* only comes in paperback.

3. In this context, I'm using the word *global* not in the sense of "world music" or "ethnic songs," but to denote songs that more broadly come from outside of your church, denomination, culture, or worship tradition.

4. Debra Rienstra and Ron Rienstra, *Worship Words: Discipling Language for Faithful Ministry* (Grand Rapids: Baker Academic, 2009), 107.

5. William Alexander Percy, "They Cast Their Nets In Galilee," © 1924 Edward B. Marks Music Corp.

6. See Marva Dawn's *Reaching Out without Dumbing Down* (Grand Rapids: Eerdmans, 1995) for an excellent discussion of being accessible without watering down the message.

7. John D. Witvliet, "The Nuts and Bolts of Worship Planning," *Calvin Institute of Christian Worship*, accessed March 4, 2016, http://worship.calvin.edu/resources/resource-library/the-nuts-and-bolts-of-worship-planning.

8. Graham Kendrick, "Why Aren't We Singing?" YouTube video, 6:39, uploaded by Graham Kendrick & Make Way Music on October 8, 2014, http://youtu.be/U4M3EhkgVPs.

9. Consider, as an example, the person who posted this request to a worship directors' forum: "Easter is coming up soon, and I am looking for a great secular song to tie into the service. I have

been scouring U2 and Coldplay all day with no inspiration . . . anybody got any ideas?" Yes, I do have an idea: let the people sing a song about the resurrection of Christ!

10. The term *a cappella* is derived from the Italian phrase "in chapel style" and has come to mean "singing without instrumental accompaniment."

11. *Strophic* means songs that have multiple verses of text under one melody.

12. The word *liturgy*—worship—comes from the Greek word *leitourgia*, which is usually translated as "the work of the people."

13. For a more complete discussion, visit Roger E. Olson, "Did Karl Barth Really Say Jesus Loves Me, This I Know . . . ?" *Patheos*, January 24, 2013, http://www.patheos.com/blogs/roger eolson/2013/01/did-karl-barth-really-say-jesus-loves-me-this-i-know/.

14. For a deeper look at including congregation members of all intellectual and emotional levels, see Barbara J. Newman, *Accessible Gospel, Inclusive Worship* (Wyoming, MI: CLC Network, 2015). Newman's work with "universal design" and disabilities in worship is also featured at the CLC Network website, https://www.clcnetwork.org/, and in Joan Huyser-Honig and Barbara Newman, "Universal Design, Vertical Habits and Inclusive Worship," *Calvin Institute of Christian Worship*, July 1, 2015, http://worship.calvin.edu/resources/resource-library/universal-design -vertical-habits-and-inclusive-worship/.

15. David W. Music and Milburn Price, *A Survey of Christian Hymnody* (Carol Stream, IL: Hope, 2011) is one of many overviews of hymns through the ages.

16. For an overview, see Greg Scheer, "Shout to the Lord: Praise & Worship from Jesus People to Gen X," *New Songs of Celebration Render: Congregational Song in the 21st Century*, C. Michael Hawn, ed. (Chicago: GIA Publications, 2013).

17. See *New Songs of Celebration Render* for an overview of the streams of song in the last fifty years.

18. For more on a diversity of singing modes, see Greg Scheer, "Perfect Harmony?: Congregational Singing Comes in Different Shapes and Sizes," *Reformed Worship*, September 2010, http:// www.reformedworship.org/article/september-2010/perfect-harmony.

19. The number of songs in a church's repertoire varies dramatically from church to church. Some have a rotation of only forty songs and others have well over five hundred. Jon Nicol, *The SongCycle: How to Simplify Worship Planning and Re-engage Your Church* (FlingWide Publishing, 2013) has some good tools for calculating how many songs your church needs.

Part 4 Practice: The Arts in Worship

1. Andy Crouch, *Culture Making: Recovering Our Creative Calling* (Downers Grove, IL: IVP, 2013), 20–24.

2. This "doctrine of sub-creation" is discussed in J. R. R. Tolkien, "On Fairie Stories," *The Tolkien Reader: Stories, Poems and Commentary by the Author of "The Hobbit" and "The Lord of the Rings"* (New York: Ballantine, 1966), 54.

3. Crouch, *Culture Making*, 24.

4. See point #6 of "Ten Core Convictions," *Calvin Institute of Christian Worship*, accessed March 4, 2016, http://worship.calvin.edu/resources/resource-library/ten-core-convictions/.

Chapter 13 The Gospel Enacted

1. Jeff Barker, *The Storytelling Church: Adventures in Reclaiming the Role of Story in Worship* (Cleveland, TN: Webber Institute Books, 2011), 53.

2. Thomas A. Boogaart, "Drama and the Sacred: Recovering the Dramatic Tradition in Scripture and Worship," *Touching the Altar: The Old Testament for Christian Worship*, Carol M. Bechtel, ed. (Grand Rapids: Eerdmans, 2008).

3. See, for example, George A. Scranton, "Rereading the Bible Again (For the First Time): Choral Readings of Scripture from the Texts of The Revised Common Lectionary," accessed March 4, 2016, http://www.covchurch.org/wp-content/uploads/sites/15/2011/11/Full-Speech-Choir-Intro.pdf.

4. Max McLean and Warren Bird, *Unleashing the Word: Rediscovering the Public Reading of Scripture* (Grand Rapids: Zondervan, 2009).

5. There are a number of good resources for improving public reading of Scripture, including Todd Farley, "Unlocking the Living Word: Tips for Reading Scripture in Worship," *Reformed Worship*, September 2008, http://reformedworship.org/article/september-2008/unlocking-living-word; Clayton J. Schmit, *Public Reading of Scripture: A Handbook* (Nashville: Abingdon Press, 2002); and Tom Long's Friends of the Groom workshop at "Enacted Word: Using Theater to Present Scripture," *Calvin Institute of Christian Worship*, January 27, 2012, http://worship.calvin.edu /resources/resource-library/symposium-2012-enacted-word-using-theater-to-present-scripture/.

6. Jeff Barker, "Enacted Prayer," *Drama Ministries Ensemble of Northwestern College*, accessed March 4, 2016, http://richdrama.com/BookStore/EnactedPrayer.htm.

7. Cornelius Plantinga Jr., *Reading for Preaching: The Preacher in Conversation with Storytellers, Biographers, Poets, and Journalists* (Grand Rapids: Eerdmans, 2013).

Chapter 14 The Gospel Embodied

1. Pope Paul VI and the Second Vatican Council, "*Sacrosanctum Concilium.*"

2. There are, of course, many ways to categorize worship dance. In Ronald Gagne et al, *Introducing Dance in Christian Worship*, rev. ed. (Portland, OR: Pastoral Press, 1999), these types of liturgical dance are listed as procession, proclamation, prayer, meditation, and celebration (p. 90). In Robert E. Webber, ed., *The Complete Library of Christian Worship: Music and the Arts in Christian Worship* vol. 4, book 2 (Nashville: Star Song Communications Group, 1994), Deena Borchers identifies common worship movements (kneeling, raised arms, and so forth), communal movement (such as folk dances), fine art dance, mime/clowning, and drama (pp. 729–30).

3. J. G. Davies, "Integrating Dance in the Liturgy," *Complete Library of Christian Worship*, 732–33.

4. Lynn Hayden, "Prophetic Dance," *Dancing for Him Ministries*, accessed March 4, 2016, http://www.dancingforhim.com/about/prophetic-dance#.Vb-juZMzaEI.

5. Tom S. Long, "Freeze Frame: Dramatic Scripture Telling Using Tableaux," *Reformed Worship*, March 2005, http://www.reformedworship.org/article/march-2005/freeze-frame-dramatic -Scripture-telling-using-tableaux.

6. Thomas Kane, *The Dancing Church: Video Impressions of the Church in Africa* (New York: Paulist Press, 1992).

7. Richard Fabian, "Jesus Wants to Dance with You at Church," *St. Gregory of Nyssa Episcopal Church*, accessed March 4, 2016, http://www.saintgregorys.org/Resources_pdfs/JesusWants.pdf.

8. Robert E. Webber, *Ancient-Future Worship: A Model for the 21st Century* (Wheaton, IL: IWS Resources, 1999).

Chapter 15 The Gospel Envisioned

1. This is not to say that "high art"—art meant for the gallery—is wrong, or that all art must be created only for worship. Artists need to follow their calling into the sanctuary or gallery, confident that their art is part of God's good creation no matter what the venue.

2. W. David O. Taylor, "Introduction," *For the Beauty of the Church: Casting a Vision for the Arts*, W. David O. Taylor, ed. (Grand Rapids: Baker, 2010), 21.

3. James F. White and Susan J. White, *Church Architecture: Building and Renovating for Christian Worship* (Nashville: Abingdon Press, 1988), 10.

4. James E. VanderMolen and Ron Rienstra, *The Transformation of the John R. Mulder Memorial Chapel, 2011–2012*, May 1, 2012, http://issuu.com/schreurprinting/docs/wts_the _transformation.

5. Excerpted from a conversation that began on the Liturgy Fellowship Facebook group, August 3, 2015, and was later published in Ron Rienstra, "Sanctuary Architecture and Theophanic Expectation," *Reformed Worship*, February 11, 2016.

6. If a congregation feels strongly that they should display a flag, consider displaying it on the outside of the building or in the church's community space. There it sends the message that the flag represents a civic affiliation rather than a religious one.

7. "The Father & His Two Sons: The Art of Forgiveness," *Calvin College Center Art Gallery*, accessed March 4, 2016, http://www.calvin.edu/centerartgallery/collection/prodigal/.

8. Sybil MacBeth, *Praying in Color: Drawing a New Path to God* (Orleans, MA: Paraclete Press, 2007).

9. W. David O. Taylor, "Discipling the Eyes through Art in Worship," *Christianity Today* vol. 56, no. 4 (April 27, 2012): 40.

Chapter 16 The Gospel Intensified

1. Variously attributed to Frank Lloyd Wright and Winston Churchill.

2. Stephen Proctor, "The Liturgy of the Rock Concert," *Illuminate*, June 9, 2014, http://illuminate .us/the-liturgy-of-the-rock-concert/.

3. For further reading on the topic of worship volume, see Thomas S. Rainer, "How Loud Should Our Church Music Be?" *Thom S. Rainer*, April 17, 2013, http://thomrainer.com/2013/04/how -loud-should-our-church-music-be/ (includes interesting insights from Disney World); Leon Sievers, "How Loud Is Your Church?" *Experiencing Worship*, October 28, 2014, http://www.experiencing worship.com/worship-articles/sound/2001-9-How-Loud-is.html; and Gary Zandstra, "Church Sound: It's A Little Too Loud, But That's . . . Good?!?" *ProSoundWeb*, November 5, 2012, http ://www.prosoundweb.com/article/worship_sound_basics_its_a_little_too_loud_but_thats_good/.

4. James F. White, *New Forms of Worship* (Nashville, Abingdon Press, 1971), 28.

5. Kenny Lamm, "Nine Reasons People Aren't Singing in Worship," *Renewing Worship*, June 11, 2014, http://blog.ncbaptist.org/renewingworship/2014/06/11/nine-reasons-people-arent-singing -in-worship/. Many people have written on this theme, citing similar problems: songs sung too high, unfamiliar repertoire, and poor acoustics for congregational singing. Lamm summarizes well the common complaint of worship becoming a concert: "What has occurred could be summed up as the re-professionalization of church music and the loss of a key goal of worship leading—enabling the people to sing their praises to God. Simply put, we are breeding a culture of spectators in our churches, changing what should be a participative worship environment to a concert event. Worship is moving to its pre-Reformation mess."

6. Kendrick, "Why Aren't We Singing?"

7. Howard Rheingold, "Look Who's Talking," *Wired*, January 1999, http://archive.wired .com/wired/archive/7.01/amish.html.

8. Proctor, "Liturgy of the Rock Concert."

Chapter 17 The Gospel in Time

1. "Fred Rogers Acceptance Speech—1997," YouTube video, 3:12, uploaded by emmys on March 26, 2008, https://www.youtube.com/watch?v=Upm9LnuCBUM.

2. Eric Shlange proposes that festival worship is primarily focused on inspiration, whereas congregational worship is geared toward discipleship (Eric Shlange, "Worship Planning: Festival or Congregation?" *The Church Collective*, October 30, 2013, http://thechurchcollective.com

/worship-planning/festival-or-congregation/). Syd Hielema identifies four contexts of worship: festival worship, congregational worship, extended family worship, and worship in solitude (Syd Hielema, "The Festival-Envy Syndrome: Four Contexts for Worship," *Reformed Worship*, March 2004, http://www.reformedworship.org/article/march-2004/festival-envy-syndrome-four-contexts -worship). In each case, they identify festival worship as an event that takes place outside the local church. While these are important perspectives, I'm limiting my focus to the different types of services that take place within a local congregation.

3. William Blake, "The Little Vagabond," *Songs of Innocence and Experience* (1794).

4. A number of people have created music videos of this sermon. A transcript of the most famous section of the sermon appears at Justin Taylor, "Well, I Wonder If You Know Him," *The Gospel Coalition*, April 9, 2009, http://www.thegospelcoalition.org/blogs/justintaylor/2009/04 /09/well-i-wonder-if-you-know-him/. The full sermon appears at "Dr. S. M. Lockridge—That's My King (Full Sermon)," YouTube video, 1:06:27, uploaded by Keith Brown on January 31, 2012, https://www.youtube.com/watch?v=4BhI4JKACUs.

Chapter 18 The World

1. *Nairobi Statement on Worship and Culture: Contemporary Challenges and Opportunities* (Geneva: The Lutheran World Federation, 1996).

2. The relationships are so tight in the Dutch Reformed world that they play a game called "Dutch Bingo." When they meet someone new, they ask where they're from and start asking "Do you know X?" until they discover some people in common. I'm proud to say that even though I'm a transplant to the denomination, I have gotten pretty good at the game too.

Chapter 22 You

1. In *Celebration of Discipline*, Richard Foster groups the spiritual disciplines this way: inward disciplines (meditation, prayer, fasting, study), outward disciplines (simplicity, solitude, submission, service), and corporate disciplines (confession, worship, guidance, celebration).

2. Walter Brueggemann, *Sabbath as Resistance: Saying No to the Culture of Now* (Louisville: Westminster John Knox, 2014).

3. For private singing/prayer of the psalms, I especially like *The Revised Grail Psalms: A Liturgical Psalter—Singing Version* (Chicago: Conception Abbey/The Grail, admin. GIA, 2010). For musical settings of *The Grail*, Michel Guimont, *Psalms for the Revised Common Lectionary* (Chicago: GIA, 1998) is immensely singable; hymnals such as *RitualSong: A Hymnal and Service Book for Roman Catholics* (Chicago: GIA, 1996) contain a wide variety of psalm settings for most of the psalter.

Ending with a Funeral

1. For a glimpse into the trials of a refugee, read the oral history of another family from my church: Robert Rozema et al., "Bent Not Broken: A Family Remembers the War in Liberia and Sierra Leone," *iTunes*, May 29, 2013, https://itunes.apple.com/us/app/bent-not-broken/id63598 9716?mt=8.

2. We sang this song, "Heaven Opened to Isaiah" (Uri Uwer'Uwer'Uwera), at Benjamin's funeral. It is a Rwandan song that I translated after learning it in Uganda. Felicite and I used to sing it while the kids played and now our church sings it regularly.

Index

Scripture Index

Boldface type indicates verses quoted in the text.

About the Author

Greg Scheer is Minister of Worship at Church of the Servant in Grand Rapids and Music Associate at the Calvin Institute of Christian Worship. His writings include *The Art of Worship: A Musician's Guide to Leading Modern Worship* (Baker, 2006) and contributions to *The Hymn*, *Worship Leader*, *International Journal of Community Music*, and *New Songs of Celebration Render* (ed. C. Michael Hawn, GIA, 2013). His music is available from GIA, Augsburg Fortress, MorningStar, in numerous hymnals, and at www.gregscheer.com.

Also Available from Greg Scheer

In the decade since it was first published, *The Art of Worship* has become the go-to book for those leading modern worship bands. This invaluable resource is utilized as a textbook in classes around the country and has been translated into Korean, Chinese, and Indonesian. *The Art of Worship* guides leaders through building teams, evaluating songs, planning services, and leading worship musicians toward a better sound. Find out what made one reviewer call *The Art of Worship* "the greatest thing since broken bread!"

LIKE THIS
BOOK?
Consider sharing it with others!

- Share or mention the book on your social media platforms. Use the hashtag **#EssentialWorship.**

- Write a book review on your blog or on a retailer site.

- Pick up a copy for friends, family, or strangers—anyone who you think would enjoy and be challenged by its message!

- Share this message on Twitter or Facebook: **"I loved #EssentialWorship by @gregscheercom // @ReadBakerBooks."**

- Recommend this book for your church, workplace, book club, or class.

- Follow Baker Books on social media and tell us what you like.

 Facebook.com/ReadBakerBooks

 @ReadBakerBooks